CAMPUS ENGLISH

A Problem-solving Approach to Study Skills

STUDENT'S BOOK

David Forman, Frank Donoghue,
Susan Abbey, Bryan Cruden and
Ian Kidd (Project Co-ordinator)

MACMILLAN
PUBLISHERS

The Centre for British Teachers

A Centre for British Teachers Project

First published 1990
Revised Edition published 1991

Published by *Macmillan Publishers Ltd*
London and Basingstoke and associated companies

ISBN 0–333–52233–8

Printed in Hong Kong

A CIP catalogue record for this book is available from the British Library

Photographic acknowledgements

The authors and publishers wish to acknowledge, with thanks, the following photographic sources, and to state that they have tried to clear copyright; in any case where they may have failed, they will be pleased to make the necessary arrangements at the first opportunity.
Agricultural Productivity and the World Market, p89
Antiquities Directorate, Iraq, p104
Barnaby's Picture Library, pp93, 100, 151
John Birdsall Photography, Nottingham, p151
Cambridge University Library, p119
Cambridge Press, pp xvii (Tass), 30, 36, 50, 103, 107, 126, 151, 161, 178
J. Allan Cash, pp67, 68, 103, 104, 151, 162
Friends of the Earth, p85
Geothermal Survey, p52
Granada Television, p152
Hutchinson Library/Michael MacIntyre, p84
Mini Levine, p155
Mansell Collection, p103
Oxfam, p97
People Magazine/Mark Edwards/Habitat, p9
Popperfoto, pp43, 104, 120
United Kingdom Atomic Energy Authority, p55
World Health Organisation, p135

Cover photograph courtesy of
Sally and Richard Greenhill

Acknowledgements

The authors would like to thank the following:
Jean Floyd, editorial consultant, The Malaysian Ministry of Education; Vanessa Lim, typist; CFBT colleagues Martha Blasek, Donald Macdonald, Jo Kukathas and Azmel Mohamed.

The publishers would like to thank The British Council and Lynette Murphy O'Dwyer, of UCLES, for their advice over the relationship to the IELTS examination.

Grateful acknowledgement is made to the following who have kindly given permission to reproduce copyright material:

American Management Association, New York, for an extract from 'White-Collar Crime' by Rod Willis in *Management Review*, January, 1986.
The Association of Commonwealth Universities for an extract from the 1984–86 edition of *Higher Education in the United Kingdom* published by Longman Group Limited for the British Council and the Association of Commonwealth Universities.
Aileen Ballantyne for the article 'Mummy's Boy who ran Amok' in *Guardian Weekly*, 30 August, 1987.
British Bio-technology Limited for the advertisement 'British Biotechnology has come a long way since 1953'.
British Broadcasting Corporation for the BBC Education advertisement 'The Changing World of Information' April, 1987.
Century Hutchinson Publishing Group Limited for extracts from *Small is Beautiful* by E.F. Schumacher.
William Collins Sons & Co. Ltd. for extracts from *The Third Wave* by Alvin Toffler.
Consumers' Association of Penang, Malaysia, for the article 'Life for the fishermen has not improved' in *Utusan Konsumer*, February, 1985.
Michael Daley for his drawing in the *Times Educational Supplement*, 5 June, 1987.
The Economist for extracts from issues dated 15 August and 26 September, 1987.
Friends of the Earth for their News sheet 'Campaign to Save Tropical Rainforests'.
Greenpeace for extracts from their Fact Sheets.
Dr. John Gribbin for diagrams from *Future Weather* (1982)
Guardian News Service Ltd. for extracts from issues dated 30 August and 13 September, 1987, of the *Guardian Weekly*.
International Atomic Energy Agency for extracts from 'Nuclear Power, the Environment and Man' and 'Facts about Energy'.
International Planned Parenthood Federation for articles 'A tale of two cities'; 'One billion people need shelter', and 'A wise head brings hope and health to squatters' from *People*, Vol. 14, No. 1, 1987.
Michael Kilraine for his cartoon in the *Times Educational Supplement*, 22 May, 1987.
Medical Research Council for their '1947–1987' advertisement.
New Internationalist Publications Limited for extracts from their 1989 Third World Calendar.
New Scientist for an illustration from article 'What makes rain forests so special' by P.Moore (21 August, 1986); extract concerning Patent Law (16 July 1987); extract 'What is a patent?' (20 August, 1987); a book review 'Computing for young superbrains' by Lynne Murray (26 March, 1987); article 'Growing up with computers' by Adrian Furnham (26 March, 1987); article 'Gene engineers fashion giant sheep' (10 July, 1986); article 'Rainforests face attack of double standards' by Catherine Caufield (5 June, 1986); article 'Altered organisms released in Australia' (30 April, 1987); a book review 'The new age of synthetic biology' by Eric Ashby (25 June, 1987); article 'Rifkin urges boycott of 'adulterated' milk' (10 July, 1986); and extract from article 'Power from hot rocks and warm water' (24 July, 1986).
Newsweek Inc. for the articles 'The Morals Mine Field' by E.Salholz, et al in *Newsweek*, 20 October, 1986, and 'Should Man make Beast?' by T.Monmaney and M.Hager in *Newsweek*, 4 May, 1987.
Julius K. Nyerere for an abbreviation of his speech at an International Conference in Tanzania, 1974.
Oxford University Press for extracts from *Science and Technology in World Development* by Robin Clarke (1985). Copyright (c) Unesco 1985.
The Panos Institute for extracts from the article 'Third World demands justice over seeds' by Andy Crump, 19 June, 1987.
Penguin Books Ltd. for an extract from *Setting Genes to Work: The Industrial Era of Biotechnology* by Stephanie Yanchinski, copyright (c) 1985, and an extract and illustration from *The Energy Question* by Gerald Foley (Second Edition) copyright (c) 1981.
Peters, Fraser and Dunlop on behalf of the Estate of Arthur Koestler for an extract from *Janus: A Summing Up*, (1978)
William Rankin and Stephen Croall for three cartoons from *Ecology for Beginners*, published by Writers and Readers Publishing Co-operative, 1986.
Routledge and Kegan Paul Ltd. for an extract from *The Clever Moron* by R.S. Scorer, (1977)
Scientific American Inc., for an illustration adapted from *Drought in Africa* by Michael H.Glantz, Vol.256, No. 6, June 1987.
SmithKline Biologicals s.a. for an extract from 'Product Profile'
Professor M.W. Thring for a graph and extract from *The Engineer's Conscience* (1980).
Times Newspapers Limited for the article 'Yuppie Puppies' by Chris Van Ormer from the *Times Educational Supplement*, 7 August, 1987, and the article 'All for IT' by Adrian Low from the Times Educational Supplement, 5 June, 1987.
University of Sussex for extract from a leaflet on B.Sc. Courses in Computer Science.
Unwin Hyman Limited for an extract from *Education and the Social Order* by Bertrand Russell, (1932).
World Health Organization for an extract from article 'Twelve yardsticks for health' in *World Health* magazine, October 1986; the article 'Village health workers and malnutrition: a project that failed' by R.N. Ratnaike, P.O'Neil and R. Chynoweth, in *World Health Forum*, Vol.5, 1984; extracts from 'Tobacco strong words are not enough' by William U.Chandler in *World Health Forum*, Vol. 7 1986; and extracts from 'A society free of smoking by the year 2000' by C.Everett Koop, in *World Health Forum*, Vol. 7, 1986.
Every effort has been made to trace all the copyright holders but if any have been inadvertently overlooked the publishers will be pleased to make the necessary arrangement at the first opportunity.

Contents

To the student

Campus English is intended for intermediate to advanced level students who need English for their studies and who are studying either in a class or on their own.

A Learning new vocabulary

The best way to learn a new word is to use it in writing or speaking rather than to memorise its meaning. You will encounter a great deal of new vocabulary in your listening and reading in this book and in your studies. You should start and maintain a system for recording vocabulary to help you use the new words in your writing and speech. A vocabulary system acts as a reminder of words you have encountered, their meanings and the situations in which they are used.

If you do not already use a system for recording new vocabulary, start one now. You will need an exercise book or loose-leaf file, access to a good English dictionary and Thesaurus (a Thesaurus groups words of similar meaning and opposites together).

Follow these tips for recording vocabulary:

- Do have a system for learning new words. It's no good writing words down if you don't use them. When you note the meaning, learn how to use the word in a sentence.
- Do organise your entries, don't just list words as they arise. New vocabulary in your subject area could be listed under subject topic headings.
- Do put words together in meaning groups or topic areas. For example, look at the article in Unit 1 on Page 9. Under the topic headings of 'Sanitation' and 'Corruption' you could list the following new words:

Sanitation	**Corruption**
piped sewage	corrupt
open sewers	profiteering
health risks	kickbacks
lack of drainage	ineffective
septic tanks	extort
sanitary latrines	
treatment plant	

  It makes good sense to group these entries together.

- Do note the relations between words. It is easier to remember vocabulary when you see how it fits into the pattern of language rather than learning the meaning of an individual word.
- Do note parts of speech and how a word changes from verb form to noun.
  For example: corrupt – vb, adj.
  corruption – n.
- Do note phrases as well as single words. It's a good idea to note how suitable adjectives match the noun.
  For example: festering slum

slight considerable major drastic	reduction

- Do list words with the same meaning and their opposites together.
- Do distinguish between essential and non-essential vocabulary. Not all words are equally useful to you. Some will be useful in your subject studies and it is helpful to have a section in your 'Vocabulary' file for subject topic areas. Don't simply look up and record every word you come across.
- Do make sure you understand the meaning of the word and the likely situations in which it may be used. Don't just copy down the meaning from the dictionary.
- Do have a system for learning and using the words after you have recorded them. You may like to set yourself a target of a certain number of new words to learn every week. Your target should be realistic. If you can't meet it, change the target.
- Do revise your vocabulary regularly. Look back over the previous week's entries.

B Using this book on your own

If you are studying on your own, *Campus English* has the following features to help you:

- A comprehensive, separate **Answer key** giving suggested answers to many of the exercises. Where answers are provided, a key symbol is given in the margin.
- The book is self-contained. You will not need to refer to any other books to complete the tasks in Sections I to III in each Unit. All the necessary information is provided in the book itself. There are some activities where you are required to work with a partner or group and to exchange ideas. It will still be possible for you to complete these activities on your own.
- There are opportunities in Section 5 of every Unit to apply what you have learnt to your area of subject study. In this Section, you may be required to use your textbooks, lecture notes, etc.
- The book aims to teach as well as practise. Language skills you will need for your subject are explained and further practice exercises are provided. See column 1 of the **Skills Matrix** on page ix for a guide to these skills.
- You can choose the skills you wish to learn. By referring to the **Skills matrix**, you can use the book according to your needs. *For example:* if you feel you need to learn how to note main points in your reading, the **Skills matrix** shows where you can learn how to do this and then practise what you have learnt.
- The book uses texts and extracts of the level you are likely to need in your studies and teaches you strategies for coping with such material.
- There is an accompanying cassette tape for use with this book. Where you need to listen to the tape to complete a task, a symbol is given in the margin.
- If you are studying for an English language qualification, such as the IELTS test, you can use the practice test at the end of the book.

Discussion among students is encouraged in every Unit. Section 4 consists of a group activity, such as a simulation or role play, which is intended to develop fluency. You may like to read this section before going on to Section 5. Interaction and discussion are an important way of improving your language skills and you should make the most of opportunities you may have for discussion in English.

To the teacher

There is a Teacher's Book available to accompany this book. It contains the following:

1 A Unit-by-Unit guide to the Student's Book. This includes:
   - an introduction to the theme of each Unit.
   - the objectives of each Unit.
   - teachers' tips for the tasks and exercises.
   - supplementary exercises for teachers to offer further practice, vocabulary extension, etc.
   - general test practice exercises for students to practise such things as interview techniques, listening skills, study skills and reading skills.
   - tapescripts for the listening exercises in each Unit.
   - extra answers to open-ended questions, in addition to those offered in the Answer Key at the back of this book.

2 Answers to the practice IELTS test (in the Examination Edition only). The practice test follows the format of the British Council/University of Cambridge Local Examination Syndicate International English Language Testing Service (the IELTS test). The test is based on extracts from the Student's Book and students will be expected to have access to this book when they take the test.

SKILLS MATRIX

Students will be able to:	This involves:	Page	Task
Unit 1			
Understand and interpret texts which describe processes.	Predicting text content from excerpts.	2	**A2**
	Working out the definition of a concept from examples.	2	**A3**
Use notes to summarise information.	Scanning a text to find particular information.	3	**A1**
	Writing notes on a process in flow chart form.	3	**A2a**
	Applying flow chart note-taking techniques to listening.	4	**A3**
	Identifying language of sequence.	4	**A3**
	Recognising the function of reference words and equivalents.	5	**B1,B2** **B2b**
	Writing a short description.	6	
	Writing a passage from flow chart notes.	6	**C1** **C2**
	Giving a short talk.	7	**A4a**
	Predicting the content of a text using clues.	9 7	**A1a**
	Skimming a text for main points and overall aim.	8	**A1b**
	Scanning a text to find relevant information.	10 9	**A4c** **A2**
	Comparing a number of texts on a similar topic.	11	**B**
	Summarising information from different sources in table form.	11	**B** **C1**
	Taking notes while listening.	11	
	Writing a short description of two contrasting problems.	11	**C2**
	Interpreting flow chart information.	12	
	Using available information to prepare a proposal.	13–15	
	Presenting a proposal in a persuasive way.	15	
	Looking critically at different solutions to a problem.	15	
Unit 2			
Collect, analyse and present information in an objective and concise way.	Drafting a questionnaire.	22 23	**C** **C4**
	Presenting the results of a questionnaire.	24	**C4b**
Understand the organisation of ideas in an argument *i.e.* cause and effect.	Presenting information in a table or diagram.	21 22–23	**B3** **C3**
	Identifying direct cause and effect relationships.	22 24	**C3** **A1**
	Scanning texts for particular information.	24–26	**A2**
	Distinguishing between objective facts and subjective opinions.	26	**A3**
	Presenting a counter argument in written form.	26	**A4**
	Presenting a paper to a seminar group.	24	**B2**

Students will be able to:	This involves:	Page	Task
	Guessing the meaning of words from context.	27	A1
	Identifying causes and effects.	28	B1
	Using notes to write a short essay.	29	B4b
	Analysing an argument.	31	D1a
	Inferring the opinion of a writer.	31	D1b
	Writing a short essay describing the causes and effects of a problem.	34	D4
	Preparing an agenda.	35	
	Briefing the chairperson and secretary.	35	
	Conducting a formal meeting.	35–37	
	Examining texts for relevant information.	38–43	
Unit 3			
Make notes from reading. take notes from listening for re-use.	Listening to realistic texts for particular information.	46	B1–2
	Identifying the main areas of a talk and formulating headings for notes.	46	B3
Arrive at solutions through comparison and contrast.	Using suitable note-taking techniques for listening.	46	C
	Picking out similarities and differences between two systems.	48	B1–3
	Summarising similarities and differences in note-form on a grid.	49	B4
	Scanning texts for particular information.	52–54	C
	Asking for specific information.	49	C4
	Learning language necessary to compare and contrast.	48	A3
		54	D1
	Writing summaries from notes in grid form.	54	D3
	Guessing the meaning of words from context.	55	A2
	Identifying attitudes.	57	B
		58	D2
	Picking out main points.	58	C1
		58	D1
	Scanning the text for relevant information.	58	C2
	Making notes from reading.	58	D3
		58	C2
	Understanding the language of comparison and contrast in listening.	58	D3
	Taking notes from listening under main headings.	58	D3
	Writing a short passage from notes.	59	D4
	Using the language of comparison and contrast in writing.	59	D4
	Reading for specific information.	59–60	A
	Making notes for a purpose.	60	D1–2
	Discussing and planning strategies to achieve an aim.	61–64	D3–4
	Negotiating to reach agreement.	61–64	D5

Students will be able to:	This involves:	Page	Task
Unit 4			
Select and use language to describe change and development, graphs and charts.	Talking at length to describe change.	67	**B**
	Listening to interviews to understand general meaning.	68	**C1**
	Listening for precise details.	68	**C2**
Use strategies for note-making (mind-maps).	Listening for the attitude of speakers.	68	**C3**
Use texts and information to prepare and assess talks.	Using the Present Perfect tense to describe change.	68	**D**
	Writing a short passage to describe a place.	68	**D**
	Talking about the environment.	69	**A1–3**
	Scanning a text for particular information.	69–70	**A4**
	Identifying the overall function of a text, graph or chart.	70	**B1**
	Identifying main points of a text.	70	**B1**
	Using mind-maps as a note-making technique.	71–72	**B3–4**
	Writing short passages to describe, interpret and predict trends from charts and graphs.	72–75	**C, D**
	Listening to identify and note main points in an interview.	76	**A2**
	Summarising notes in mind-map form.	76	**A3**
	Identifying predictions made by a speaker.	76	**A4**
	Examining the degree of certainty of predictions.	76	**A4**
	Predicting the content of a text from its title.	77	**B1**
	Comparing and contrasting in chart and written form.	79	**C3**
	Preparing, giving and assessing a short talk.	79–81	**E**
	Reading longer texts for specific information.	81	**A1**
	Identifying the writer's point of view.	81	**A2**
	Noting main points in an appropriate way.	81	**A3**
	Referring to texts to prepare a presentation.	82–85	**B**
	Delivering a presentation to a group.	82–85	**B**
	Participating in a discussion.	82–85	**B**
	Writing a report from a given angle.	86	**C**
Unit 5			
Give clear and persuasive explanations in written and spoken form.	Predicting text content from the title.	89	**A2a**
	Scanning text to check predictions about content.	89	**A2b**
Understand new vocabulary using available clues.	Making outline notes from a text.	91–92	**B1,B2**
	Taking notes while listening.	92	**A1**
	Explaining using the language of cause and effect.	92	**A2**
	Using notes to present ideas.	93	**B1,B2**
	Speaking persuasively.	94	**B2**
	Making notes from reading.	94	**A2**

Students will be able to:	This involves:	Page	Task
	Presenting a proposal to a group.	96	A3
	Guessing the meaning of unknown words from word-formation and context.	96	B1,B2
	Identifying important words.	97	B3
	Designing promotional literature to explain and persuade.	97	A
	Preparing and presenting an argument in a formal situation.	100–101	B
	Assessing arguments to reach a decision.	100–101	C1
	Commenting on a decision.	101	C2
Unit 6			
Recognise bias in reading and listening.	Recognising emotive language.	105	B3
	Assessing the power of emotive language.	105	B4
Identify the force of language, purpose of text and target audience.	Employing negative emotive language in writing.	105	B5
	Describing a graph, summarising trends and explaining predictions.	106	C
	Identifying optimistic language in reading and listening.	107 110	C3b,c B4
Increase power of expression to make writing and speaking more effective.	Skimming texts for specific information.	108–109	B2
	Examining the organisation of a text.	110	B3a,b
	Making notes in mind-map form.	110	B3c,d
	Identifying the purpose and target audience of a text.	111–113	D3–5
	Differentiating between fact and opinion.	112–113	D2,D4,
	Employing emotive language in writing.	115	D7
	Identifying the attitude of speakers through language and tone.	115–116	B
	Anticipating what a speaker will say.	117	C2
	Identifying bias in texts.	118–127	D2
	Agreeing and disagreeing appropriately.	127	E1–2
	Giving views in a meeting.	128	E3–4
	Writing concise opinion.	128	E5
	Discussing and debating.	128–131	
	Writing to present a point of view.	128–131	
	Responding to biased writing.	128–131	
	Making oral presentations.	128–131	
Unit 7			
Evaluate data from a variety of sources to write a report.	Scanning a text for information.	133 134 139–141 145–147	B2 A2 A1 A1
Assess progress objectively.	Conducting an investigation using reference materials.	135	A4,B1
	Recording information in grid form.	136	B2,B4
	Writing a short passage based on notes	136	B4c

Students will be able to:	This involves:	Page	Task
	Suggesting solutions to problems.	136	**C3,C4**
	Writing a report.	137–139	**D–G**
	Reporting on a project and suggesting improvements.	141	**B**
	Establishing criteria for evaluation.	141–143	**C1,C2**
	Interpreting trends from statistics.	143–145	**D1,D2**
	Conducting group discussion.	148	**A2**
	Designing effective promotional literature.	149	**B**
Unit 8			
Communicate accurately and appropriately.	Giving views in discussion.	151	**A2**
	Skimming for precise information.	152	**B1**
Use active and passive skills taught and practised in the book.	Devising and putting questions to obtain information.	153	**B2**
	Presenting the results of a survey.	153	**B3,B4**
Compile a report in a group.	Comparing two reports.	154	**C**
	Reading and listening for main points and attitudes.	154	**A1,A2**
	Using notes to give short talks.	155	**A3**
	Identifying speaker's position.	160	**B1**
	Using discussion techniques (interrupting/changing direction/agreeing and disagreeing).	161	**C2**
	Writing an essay giving an opinion.	161	**C3**
	Compiling a report:	162–177	**B**
	– finding relevant information		
	– organising group work		
	– reporting to a group		
	– collating materials and ideas	162–177	
	– planning a report		
	– writing a group report	162–177	
	Conducting a discussion.	177	**A1,A2**
	Presenting a plan.	178	**A3,A4**
	Assessing a plan.	178	**B1,B2**
	Writing a report to compose plans.	178	**C**

STARTING ON CAMPUS ENGLISH

Look at the front cover of the book. Can you tell from the title what it is likely to be about?

The 'blurb' on the back cover of books usually gives a broad outline of what you are likely to find inside. It helps you to decide whether you think the book is likely to be useful to you. If you haven't read the 'blurb', turn to the back now and read it before you go on.

A1 Working in pairs, glance quickly through the book to decide whether you think the following statements are true or false:

a This book will help you to improve your ability to study more effectively.
b This book will help you to improve your English.
c This book will help you to improve in your field of study.
d This book will help you to improve your performance in a language test.
e The book aims to help you pass your subject exams.
f The book uses authentic material.
g The book will help you to integrate skills.

A2 Now check your answers by reading the following passage.

This book aims to improve your English by looking at the type of material you may encounter in your studies. There is a great deal of variety in the subject matter chosen. You may come across some, but not all of these topics in your chosen field of study, but this is not a subject textbook and it isn't written for students on a specific course. You may encounter a lot of material which is not directly relevant to your own subject area but it will be used to practise the kind of skills you will need in your own studies.

In your field of study you will need to write reports or essays, listen to lectures, participate in seminars, locate relevant information, read for 'gist' and understand texts. In this book you will practise the skills which enable you to do these things more effectively. These skills are not used in isolation. *For example:* you may need to interpret a graph in order to write an essay or take notes in order to give a talk. This book gives you practice both in using individual skills and in integrating them.

Your subject texts will give you the opportunity to study a relatively narrow field in depth. In contrast this book draws on many different disciplines and subjects, which have been chosen for their topicality and interest. As a result, you will be introduced to a broader field of inquiry than you would normally encounter in a narrow specialist field. It is hoped that the book will help to broaden your horizons.

The theme of the book is 'Problems and their solution' and each Unit explores this theme through an examination of contemporary issues which are of interest and concern to both arts and science students. Such issues as whether Man has the right to create animals, what is the best type of education system, the problem of improving agricultural output and the causes and effects of crime are all considered in different Units. Each Unit is divided into five sections. In the first Section you will be asked to consider the topic of the Unit, drawing on your own knowledge. Section II contains the main teaching element of the Unit, with further practice in Section III. Section IV will give you the opportunity to integrate the skills you have learnt by participating in a seminar, role-play or simulation. In this Section, you may be confronted with a problem faced by a section of society and asked to look for a solution. In Section V, there is a summary of the skills practised in the Unit and there will be an opportunity for you to consider the language skills you have practised in relation to the subject you are studying.

The source material in each chapter is drawn from a variety of specialist magazines, subject textbooks, newspapers and journals. The sources are listed in the bibliography at the back of the book. There is also an audio cassette of realistic material which should be used in conjunction with this book. There is a in the margin when you need to listen to the cassette.

B1 Study the Skills Matrix on page ix. Look down the left hand column and decide in which of these skills you need most practice.
Which unit offers most practice in these skills?

B2 Look back to the Contents page and find out in which Units and Sections the issues mentioned in paragraph 4 in the above passage will be raised. Check your answers by turning to the relevant Section.

B3 Now discuss the following questions with a partner. Decide which you think is the best answer.

a This book will help you to:
A improve in your field of study.
B learn about developments in genetic engineering, ecology, etc.
C improve your English language skills for study purposes.
D use English in everyday life.

b This book is mainly intended for:
A non-native speakers.
B non-native speakers who are studying one or more subjects in the medium of English.
C native speakers of English who are studying one or more subjects in English.
D non-native speakers who are studying English.

c Practising the skills on pages ix to xiii will directly help you to:
A get more marks.
B write better essays.
C understand your subject.
D improve your language ability.

d These skills are important because:
A they are used everyday.
B they are used in order to study a subject.
C they are necessary to improve English.
D they need to be integrated.

Compare your answers with another group. Multiple-choice questions of this type usually have only one correct answer (or one that is better than the others), but it is possible that there is more than one correct answer here.

C Book talk

In this book you will be asked to take part in simulations and role-plays. You will have a job to do, an aim and some information to help you. You will not be required to act as if you were in a play. A simulation is neither a drama nor a game. You will be expected to discuss, argue, explain, ask questions, report and co-operate as a member of a group. Simulations and role-plays are a very useful way of putting into practice what you have learnt and they are also a lot of fun. The aim is that you will enjoy learning as you will have to communicate with your own group and with other groups.

In a role-play, you are given information about the character you are expected to be or the role you will play, whereas in a simulation you can choose your role.

C1 The class is now going to divide into four groups. Each group will represent one of the following:

- Representatives from Macmillan Publishers
- Officials at the Ministry of Education
- English teachers
- Students who want to improve their English

These four groups between them are going to decide on a textbook to buy for a Study Skills in English course for non-native speakers of English who will be going on to study at an English-medium university. Students require an English language qualification for admission. Imagine you will have to sit the British Council/University of Cambridge IELTS test to meet this requirement.

a Decide which group you are going to represent.
b Read the information for your group.
c You should ensure that you spend sufficient time on this to prepare your case fully.
d Hold a meeting and decide which book you are going to buy.

Publisher's representatives
You are trying to promote this book.
You feel that it is:
a good value
b appropriate for the course
c up-to-date
d relevant for the IELTS test
e suitable for both arts/science students
In the meeting, try to persuade the other groups to buy this book for their course.

Ministry officials
You work in the Ministry of Education and it is your job to purchase a set of textbooks for this course. You are interested in what other groups, especially the teachers, have to say, but you feel that this book is rather expensive. Choose another English textbook with which you are familiar and compare it with this book in terms of content, layout and price. (Check with the teachers and make a different choice from their group.) At the end of the meeting, you will announce which book you have decided to purchase. One of you will act as Chairperson and should read the note for the Chairperson.

English teachers
You will be teaching this course so you are anxious to persuade the Ministry that they should buy the most appropriate book. Choose another English textbook with which you are familiar and compare it with this book. (Check with the Ministry officials and choose a different book from their group.) Decide what you think are the advantages and disadvantages of each from your point of view.

Students
Decide what course you will be studying at university and which English textbook would be most appropriate for you to prepare for such a course and the IELTS test. Compare this book with any others you are familiar with. In the meeting, say why you think the book you have chosen is the most appropriate.

Chairperson
The chairperson's job is to ensure that everyone has a chance to speak and that a decision is reached at the end. The Chairperson should not put the point of view of any group, though he or she may be a member of the Ministry officials group during the preparation.

C2 Evaluation

- Which book was chosen and why?
- Which group presented the most persuasive arguments?
- Was this a simulation or a role-play?
- What do you think was its purpose?
- Did it achieve its purpose?

In simulations and role-plays there is a job to do and a problem to be solved. The purpose is to integrate skills, to give students an opportunity to put together and use skills which may have been learnt or practised. In later units, the simulation or role-play will give you an opportunity to consolidate and integrate the skills learnt and practised in that chapter.

UNIT 1 · *Help yourself*

SECTION 1 *INTRODUCTION*

A Here are two examples of technology, one considered appropriate for a rich, developed society, the other for a poor, developing society.

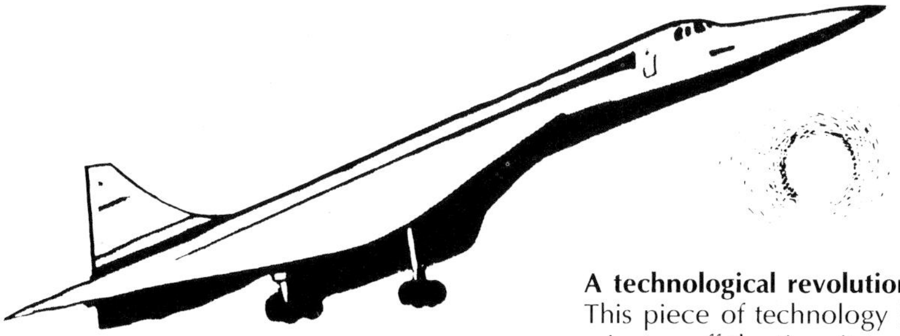

A technological revolution
This piece of technology knocked 200 minutes off the time it took to transport 100 people from London to New York. It has sonic boom. It cost $40 000,000.

Another technological revolution
This piece of technology knocked 14 hours off the time it took to transport a day's supply of clean water for a village from the well. It has no sonic boom. It cost $42.

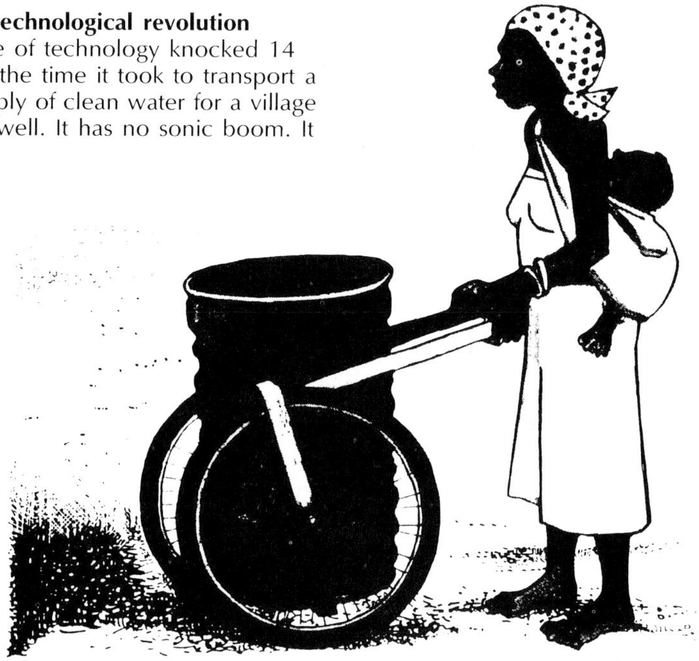

A1 For discussion

- In what respects are these pieces of technology appropriate?
- What do they imply about the world distribution of wealth and the expectations of citizens in the two societies?
- Why do you think the writer uses the word 'revolution'?
- The contrast he draws is in some ways an extreme one – how appropriate does he consider each piece of technology to be?

A2 What is 'Appropriate Technology?'

a You may have heard of, or read, E.F. Schumacher's influential book *Small is Beautiful*. Read the quote below from this work.

> Give a man a fish, as the saying goes, and you are helping him a little bit for a very short while; teach him the art of fishing, and he can help himself all his life.

Schumacher goes on to develop this saying in the context of fishing.
– What do you expect him to write?
Now read on and see how close you were to Schumacher's development.

> On a higher level: supply him with fishing tackle; this will cost you a good deal of money, and the result remains doubtful; but even if fruitful, the man's continuing livelihood will still be dependent upon you for replacements. But teach him to make his own fishing tackle and you have helped him to become not only self-supporting, but also self-reliant and independent.

b Schumacher uses a saying about fishing to introduce an idea with much wider application. Study the extract again and try to rewrite it in more general terms of developed countries extending aid to developing countries.

c Discuss in pairs:
- What organisations or professions do you think might have been influenced by Schumacher?
- What kind of changes might have occurred under his influence?
- Does there seem to be a connection between the title of his book and the idea in the extract?
- Can you draw a connection between this idea and the water-transporting device on page 1?

A3 *a* Look at the following statement from the author of the comments on Concorde and the water carriers.

> Western technology often doesn't match the needs of developing countries. It is expensive, wasting precious foreign exchange; spare parts for the machinery will need to be imported; and it can mean fewer jobs available locally. An appropriate technology would be one that fitted local conditions, local needs and local purses.

– Does this reflect Schumacher's theme?

b Towards a definition.
Using the idea from both these extracts, try to write a definition of the term 'Appropriate Technology'.

SECTION 2 *PRINCIPLES INTO PRACTICE*

A1 Read the following text about a poor African village. Identify the problem faced by the villagers and note down the various kinds of help offered to them.

The right machine for the job

In the beginning, before the white people came, the women in the village worked in the fields with hoes and spades. The men would help sometimes but usually only supervised and sold what produce was left at the end of the season. The work was hard and broke their backs. But everybody grew enough to eat.

Then came the first expert. He talked of progress and modernisation, a world where work would be easy and money plentiful. His organisation donated a tractor to the village. It roared and spluttered impressively and the men were so interested that they decided to take over the preparation of the land. But after three weeks the tractor broke down. The government officer in the town said he'd send a mechanic but it would take two months. When the mechanic came after four months he said it would need spare parts from Canada. Meanwhile the women had gone back to preparing the ground and the men to supervising. The tractor is still rusting over there by the trees-children come from miles around to play on it, and girls now get to sit in the driving seat as their mothers had not been allowed to do while the machine was working.

The second expert came ten years later. He told the villagers how western Technology was no good for African people, how it put them into debt. They told him about the tractor and he nodded his head, saying 'You see?' They did. He promised to bring them a simple machine made with local materials that they could use to grind their own flour instead of paying to have it done ten miles away. When the mill arrived it looked very impressive but it was powered by someone riding a bicycle. And in the village only women grind flour and only men ride bicycles – bicycles aren't as good as tractors at persuading men to work. Now the mill is rusting over there by the trees, too.

Then a third expert came to the village. She stayed for three weeks, not just a morning. And instead of describing her wonder machine she simply asked 'What do you want?' She asked the women as well as the men and sat with them talking about their life and how it could be improved. Eventually the village decided that what it wanted most was hoes and spades that didn't break. They discussed how to get them with the outsider – could the village smith be trained to make better tools or should they buy them from the town? It seemed best in the end to do both. The village forge wasn't sophisticated enough to produce the stronger tools necessary, so the expert's organisation agreed to pay for a batch to be made in the town. But the village smith went to the larger forge and helped them to make the right kind of tools – so his own skills were improved for the future.

Now the women prepare the fields with tougher hoes and spades. The men still supervise. The work is still hard. And it still breaks backs – but not spades.

VSO Third World Calendar 1986

A2 *a* Look again at the description of the first attempt at overcoming the problem, the donation of a tractor. We can break this section down into a series of important steps which are as follows:

the women hoed the ground
the expert came to the village
the expert donated a tractor
the men prepared the land
the tractor broke down
the government officer sent a mechanic
spare parts were needed
the women hoed the ground

It is often useful to store or present this kind of information, which describes a sequence or a process, in the form of a **flow chart**.

[women hoed ground] → [expert donated tractor] → [tractor broke down] → [spare parts needed]

→ [expert came to village] → [men prepared land] → [gov't officer sent mechanic] → [women hoed ground]

This can be a very convenient technique for the writer or student and can make the reader's interpretation of the information much easier.

b Working with a partner read the article again and decide on the following:
(*i*) Which of the three attempts to help the village was successful?
(*ii*) What were the important steps involved?
(*iii*) Use the steps to make a flow chart.

c The first and second attempts failed. The third succeeded. Why?

What difference in the respective approaches of the three 'experts' can you discern?

d Let's consider not only the various steps involved but also 'the principles' behind those steps.

Below is a suggested list in random order of the principles which reflect the nature of the successful process:
- isolate a problem
- nurture idea of self-help
- work together to alleviate or overcome problem
- discuss problems
- propose remedy
- ask questions
- gain local support and confidence

Working with your partner, establish the order which corresponds best with the flow chart you've made.

Now make a flow chart for this information. Your first box should contain 'ask questions'.

A3 The technique of making flow charts as a note-taking skill can be applied when listening to lectures as well as using textbooks.

a As an example, listen to the brief extracts on the tape. Each contains a description of a process. As you listen, note down the sequence of the process in the form of a flow chart.

The first describes peanut farming.

The second extract is concerned with the construction of an efficient stove in Burkina Faso.

In the third, **three** ways in which poverty leads to further poverty are discussed.

In order to make sense, a flow chart obviously relies on the sequence of a process. In the listening extract about peanut shelling, the speaker helped us to understand the sequence by using the following words and phrases: *before sowing/then/after harvesting.*

b Listen to the tape again. How did the other speakers emphasise the order of the steps for the construction of the stove and for the poverty cycle?

c Look through the article about the African village again and note down the words or phrases the author used to make this kind of emphasis.

Try to think of more examples of 'sequence-markers' to add to these.

B1 In demonstrating the interrelationship between ideas and information, a writer often links ideas by using simple words to refer to a person, object or idea in another place in the text. In this way he avoids repetition.

a Read the text below. What do the words in italics refer to?

One billion people need shelter

More than one billion people, a quarter of the world's population, are either literally homeless, or live in extremely poor housing and unhealthy environments. About 100 million people have no shelter whatsoever; *they* sleep in the streets, under bridges, in vacant lots, alleys and doorways.

In the developing world, approaching 50 per cent of the urban population lives in slums and squatter settlements. In some cities *the figure* approaches 80 per cent.

The housing situation is made worse by the urban growth rates. Cities in developing countries continue to grow at a rate of over 3.5 per cent per year; *this* means a yearly growth of around 49 million people. By the year 2000, *these cities* will be expanding by some 78 million people a year – more than 214,000 every day.

By 1985, the number of people living in the cities of developing countries had reached nearly 1.2 billion. In the next 14 years, an estimated 800 million people will be added to the already rapidly expanding cities of the developing world. Given *these trends*, countries would have to double their shelter, infrastructure and services capabilities simply to maintain the status quo.

The growth rates of slums and squatter settlements are even more dramatic. Overall, the population of *these settlements* is increasing at twice the rate of the cities themselves, and four times faster than world population growth.

The developing countries face a formidable challenge. *They* have the task of providing shelter, services and work in cities for an additional 150,000 people every day. *They* must seek to do this when more than 300 million are already jobless, 700 million people live in absolute or relative poverty, and development prospects appear more constrained than ever before.

In the countryside, housing conditions continue to be marked by mass poverty, malnutrition, dilapidated housing, poor water supply, inadequate sanitation, and a lack of services.

This situation, coupled with lack of employment opportunities, continues to drive rural people away from their homes, in the hope of improving their lot in the cities. The decline of traditional agriculture, rapid population growth, absence of alternative centres to disperse migratory flows, the concentration of economic activities in a few major cities – *these factors* will guarantee that the urban population of primate cities will continue to expand rapidly, this leading to the further expansion of slums and squatter settlements.

Habitat

People Vol. 14 no. 1 1987

b Select a short piece of text from your own subject area and underline the reference words it contains.

c Test your partner's ability to detect what the writer is referring to.

B2 As well as being aware of the need to refer back to information already mentioned, a good writer does not like to use the same word over and over again. He will try to find different words to correspond with the word which is being 'avoided'. The purpose is to make the text more stimulating in order to retain the reader's interest.

a Study the extract below and note down all the different words and phrases the writer uses to refer to Dr. Tomas Perreira.

When an elderly man started appearing regularly in the streets of San Rom, a sprawling squatter area about a half-an-hour's drive from the centre of Bonavista, few residents showed any interest.

Politely, they answered his questions about their daily routine. How was their health? How did they cope with sanitary matters in their home? Could they afford to visit the doctor when someone in the family fell ill? Here was another official who would surely find an excuse to extort money on the pretence of providing services.

But this time they were wrong. Dr Tomás Perreira, an active man of 73, was visiting one of South America's largest urban slum areas at the invitation of the head of the Bank of Credit and Commerce International. Dr Perreirá turned down the initial request to establish philanthropic work in San Rom. As a veteran of rural development work and a respected academic figure who has taught in several South American countries and the United States, he believes firmly in establishing self-help programmes.

Adapted from 'People' Vol. 14 no. 1 1987

b Write a short paragraph describing the life of a major figure in your field of study.

c Exchange descriptions with your partner and see if you can improve the readability of the text by making the references to the person more interesting.

C Putting it all together

C1 Getting groundnut production off the ground

In many areas of the world climatic conditions and poor soil limit the choice of crops which can be grown by farmers. In Northern Thailand one of the few crops which can do well is groundnuts. These are grown by small farmers who have faced difficulties in processing the nuts efficiently and economically.

Below is illustrated a groundnut-shelling machine developed by the Faculty of Engineering of Khon Kaen University in response to local needs and at a low price – one might almost say 'for peanuts'!

Peanut sheller developed at Faculty of Engineering, University of Khan Kaen, Thailand

(1) Machine open **(2) Machine in operation**

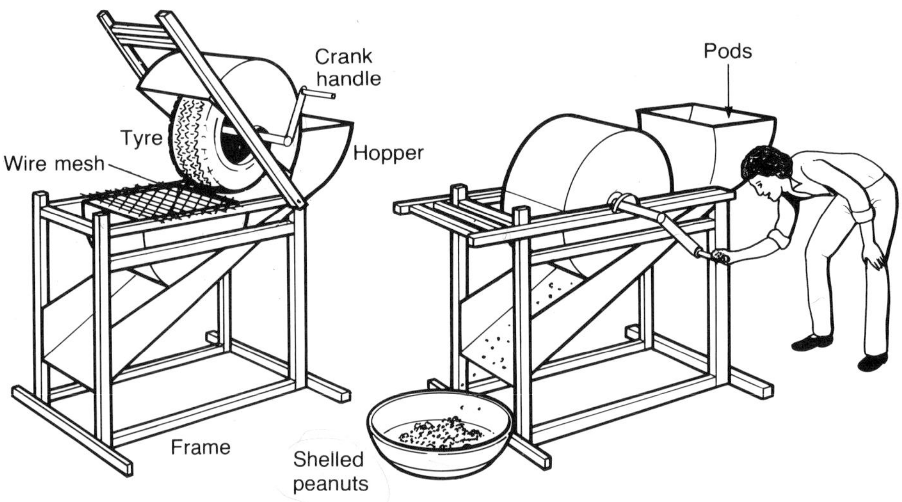

a Working in pairs or groups, study the illustration and discuss how the machine works.

b Jot down your ideas in a flow chart.

c Now write this up as a piece of continuous prose, remembering to use sequence-markers and reference words where you think necessary.

C2 'Do it yourself'

Work in groups.

SCENARIO You work in the engineering department of a university in a developing country. Your department is committed to the principles of Appropriate Technology.

You have been asked to look into the following problems:

(i) Farmers along the banks of the river in your area are now experiencing difficulties in producing successful crops because the irrigation scheme which depended on a single massive pump was the only means of providing water for their fields. The pump lies useless awaiting replacement parts, but there are strong reasons to suppose these parts will never arrive.

(ii) The government recently built thousands of pre-frabricated houses in the city as part of a project to alleviate the problems of over-crowding. Unfortunately, no heed was paid to the exact location of each group of houses and a uniform design for their construction was used. People who live in areas which are prone to mild seasonal flooding are concerned because the structures, which have no foundations, are made of wood.

(iii) As plantations are being established higher and higher up the mountainside, the Forestry Department has run into trouble. A helicopter has to be used to supply workers at a remote base camp with food and other essentials. Even the most sophisticated four-wheel drive vehicles cannot cope with the gradient. The nearest supply road is 1,000 metres below the camp.

(iv) Students in your own halls of residence complain that at certain times of year the reading lamps in their study rooms attract so many insects that it is almost impossible for them to work at night.

a Discuss these problems and try to remedy **one** of them using an 'appropriate' solution. If possible **draw** the device or system with which you propose to remedy the problem.

PRESENTATION

b Select one member of your group to present your solution, using the blackboard, to the rest of the class. While the other groups are making their presentation, listen carefully to what the spokesperson is saying and make a flow chart of their proposed solution.

c When you have heard all the presentations, compare your flow charts with those of other students.

SECTION 3 *SUCCESS AND FAILURE*

A1 It is important to be able to assess quickly the contents of a chapter in a book or an article in a magazine or journal without wasting time in detailed reading. You can get an overall impression of content by doing the following:

– Look at the title, illustration and introduction below.

a What do you think this article is going to be about?

A wise head brings hope and health to squatters

In Orangi, the largest of several hundred squatter colonies around Karachi, a unique project has transformed the lives of several thousand families through the introduction of sanitation and sewage facilities.

A bird's-eye view of the Orangi 'lanes'.
From 'People' Vol. 14 no. 1 1967

You can find out more about the main points in such an article as this by **skim-reading**. This involves:

– reading the whole of the first paragraph.
– reading the first sentence in each subsequent paragraph.
– reading the whole of the final paragraph.

b Do this with the article which follows.

When an elderly man started appearing regularly in the lanes of Orangi, a sprawling squatter colony about a half-an-hour's drive from the centre of Karachi, few residents showed any interest.

Politely, they answered his questions about their daily routine. How was their health? How did they cope with sanitary matters in their home? Could they afford to visit the doctor when someone in the family fell ill? Here was another official who would surely find an excuse to extort money on the pretence of providing services.

But this time they were wrong. Dr Akhtar Hameed Khan, an active man of 73, was visiting one of Asia's largest urban slum areas (known in Pakistan as *katchi abadis*) at the invitation of the head of the Bank of Credit and Commerce International, Aga Hasan Abidi.

Dr Khan turned down the initial request to establish philanthropic work in Orangi. As a veteran of rural development work and a respected academic figure who has taught in India, Bangladesh, Pakistan and the United States, he believes firmly in establishing self-help programmes.

And this explains why he spent several months wandering around Orangi in 1981 – to find out what the people themselves wanted as a prelude to setting up a research project to promote development through community organization. No targets were set. The programme evolved from the response and willingness of the residents – who presently total 800,000 in an area of about 5,000 acres.

Within a short time, Dr Khan saw that the absence of piped sewage services in Orangi meant that after it had rained, children and their mothers waded through virtual open sewers in the lanes around their homes, exposing themselves to serious health risks.

Common health problems ranged from malaria, typhoid, cholera and dysentery, to parasitic infestations. His chief concern was that as more people poured into the community and the population reached a density of 200 per acre, with millions of gallons of water being used daily, the lack of drainage and a sewage system would turn the area into a festering slum.

Dr Khan set about finding out how the people of Orangi could be helped to put their own lives in order. Residents, he learned, felt it was their right to have sanitation provided by the Karachi Development Authority and the Karachi Municipal Corporation, the two local bodies which provided such things for more affluent areas. Officials told him such services were never free and where they existed, residents paid between R150–200 per square yard of plot area for water and sewage services.

Clearly, slum dwellers could not be expected to pay what would work out at an average R25,000 for similar services. Various solutions were suggested but Dr Khan found them all inadequate or too costly. Dr Khan discovered that KDA charges were at least four times the actual cost of labour and building materials because of contractors' profiteering and kickbacks to government officials. He set about designing a cost-efficient sewerage system that would be paid for, installed and managed by residents to cut out all overheads.

Under the Orangi Pilot Project (OPP) the community was divided into units of organization based on the lanes, which comprise 20–30 houses. In such a grouping residents knew and could trust each other. The consensus was that the existing leadership had proved corrupt and ineffective.

One of the toughest challenges for the OPP's social organizers was to persuade residents that their lane was part of their home. With a sanitation system, the lane would be cleaned and raise the value of their houses. Further, their children's health would improve and they would save money on medical bills.

Slowly, they won the people's support and confidence, primarily by introducing more appropriate technologies that reduced construction costs. This put an acceptable measure of sanitation within the reach of the poorest of Orangi. Apart from the substantial decrease in costs which was possible by eliminating cutbacks and the middlemen, drastic reduction was made possible by improving the design of the manholes and septic tanks.

Today, the project workers are inundated with requests and individuals often get on with the work themselves following designs of the OPP. Since September 1981, the project has developed, 1,676 lanes out of the 3,181 in its sector. . .

c The article is about:
A disease in squatter areas
B establishing a self-help programme
C constructing low-cost houses
D living standards in Karachi

Discuss your answer with other students. Are your answers the same?

A2 Now read the article in more detail and make brief notes on the steps involved in this project.
– Could these points be presented as a flow chart?

A3 Read the next part of the same text to decide whether the information it contains could be recorded in a flow chart.

. . . But the story is not one of unconditional success. For Orangi was divided into two sectors when the project started, with the OPP having responsibility for one and a UN community development programme the other. And sadly, the two programmes were unable to co-operate. It is perhaps a classic example of the divergence of approach between international development agencies, geared to target-oriented aims, and small-scale bodies which tend to involve the people and work through trial and error.

Arif Hasan, OPP's architect and consultant, confirmed the division and said that neither group could agree on work methods. The Bank allocated a sector of Orangi to the UN agency and set up the project for them. But it had now been wound up after $625,000 had been spent on developing 35 lanes in three years, he explained.

Dr Khan and his team have fulfilled their aim to reduce costs, and involve home owners in managing and paying for sanitary latrines in their homes and underground sewerage in their lanes. But Dr Khan wants to persuade the KMC to look after the external drains and the treatment plants. These require a master plan and centralized execution and management, he says. He thinks the Orangi people would gladly pay in reasonable instalments provided they are convinced that the work has been done economically and contractors have not stolen too much money.

b If you feel a flow chart is inappropriate in this case, note, in another way, the main points in the U.N. project collapse as concisely as you can.

c One project succeeded, one failed. Discuss to what extent the successful project reflects the principles of Appropriate Technology which we looked at earlier.

A4 You are a researcher interested in the planning and costing of development projects.

a Preview the following article and discuss with a partner whether it is likely to be about:
A Architectural techniques in Bombay.
B Different approaches to low income urban housing.
C The population explosion in Bombay and Madras.
D The success story of planners in India.

A tale of two cities

India is set to have the highest urban population in the world by the year 2000 yet her city planners still have many important lessons to learn. *Darryl D'Monte* visited two contrasting metropolitan housing developments in Bombay and Madras, where housing for the poor has had very different results.

Contrasting urban solutions in New Bombay and Madras.

b Now skim-read the article to see if your expectations are correct.

c Having previewed the article you decide it could contain some relevant information. Scan the article to find the various planning organisations involved.

If you go house-hunting in New Bombay, now being built on the mainland opposite the old city on the peninsula, the chances are that you'll take one look and never come back. There are rows and rows of squalid, decrepit houses, which look as if they have been abandoned but are in fact only a few years old.

Two of the worst sectors are in the township of Vashi, where the blocks have cracks in the walls and perennial leaks. According to Mr Bishanchand Agarwal, whose brother, Kailash, occupied a 'low-income group' tenement two years ago, the houses are full of serious faults. 'There is a great deal of leakage in the latrine. The water just keeps oozing out of the ceiling. There wasn't even a cooking platform built when we moved in.'

The City and Industrial Development Corporation (CIDCO) of Maharashtra state, of which Bombay is the capital, has built about 36,000 houses in the new city since the 1970s. Several blocks have been built privately. Of these houses, 44 per cent belong to the so-called 'economically weaker sections and low-income group.

However, the desperately poor have not yet been accommodated in New Bombay as the first townships were intended for blue collar workers from nearly industries. In the Indian context, to be lower than 'economically weak' is not to have a permanent job.

Mr J.B. D'Souza, former managing director of CIDCO, recalls that one of the innovations in Vashi was to reduce conventional building standards. Ceilings were lowered from 10 to eight feet forcing occupants to lower overhead fans and keep doors open in summer because of the lack of ventilation. On the other hand, some blocks had as many as five 'open-to-sky' terraces and staircases, but these aggravated the leaks during the rains.

New Bombay's own planning practices are based on national official policy and are inspired by Soviet and Western experience. The emphasis is on the structure rather than its suitability for occupation. In other words, housing boards and public works departments firmly believe that the only way to house the masses is to fit people into a preconceived design. Public authorities appear to be convinced that the urban poor cannot afford to build their own homes.

But this article of faith is being challenged 1,000 miles south-east of Bombay – in Madras. Since 1977, the smallest of India's four metropolises has been running an entirely different kind of housing scheme. Residents start out with the bare minimum and add their own refinements to the houses if and when incomes permit.

Mr Evan Rotner, of the World Bank, who helped to establish the programme, said: 'The size and scale of this operation has never been undertaken before by the public sector. It reaches out to 60 to 70 per cent of the poverty group.'

The government of Tamil Nadu now aims to commit almost 80 per cent of its housing funds to economically weaker and low-income sections. Called the Sites and Services scheme, it reflects concern for improving shelter possibilities for the poor and both the people and the government can afford it. A site in Madras costs only $90 compared to $500 for the cheapest low-income unit in New Bombay.

Arumbakkam, 8 km from the centre of Madras, was the first location for the scheme. Today, it looks clean and well laid-out, with a mixture of poor and middle-class homes. It has a bustling market, school and playground and a purposeful air – in sharp contrast to the deserted atmosphere of New Bombay. This is partly because Arumbakkam is within commuting distance of offices and factories, whereas New Bombay has become a dormitory town for people working in the old city.

'I never dreamt I would ever live in a place like this,' Mrs Shanti Dakshinamurthy, aged 25, said. She lives in a smart two-storey house in Arumbakkam, having moved in five years ago with her family of five. They have completed their payments to the Madras Metropolitan Development Authority (MMDA) of Rs22 a month (under $2) as loan instalments. With further loans the family has built a first floor.

'We lived in a hut nearby previously, paying Rs50 ($4) rent monthly. I studied up to the school leaving certificate but couldn't ever hope to find a job. Here, I buy cloth from wholesalers and sell it locally. This has helped us repay our debts,' Mrs Dakshinamurthy said. Like her neighbours, her joy centres on the fact that her family now own their own home.

Around 30,000 people have received sites in the first two phases of the Madras scheme, which may be extended this year to a third. Now, 80,000 families have had their existing slum homes improved instead of removed.

d Working with a partner read the article in more detail. One of you note down details of the Bombay development, the other the Madras development.

e Discuss the similarities and differences:
(i) between these two schemes;
and *(ii)* between these two schemes and those in the previous article.

B Work in pairs. Refer to the notes you've made on all the projects and draw up a **table** to display the nature of the various planning processes. In addition, consider also the Peanut Sheller from Section 2, page 6. You should give details of the environment, the scale, size and type of problem involved in each case and the sort of approach adopted to try and rectify it.

You might make your first column like this:

	African village	
Scale	local / small scale	
Type of problem	Lack of good tools	
Approach	discussion → consensus → self help	

When you have completed your table, show it to other pairs and check that your entries are similar to theirs.

C1 *a* You are going the hear part of a discussion with a U.N. housing specialist. As you listen, take notes on:
- *(i)* the nature of the problem he refers to.
- *(ii)* the scale of operation he is considering.
- *(iii)* his view of the approach necessary.

b Now use your notes to add a final column to your table.

c Listen again to the discussion in order to answer the following questions:
- *(i)* Do the opinions of the interviewer and the specialist differ?
- *(ii)* Who is closer to the principles of Appropriate Technology?
- *(iii)* How does the other regard these principles?

Discuss your answers to these questions.

C2 Using your completed table as a source, select two contrasting problems. Write a brief description of these problems, the remedies adopted and the results.

SECTION 4 *LIMITED FUNDS*

Although Appropriate Technology is often comparatively cheaper than other more conventional types of technology, governments still have to make painful choices regarding the allocation of scarce resources as the following activity demonstrates.

SCENARIO Four villages are experiencing various types of problems. They have proposed answers to them but need financial, and perhaps technical, assistance from the State government in order to implement their solutions. To this end they will each make an oral presentation to the State government backed up by plans, maps, estimates of cost, etc. (details below). The State government, however, does not have the financial resources to assist all the projects; indeed it is likely they will only grant assistance to **one**. The State government's choice is a difficult one – all the problems are serious but none is an emergency. The final decision will be based on certain fixed criteria which are explained in full below. However, a coherent and forceful presentation by the villagers of their respective schemes will obviously impress the government and, hopefully, influence the final choice.

This activity requires the class to divide into five groups of roughly equal size, one group to represent the State government and one group for each of the four villages, Hamton, Norby, Westham and Cuddon.

Now study the flow chart which shows diagrammatically the organisation of this activity.

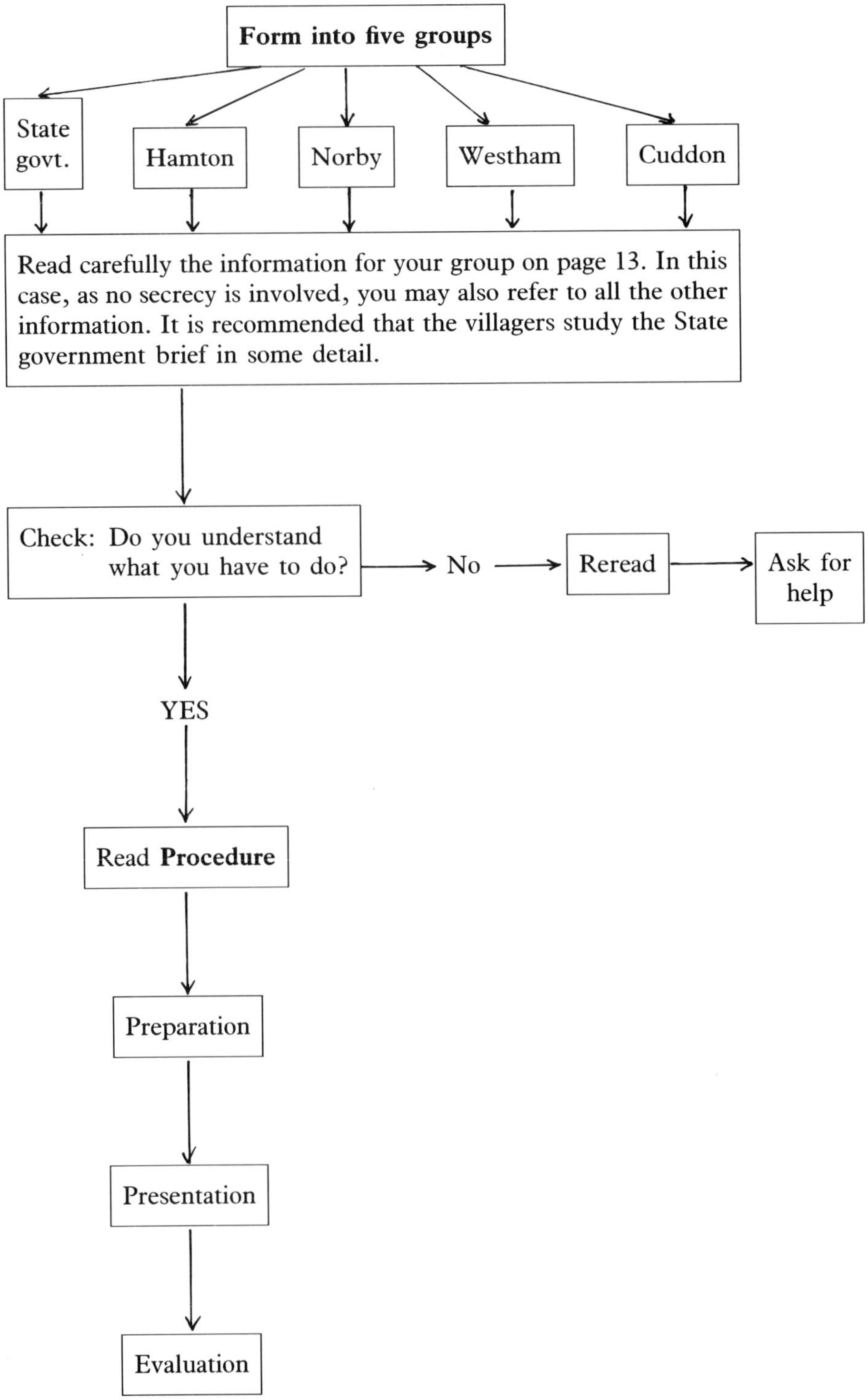

FORM INTO GROUPS Now form five groups as described above and study the following information.

READ INFORMATION The villages

Hamton	Norby	Westham	Cuddon
Your village is located in a coastal area of the state and is heavily reliant on fishing for its income. Unfortunately you do not possess a natural harbour and consequently face the problem of boats being damaged and sometimes lost during excessively high tides.	Your village is in the arid uplands and relies for its income on the staple agricultural crop of your area. Whilst crop yields have been quite good over the years you feel production could be improved considerably by the provision of irrigation facilities.	You represent a group of villages in the remote northern regions of the state. Up until now there has been no secondary school in your area and you feel that this has caused some of your most able young people to study in the south and never return.	Your village is lucky enough to have three well-trained health workers. Unfortunately the lack of an adequate building to house the clinic considerably lessens their effectiveness in successfully treating some patients. As a result certain patients have to be transferred to the National Hospital by ambulance.

State Government

In considering the proposals you will receive from the villages, you should be aware of the following criteria:

1 As your area possesses limited resources for development, high priority must go to the scheme which utilizes available resources in the most efficient way.
2 There exists a considerable gap in income distribution between villages close to the capital and those further away, the former being much better off. You wish whenever possible to help to right the balance.
3 You will favour a scheme which reflects the aspirations of the local people and ensures their active co-operation in its completion.

PROCEDURE

1 **Villagers** Your job is to persuade the state government to approve the scheme you propose. In trying to persuade them you must bear in mind the following:

(i) You should impress the needs of your people upon them to make them more sympathetic towards the villagers' problems.
(ii) You must convince them that you are able to make use of the available resources in a cost effective manner with the minimum of wastage. Although the exact quantities of material available from the government are not given you should specify the estimated quantities you intend to use.
(iii) Your proposal must be feasible from a technical point of view. A series of plans or diagrams may aid the effectiveness of your presentation.

2 **State Government** Your job is to allocate government funds wisely. In order to do this you have to listen to each presentation.

(i) Devise a series of appropriate questions for each village to determine
- the necessity of each project.
- its economic viability.
- its technical feasibility.

(ii) Listen to the presentations and ask your questions.
(iii) Assess the merits of each proposal.
(iv) Decide which proposal will be allocated funds.

PREPARATION

Working in your groups prepare your case thoroughly. In the newspaper articles all five groups will find background information which may be of assistance, particularly in suggesting ways in which you could develop your case and also in showing you clues as to the likely arguments of other groups. Then the groups should come together to make their presentation to the State government.

ARTICLE A

I'll get the grant or stand down! – Councillor

Hamton (Sun.) The outcome of the forthcoming meeting on proposed harbour facilities with State Treasury and Department officials will decide whether long-serving councillor A.T. Phan is to be a contender in next month's local elections.

Phan (62), former leader of the regional Fisheries Union, has served Hamton for over 30 years and has announced that he will not run for re-election if he fails to bring home the government cheque. 'We've been arguing for proper harbour facilities in this village for longer than I care to remember,' says Phan, a stocky sextagenarian wordsmith, 'and this Prime Minister's recent statement on trade, together with the Rural Priority Policy (R.P.P.), seems to me to make this a particularly timely moment to put forward our proposals again.'

Optimistic

Asked if the allocation of funds by the government to nearby Dorsal, Carping and Ikan Baru in the last few years was likely to weaken Hamton's case, Phan replied that he thought these examples would actually strengthen his case. 'Who pioneered the whole discussion on assistance for the fishing industry in the first place? We did. Whose people are the most dependent on fishing and I mean actually going out there in a boat to get the stuff, for a livelihood? Ours. Ikan Baru and the others have natural harbours – they were given cash to set up processing and canning factories. This took a lot of their men off the boats and increased the industry's reliance, in this area, on us to catch the fish. Yet we continue to be expected to operate at great physical risk without a harbour. I'm optimistic that the government can be persuaded to provide what we want and what the fishing industry as a whole needs.'

Overlooked

'We're asking for primary facilities. Carping and Ikan Baru were given very costly, ultra-modern plants. We're not after that – we're talking about basics here. I think we've been overlooked. The government was keen to demonstrate its commitment to the remote areas in the early days of R.P.P. And the new factories were ample demonstration of that. But the time for prestige projects is past. And the Hamton proposal is exactly what R.P.P. is all about: helping to reduce the flow of people from the rural areas to the capital by bolstering local industries.'

Mr. Phan went on to outline the proposals he and his team will make when they meet with ministers on Thursday.

ARTICLE B

R.I.P. R.P.P.? Gov't commitment to Rural Priority Policy under question

by Gaston Hick

Next week's meeting between government department bosses and local government leaders is being regarded in many quarters as a critical one for the future of the Rural Priorities Policy (R.P.P.), introduced 11 years ago.

Against claims from opposition members that the government has lost sight of the original aims of R.P.P. (increasing the prosperity of outlying areas and reducing migration to the capital for employment), Home Affairs spokesman Frank Lee DuBios said that government commitment to helping rural and particularly remote areas to increase their standards of living had never been stronger.

Speaking at the opening of the extension to the University Teaching Hospital at Disheville yesterday, Mr. DuBios said that the opposition's claims were ill-founded and designed to mislead the public.

'The R.P.P. was introduced to help needy areas, but not at the expense of the overall development of the country's trade, nor of the general improvement of living standards nationwide,' he said. The opening of the Hospital extension was a good example of how government funding had to be carefully planned and a great deal of budgeting done before decisions could be made about allocation of financial assistance. 'This hospital is in the capital. We need doctors, we have to train them. That has to happen in the capital because this is where existing resources are centred. Critics who use this new extension as an example of our so-called neglect of other parts of the country are forgetting that aspect of our planning – that we allocate funds according to necessity for the immediate locality firstly, then according to how the proposed project will be of benefit to the nation as a whole and then, obviously, according to how the existing infrastructure can deal with the envisaged project. Yes, there are claims from rural clinics that they are under-resourced. We are continually looking at the possibility of funding health service improvement schemes nationwide. But the health budget can only stretch so far. To the people in rural areas we say, "Be patient. Your concerns are our concerns."'

Future of R.P.P.

Asked to comment on how the 'concerns' of the rural population were being dealt with, Mr. DuBios assured reporters that the government was constantly looking into ways of supporting initiatives from the non-metropolitan area. 'Indeed, we will be in consultation next week with interested parties from these regions in order to gain fresh insight into their needs and to decide on ways of overcoming, or rather – and this is important to note – ways in which we can help them to deal with their problems.'

ARTICLE C

Services 'never better'. Trade 'on the up' – P.M.

While the trade figures of our neighbours describe a steady decline over the last six-month period, our economy continues to thrive. This was announced by the Prime Minister yesterday. 'In this, I would say that the ends have justified the means. By single-mindedly and doggedly pursuing our goal of achieving economic stability, we have made great progress. The key 'traditional' industries show improvement all round, fisheries and agriculture having re-asserted themselves as the foundation of the economy.'

More Cash For Agriculture, Fisheries

In acknowledgement of this, the government will continue to regard these sectors of the economy as a top priority.

'But not at the expense of the overall development of the economy. We need to continue the drive towards modernization and innovation. This is happening in industry and with impressive results.'

'And now look at the services now available to the people. More schools, more hospitals and clinics. Improved training facilities for industrial as well as educational and medical expertise.'

Services Never Better

'Indeed, we say to our critics – when in the past could you ever find the array of services now available? When in the past did the rural areas enjoy such a standard of living as they now do? Was there an urban housing plan before? No. I think this government can honestly claim that services have never been better.'

To suggestions that this general improvement in services obscured the fact that the government's pledge to the rural population as laid down in the Rural Priority Policy had been abandoned, the P.M. issued a categorical denial and reaffirmed his government's commitment to the R.P.P.

PRESENTATION Once each team has completed its preparation, the villagers should present their case to the State government and answer the questions put to them.

EVALUATION The State government should hold a brief meeting, come to a decision and announce the result.

When you have finished, discuss the following questions:

- Which group made the most convincing case?
  – What made it convincing?
- On what basis did the State government make its decision?
- Was their decision fair?
- What important factors (if any) did they neglect?
- Did everyone participate in the discussion?
- Which groups had the most active participants?

SECTION 5 *SELF-HELP*

In this Unit you have practised a number of skills which can be applied to various areas of study. Let's look at some of these again and see how they can be used in your own work.

	Skill taught/ practised	Study techniques	Application
1	DEFINITION →	Stating exactly the meaning, nature or limits of something →	While this would appear to be a simple enough skill, it's sometimes difficult to be exact, comprehensive and concise. Think of some vocabulary items from your main subjects. Write down your own definition of them, then check with: *a* a general English dictionary; *b* a specialist subject dictionary. Try this test of your own ability often, especially with new vocabulary which crops up in your studies. Get together with other students and test each other's ability to produce definitions in the same way.
2	SEQUENCE MARKERS →	Showing the order or chronology in a process or chain of events →	When you describe a process or chain of events, make sure you are able to use as many of the markers we've identified as you can. And when you're listening to a lecture or talk be aware of the importance of these words. After your next lecture, look at your notes and underline all the sequence markers you've noted down.
3	FLOW CHART →	1 Storing your notes on processes or sequences/ events coherently →	When you re-read your notes try to consolidate them and reproduce them in an easily readable way by converting them into, or supplementing them with flow charts. Choose some important processes or sequences from your own field and make flow charts for them.

Skill taught/ practised	Study techniques	Application
	2 As a first-hand note-taking skill →	Try to practise making a flow chart when you're taking notes on processes or sequences. When the lecturer says, for example, *firstly*, start taking notes but don't draw your box. Only when he moves on to the next stage *secondly*, *next*, *after this*, etc. should you box off the first stage. Similarly, use flow charts, as appropriate, when making notes from textbooks, again boxing off only when you're sure one stage is completed.
		Remember always to think carefully about **how much** to include in one box; usually careful attention to the use of '**sequence markers**' in your source will indicate the extent of the information to the written in any one box.
4 DESCRIBING PROCESS →	Giving a written or oral account of how a thing works or happens →	How a machine works, how a mountain is formed, how inflation occurs, how a corporal becomes a field-marshal. These are all processes. Select a topic from your subject textbooks and see how many processes are involved in it. If the authors of the textbook haven't done it for you, research all the steps involved and write up the process.
5 REFERENCE WORDS →	Avoiding unnecessary repetition →	Next time you're listening to a talk or reading a textbook, note down the different ways the speaker or author refers to a particular item or topic. Select an item or topic from your field and write a brief description of it. Try to avoid using its name or title again after introducing it once.

	Skill taught/ practised	Study techniques	Application
6	TEXT ATTACK →	Anticipating content by previewing title, introduction, illustrations (if any), etc. →	You can practise this very easily by referring each day to the newspaper. But try also to use this skill in a more academic context. Look at a textbook you haven't used. Go to the beginning of a chapter – from the title, introductory paragraph and illustrations (or diagrams, graphs, etc.) try to decide what it's about. Now skim the chapter to see if you were right.
		↓	↓
		Skimming the text to establish general topic content. →	You can do this by referring to a subsection from a textbook chapter, an article in a journal or a newspaper article. The speed at which you skim a text may improve if you adopt the following technique: **1** Read the whole of the first paragraph. **2** Read the first sentence of subsequent paragraphs. **3** Read the whole of the concluding paragraph.
		↓	↓
		Scanning the text to discover specific information. →	You already practise this skill every time you consult a TV and radio guide in your newspaper. You can practise this in your studies in the following way: **1** Turn to a new chapter in your textbook. **2** Select a topic you think will probably be dealt with. **3** Scan the chapter to see if the topic is actually referred to.

	Skill taught/ practised		Study techniques		Application
7	SPEAKING TO THE CLASS	→	Addressing the class. Making thorough preparation and reference to your own notes and other textbooks, etc.	→	Ask your teacher if you and your colleagues can make brief presentations of subject-related material to the rest of the class. Try to establish this as a regular class-time feature. Limit each presentation in range and timing. Aim to give short talks of about three to five minutes. Select topics of relevance and interest to your fellow students and/or ask your teacher for his/her ideas on what you could speak about. (Ideas might be 'How a fridge works', 'Some causes of soil erosion', 'The development of television technology' by J. Logie Baird, and the ideas in **4. Describing Process** above, and so on.) As an oral presentation, this activity should encompass **all** the main skills referred to in **1–5** above. Make full use of the blackboard to illustrate what you are speaking about, but prepare suitable diagrams, tables, etc, which are helpful and which can be sketched on the board quickly so that your time in front of the class is properly used to communicate your information.

UNIT 2 · *Arresting stuff!*

SECTION 1 *IT'S NOT REALLY BREAKING THE LAW, IS IT?*

A One of the purposes of law which renders it indispensable to any society is the maintenance of order.

- What do you understand by the term order?
- What would a society be like without order?

Although all societies need laws to preserve order, the exact definition of what constitutes order and the precise nature of the laws needed to enforce it will vary from society to society.

- Why do you think laws vary from one society to another?

Sunday Express Colour Supplement

- What do you think has caused the man in the picture to behave and dress in this way?
- Do you think he represents a threat to order?
- Explain why behaviour of this kind would or would not be acceptable in your society.
- Try to list some actions which are legal in the society you are living in but are against the law in other parts of the world.

B1 Nearly three million British people break the law each year. The vast majority of them do not realise it and very few care anyway. A 200-year-old Act of Parliament makes it illegal to charge admission for watching sport on Sundays. Yet almost every Sunday people do watch and do pay. On the whole the police and legal authorities turn a blind eye to this.

a Why do you think it is against the law to watch professional sport in Britain on Sunday?

b Why do you think the police do not try to enforce the law?

Of course this does not mean that law and order in Britain is breaking down nor would spectators peaceably watching a game of cricket regard themselves as criminals. Nevertheless, it may be seen as a dangerous precedent for 'honest' citizens to believe it is acceptable to break the law.

c Do you think it is dangerous? If so, why?

B2 Look at the following questionnaire. Answer on a separate sheet of paper – as honestly as you can!
– Have you ever been guilty of any of the following offences?

	Often	**Sometimes**	**Never**
a Dropping litter			
b Exceeding the speed limit			
c Riding a bicycle at night without lights			
d Smoking a cigarette in a non-smoking area			
e Taking a coin from a public telephone and using it yourself			
f Failing to pay bills on time			
g Disturbing your neighbours			

B3 The results of any questionnaire must be collected and analysed for some purpose. For the above questionnaire, the purpose is to find out the most law-abiding members of the class!

Form into groups of five or six and discuss your answers. Establish which of the above offences the members of your group committed **often**, **sometimes** or **never**. (It would be useful to elect one member to act as 'recorder' and draw up a data sheet for this information.)

Are there any other technical offences which members have committed? If so, add these to the list from the questionnaire and include the results in your data sheet.

Decide upon a method of presenting the information in tabular form that is acceptable to the whole class.

Ensure that the data collected by all groups is clearly displayed.

B4 Can you agree on an order of 'seriousness' for the offences?

Do you, as honest citizens, feel that committing these offences constitutes a serious and dangerous breach of the law?

What is the difference between a technical offence and a criminal offence?

What would happen if many citizens often committed these offences?

What would happen if most citizens **always** committed them?

What causes citizens (including yourself perhaps!) to commit them?

C It is also important to think about what kind of questions you want to ask and how you are going to ask them. A questionnaire must be designed with care, otherwise the information you obtain from it cannot be used effectively.

C1 Look at the following two styles of asking questions and recording answers: *(i)* and *(ii)* below.

a Which gives you more detailed information?
b Which answers would be easier to show in diagrammatic or table form?
c Which question-type do you think would be easier to administer?
d Which question-type would provide you with the most easily quantifiable data?
e Which question-type would provide you with the most detailed picture of public opinion?

(i) Question: Do you think the implementation of the death penalty for the following crimes serves/would serve as a deterrent?

	Murder			**Drug-trafficking**			**Terrorism** (incl. Hijacking)			**Kidnapping**		
	Yes	No	Don't Know	Yes	No	Don't Know	Yes	No	Don't Know	Yes	No	Don't Know
1st reply		√			√				√			√
2nd reply	√					√	√			√		
3nd reply		√			√			√			√	
4th reply	√			√			√			√		
5th reply			√		√				√			√
6th reply	√				√		√				√	
Total	3	2	1	1	4	1	3	1	2	2	2	2

Total 'Yes' : 9
'No' : 9
'Don't Know' : 6

(ii) Question: Which crimes do you think would occur less frequently if the death penalty were imposed on those who commit them?

1st reply	none
2nd reply	murder, perhaps drug-trafficking
3rd reply	none
4th reply	terrorism, murder, rape, adultery, kidnapping, hijacking, drug-trafficking
5th reply	none
6th reply	murder and terrorism

C2 Working alone, note down which serious criminal offence you believe is most commonly committed in your town/area. (Your response need not be one of the crimes listed above.)

C3 Now divide into groups and identify the **two** offences mentioned most frequently by the students in your group.

Try this exercise:

I have spilled hot coffee on your arm. It burns you because:
A you knocked the jug.
B it is hot.
C I missed the cup.
D you were not wearing sleeves.

You are being asked to distinguish the cause of burning from possible causes of the accident (*D* is neither).

A man steals two TV sets from a warehouse one night. What was his motive?
A He is a thief.
B He needed a TV.
C The warehouse was unlocked.
D He intended to sell them.

In looking at the causes of crime we are concerned with motives.

With the findings from your group, work individually again, using a separate piece of paper, and draw up a table like the one below with the two offences 'chosen' by your group. Try to decide what the three most likely factors are which cause people to commit these crimes. You might think of such motives as: boredom, social group and so on. Enter this information in the 'Cause' sections.

In this exercise, we want to examine not the **incidence** of crime, but its **causes**.

Crime One	**Crime Two**
Cause: 1 2 3	**Cause:** 1 2 3

After filling in the table collate the responses of your group and transfer the tabular data to a bar graph.

Now compare your bar graph with those of other groups. Nominate a member of your group to sketch your graph on the blackboard.
– Did each group select the same crimes?
– If not, why not?
– How wide was the variety of causes mentioned for a particular crime?
– Do you think your results give a reliable indication of wider public opinion?
– If not, why not?

C4 You have investigated the opinions of your class on the causes of crime. Let's now consider the **effects** of crime.

You are now going to find out the opinions of a group of other people by asking them questions about the effects of the two major crimes identified by your group.

You have already examined a question sheet for the causes of crime, now draw up a question sheet to find out the effects of these two crimes.

Discuss in your group what sort of question sheet you should use. You could leave the question open: 'What are the three main effects of (Crime 1)?' Or you could limit the choice, by providing guided responses. When you draw up the question sheet, consider how you will collate the answers.

When you are ready, decide who you will interview and how many answers you will need.

Administer the questionnaire.
a Compile your findings as a group.
b Present them to the rest of the class.

SECTION 2 *WHAT KIND OF PEOPLE COMMIT CRIMES?*

In furthering your studies at university level you will be required to read and comment on the work of writers with whose opinions you do not agree. To do this effectively you must be able to distinguish between **objective** facts and **subjective** opinions.

Unbiased objective writing consists of facts which are uninfluenced by the author's personal thoughts or feelings. A subjective view is more likely to be biased as this will include the author's own opinions on a particular issue.

The question of bias is particularly relevant to any discussion of causes and effects. Whilst effects are on the whole easily identifiable it is difficult to pinpoint causes with the same degree of certainty.

Two or more events may occur at the same time. They may be:
- completely unrelated.
- two or more effects stemming from the same source.
- linked to each other in a direct cause/effect relationship.

A1 *a* Which diagram represents each of these relationships most effectively?

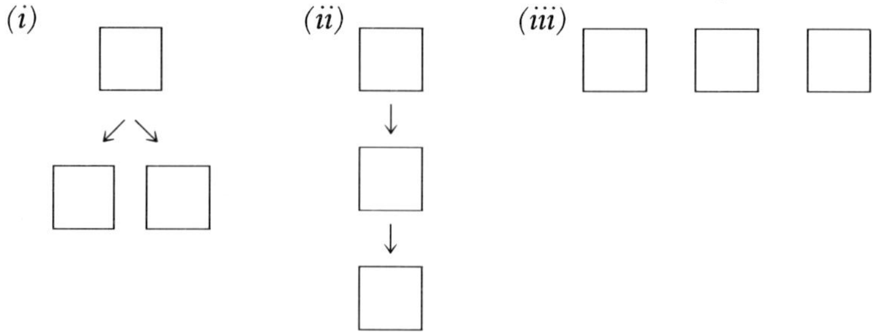

b Match each of the following sentences with the appropriate diagram:
A The 1960's saw rising crime rates, overcrowding in prisons and an increase in prison riots.
B The 1960's saw rising crime rates, rising living standards and the first man on the moon.
C The 1960's saw rising crime rates, overcrowding in prisons and an increase in police recruitment.

Even when statistics seem to suggest that two or more events are directly connected, this is not always the case. Sometimes writers **manipulate** statistics to make their subjective views appear more factually objective.

A2 'Well, it's just what you would expect from that kind of person, isn't it?'

In presenting his views of the causes of crime the writer of the following extracts portrays a stereotype of the 'typical criminal' which is deeply offensive to various groups in society.

a Scan the text to find out which of the following groups of people are discussed by the author.
(i) people living in warm climates
(ii) the unemployed
(iii) women
(iv) the less well-educated

(*v*) strikers
(*vi*) football hooligans
(*vii*) illegitimate children
(*viii*) people who live in cities
(*ix*) drug addicts
(*x*) single people

b Now, in pairs, make brief notes on why the author believes the groups he refers to are likely to commit crimes.

The objective causes of crime may be divided into causes in the physical environment and causes in the social environment. The causes in the physical environment are relatively unimportant, but are worthy of note as showing how many various factors enter into this social phenomenon of crime. Climate and season seem to be the two chief physical factors that influence crime; and in connection with these we have two general rules, abundantly verified by statistics; namely, the ratio of crimes against the person is higher in warm climates than that of crimes against property; and also the ratio of crimes against the person is higher in summer than in winter, while crimes against property are relatively more numerous in winter than in summer. All this is probably an outcome of the effect of climate and season upon general living conditions.

The causes of crime in the social environment are of course much the most important objective causes of crime, and, many students think, altogether the most important causes of crime in general. Let us briefly note some of the more important social conditions that give rise to crime.

(1) Conditions connected with the family life have a great influence on crime; indeed, in as much as the family is the chief agency in society for socializing the young, perhaps domestic conditions are more important in the production of crime than any other set of causes. We have already seen in former chapters that demoralized homes contribute an undue proportion of criminals. It is estimated by those in charge of reform schools for delinquent children that from 85 to 90 per cent of the children in those institutions come from more or less demoralized or disrupted families. Illegitimate children notoriously drift into the criminal classes, while dependent children who grow up in charitable institutions are prone also to take the same course. Domestic conditions also have, of course, an influence on the criminality or noncriminality of adults. This is best shown perhaps by the fact that so large a proportion of criminals in our prisons are unmarried persons. Thus the United States prison census of 1939 showed that 51.9 per cent of all the prisoners were single persons. Statistics from other countries are practically the same. This means that, on the one hand, the family life is a preventive of crime, and on the other that the socially abnormal classes who drift into crime are not apt to marry.

(2) Industrial conditions also have a profound influence upon criminal statistics. Economic crises, hard times, strikes, lockouts, are all productive of crime. Quetelet, the Belgian statistician, thought that the general rule could be laid down that as the price of food increases, crimes against property increase, while crimes against persons decrease. At any rate, increase in the cost of the necessities of life is very apt to increase crimes of certain sorts.

The various industrial classes show different ratios of criminality. In general among industrial classes the least crime is committed by the agricultural classes, while the most crime is committed by the unemployed or those with no occupation. The prison census of 1923 showed that 31 per cent of all prisoners committed that year were unemployed at the time their crimes were committed, or were persons of no occupation.

The investigations of the Wickersham Commission on Law Observance and Enforcement showed that there was a very close connection between unemployment and crime. From forty to fifty per cent of the men admitted to Sing Sing Prison in the year ended February 28, 1930, were found to have been unemployed. Lack of employment seemed especially to conduce to crimes against property, such as robbery, larceny, and burglary. Another investigation in Cincinnati about the same time showed that 40 per cent of all misdemeanor arrests were of the unemployed classes, although it was estimated that the unemployed at that time constituted only 8 per cent of the total population of Cincinnati.

(3) Urbanization and other conditions concerning the distribution and density of the population have an influence upon crime. In general there is more crime, in proportion to the population, in the cities than in the country districts. The statistics of all civilized countries seem to show about twice as great a percentage

of crime in their large cities as in the rural districts.

(4) Educational conditions have undoubtedly a great influence upon crime. While education in the sense of school education could never in itself stamp out crime, still defective educational conditions greatly increase crime. This is shown sufficiently by the fact that illiterates are much more likely to commit crime than those who have a fair education. The prison census of 1923 showed that 10.7 per cent of the prisoners were illiterate, while only 7.1 per cent of the general population twenty-one years of age or over were illiterate. Of major offenders a still higher per cent are generally found to be illiterate.

The defects in our educational conditions which especially favor the development of crime in certain classes are, chiefly, lack of facilities for industrial education, lack of physical education, and lack of specific moral instruction. The need of these three things in a socialized school system need not here be more than emphasized.

The influence of the press and the motion picture as popular educators must here be mentioned as among the important stimuli to crime. The excessive exploitation of crime in the sensational press and in motion picture shows conduces to increased criminality in certain classes, for it has been demonstrated that crime is often a matter of suggestion or imitation. When a large proportion of the motion picture shows are taken up with depicting crime and immorality, it is not to be wondered at that the contagion of crime is sown broadcast in society.

(5) The influence of certain social institutions in producing crime must be mentioned. Here comes in especially the lack of opportunities for wholesome social recreation among our poorer classes, particularly in our large cities. Lacking these, the masses resort to the saloons, gambling houses, cheap music and dance halls, and vulgar theatrical entertainments, while their children have to play in the streets. The influence of all of these conditions is undoubtedly to spread the contagion of vice and crime.

From C.A. Ellwood, *Sociology Principles and Problems*, American Book Co., 1924. Adapted.

A3 If you disagree strongly with an opinion, you should be able provide convincing counter arguments. In order to argue against the views expressed by C.A. Ellwood, you should do as follows:

a Carefully examine the notes you have made and consider which of the author's views you disagree with most.

b *(i)* Why do you think he makes these claims?
(ii) Look for the contradictions and illogicalities in the arguments he uses to justify these views.
(iii) Note down any ways in which he makes use of statistics.
(iv) To what extent do you think the data is used in a valid way to draw the conclusions reached?
(v) What do you think is the difference in meaning between subjective and objective?
(vi) What do you think is the difference between a statistic and a fact?

A4 Provide counter arguments of your own to refute the writer's claims.

A5 Use the notes you have made to write a short paper which critically examines the author's views. This paper should provide the basis for a seminar.

B1 Read the following paragraph and discuss the questions that follow:

A seminar usually involves co-operation among its participants. A particular topic is examined from various points of view and any conclusions drawn from the discussion are expressed tentatively and politely to avoid confrontation. In a seminar, broad generalisations are less appropriate than specific data and examples which are directly relevant to the topic under discussion. The basis for discussion in a seminar is usually provided by the main participants delivering a short paper outlining the principal points that justify the position they seek to adopt.

From what you have read above, can you now express the differences between a seminar and a debate?

How should presenters and participants behave in a seminar?

B2 You will now be required to organise a seminar based on the following topic:

Critically examine C.A. Ellwood's theories of the causes of crime.

A representative from each group should read out their group's paper. Remember to:
– make sure all the points will be clear to your audience.
– stand up.
– speak slowly and clearly.
– make sure everyone can hear you.
– look at your audience, don't just read with your head down.
While a paper is being delivered, members of the other groups should note the key points.

Refer to these notes to determine any points of disagreement between the different groups.

B3 Discuss the criticisms of Ellwood's views. To what extent have the groups avoided sweeping generalisations and false use of statistics?

SECTION 3 *WHY DO PEOPLE BREAK THE LAW?*

A Although it is possible to discuss the causes of crime in general, sometimes expert and layman alike find it difficult to explain certain crimes. Such a crime occurred in Britain in August 1987 when a man ran 'amok' and shot dead sixteen people, including his own mother.

A1 Quickly read through the following article and try to guess what 'Mummy's boy' and 'ran amok' mean.

'Mummy's boy' who ran amok

By Aileen Ballantyne and David Rose

UNTIL Michael Ryan brought the violence of the streets of Detroit to the sleepy, closely-knit community of Hungerford last week he was a man nobody noticed.

All that neighbours remember as particularly remarkable about the polite, shy 27-year-old man, who lived with his widowed mother, was that he kept a formidable armoury of guns in the shed at the bottom of his garden and tended them in the way most people tend plants.

An only child, whose 80-year-old father died two years ago, Ryan was described by one woman neighbour as a 'mummy's boy.' Mrs Dorothy Ryan, who became her son's second victim, appeared to idolise her son, according to Mrs Iris Watts, who worked with her.

Mrs Ryan, aged 63, worked as a dinner lady at the local primary school and as a part-time silver service waitress at the Elcot Park hotel on the outskirts of Hungerford. It was her regular employment which appeared to pay for her son's luxuries.

Brian Meikle, aged 27, a security guard who grew up with Ryan, said that when Michael was a boy his mother used to give him everything he wanted. 'He had the best clothes, the fastest cars and the latest records.' The pattern appears to have continued into his adult life.

Mr Stephen Ballard, aged 30, remembered Ryan at the John O'Gaunt secondary school, where Ryan was finally cornered by police. A few years ago Ryan owned an antique gun shop in Marlborough, but the business closed because of financial difficulties. Since then, Mr Ballard said, Ryan had been unemployed – but the new car he would appear with each year, always with the latest registration plate, appeared to have been purchased by his mother.

She is also thought to have paid for his clothes and guns as Michael's only source of income was from occasional labouring and gardening jobs. Apart from his love of guns the main interest in the life of a man described by all as a loner, appears to have been his Labrador dog, Blackie – which he shot immediately after shooting his mother.

People living near Ryan's home in South View attested to his solitariness and his relationship with his dog. Mrs Sue Swain, whose house was damaged by gunfire, said: 'I used to see him with the dog every evening, going out to the common. He wouldn't offer verbal commands but just clicked his fingers, and the dog would do what he wanted.'

Sometimes, she said, he would go for a drive in the evening in his new grey Vauxhall Astra, but always alone. 'You never saw him with friends. The only one I ever saw him with was his mum.'

Her son Alan, aged 14, told how he and other teenage boys would sometimes kick a football on the common with Ryan and the dog. Alan said: 'He used to shout at kids if they went up his driveway.' The Rambo figure that burst on to the small market town's streets wearing a headband and paramilitary gear and with guns blazing from each hand may have been the man Ryan saw in his fantasies, but there was nothing aggressive or heroic about him in reality.

The fair-haired, bearded Ryan was of medium height and medium build. Mr Denis Morley, aged 65, a self-employed builder who worked with him on a recent job, said: 'I thought he was a wimp. He wasn't the sort to get mixed up in a punch-up. He wouldn't even go up a ladder.'

Ryan was a member of a shooting club in Devizes, Wiltshire, where Mr Andrew Barnard, a partner in the club, said: 'He was certainly not the sort of bloke you would be very conscious of. The most remarkable thing about him is that he was totally unremarkable.'

From Guardian Weekly, Aug. '87. Adapted.

A2 Refer back to the notes you made during the seminar. Could any of the factors mentioned there help to explain Ryan's act?

A3 Discuss with a partner any additional ideas of your own which may suggest what caused the tragedy.

A4 Quickly read the article again and try to predict the most likely effects on government policy subsequent to the disaster.

B Read the following synopsis of an article which appeared a few days later in the same newspaper.

B1 What were the **actual** effects on British government policy?

B2 How closely do they match the effects you predicted above?

The Rambo of Hungerford

The British Home Secretary, Mr Douglas Hurd, has ordered an urgent review of the operation of firearms law and practice in the wake of the Hungerford killings last week when a gun fanatic shot dead 16 people in the small Berkshire town. The BBC and ITV are also expected to have talks on long-term measures to deal with screen violence; both have withdrawn or postponed some violent programmes since the shootings.

Guardian Weekly', Aug. '87.

Not all crimes of violence are committed by individuals. Sometimes they are committed by large groups.

Unfortunately, in recent years English football fans have acquired a reputation for committing acts of violence, in both their own country and the rest of the world.

B3 *a* Why do you think people misbehave at sporting events?
b Do such incidents occur in your own country?

c Why do you think the misbehaviour of English fans attracts such a lot of publicity?

B4 On the tape you are about to listen to, Dr. Foster, an academic with a keen interest in football, is discussing how to deal with the problem of football violence.

a Take notes under **one** of the following headings:
(i) The causes and effects identified by the speaker
(ii) The problems he mentions and the solutions he advocates

b Try to organise your notes clearly. Then:
Exchange them with a student who listened to the tape from the other perspective and use the other student's notes to write a short paragraph on **one** of the following topics:
(i) Discuss the factors that led to the introduction of the Luton town membership scheme for football supporters.
(ii) Examine the effects of the introduction of the 100% membership scheme.
(iii) Identify the problems posed by a rise in football violence.
(iv) How has the introduction of the 100% membership scheme solved the problem of football violence?

c Exchange what you have written with the student whose notes you used and discuss whether you have satisfactorily summarised each other's points.

C In the following editorial the writer is concerned with an issue which emerged in the aftermath of the Heysel Stadium disaster mentioned on the tape.

C1 Identify the problem.

C2 In the underlined sentences in the text the author shows his attitude. In each case pick out the words or phrases which do this. *For example:* 1 properly

---

AFTER more than two years of legal argument, Mr Douglas Hurd has put his signature to 26 extradition warrants against Liverpool football fans wanted by the Belgian authorities as a result of the 1985 Heysel Stadium disaster. Some time this week, therefore, the accused will be flown to Belgium where, after yet further delays, they will eventually stand trial for manslaughter. Any unease at the numbers involved in the extradition and at the length of time which it has taken to bring them to trial clouds but does not outweigh the belief that the
1 26 have been properly treated.
2 The cases have been very thoroughly examined: first, in the investigation of large amounts of video and photographic evidence; second, in the fulfilment of the requirement for our domestic courts to be satisfied of a *prima facie* case against them; third, in the Home Secretary's review, and finally, at one remove, in the procedural challenges which have occupied the courts this year. Proper procedures have been properly invoked.
3 The objections against the extradition are frivolous. Seri-ouscrimeswerecommittedat
4 the Heysel. There is high quality documentary evidence of them which can be put to the test in the courts. Belgium is quite
5 obviously the proper place for
6 the trials. To say that British suspects will not get a fair trial there is simply to display
7 shameful xenophobia. Criminal procedure in Belgium, though different in certain key respects from ours (there will be no jury in this case, for instance), is in no decisive sense inferior. Language problems are everyday matters for courts throughout Europe, and particularly in a bi-lingual country such as Belgium. British lawyers, if the accused want them, have rights of audience in Belgian courts. The claim that the judges will be subject to pressure from public opinion is as true or as untrue of Britain as of Belgium. Of course, the suspects will be far from home. That will be difficult for them and their
8 families. But it is hardly an argument against extradition. And the remand wing in Louvain is almost certainly superior to the remand wing in Wormwood Scrubs where many of the 26 have been held for so long.

None of this is to ignore the possibility of improper considerations in some minds at some stages of the hearings in this country. Mr Eric Heffer has argued that the football authorities have put pressure to extradite, so that the Heysel affair can be finally laid to rest and English clubs allowed back into European competitions. A much more serious thought is that the British Government is operating the policy that one good turn deserves another. Britain is politically predisposed to extradite to friendly states like Belgium, without necessarily always looking at the individual facts, because its overriding concern is to encourage those states to extradite IRA fugitives in turn when Britain wants them back. The irony of the Heysel cases is that they were determined under tough rules of proof which the Government, in its Criminal Justice Bill, intends to abolish. Those rules – particularly the need to establish a *prima facie* case in the British courts before extradition can be agreed – are what guarantee the propriety of the Heysel warrants. They are there to protect the suspect against any temptation of Mr Hurd to succumb to political considerations. By next year, though, those protections will have been abolished.

Guardian Weekly, Sept. '87

D Many people believe that one of the key factors in starting trouble in the Heysel stadium was the excessive consumption of alcohol.

Heavy consumption of alcohol is a problem in many societies. In Britain, for instance, about one million people have a drink problem; 10 million working days are lost each year through alcohol-induced absenteeism; half of all violent crime is committed by people who have been drinking; a third of drivers killed in car crashes are over the legal alcohol limit. The social costs of alcohol abuse in Britain probably amount to over £2 million a year.

The debate over the causes and effects of alcohol abuse in society has sparked off a lot of controversy with many differing opinions being held.

In your studies it will be necessary to consult a range of books. In doing so you must be aware that writers may express opinions or ideas that are inconsistent with your own. Your attitudes to a topic could conflict and the writer's perspective may be different from your own; in other words the way he looks at something may be influenced by experiences which you do not share.

D1 *a* Let's now look at an example. In Text 1 below the writer says:

'Alcoholic beverages and some narcotics have been so productive of antisocial conduct that practically all civilized governments have attempted some form of restriction of their use.'

- According to the writer, what does alcohol produce?
- Which governments have attempted some form of restriction of their use?
- What is the writer's view of governments which have not attempted such restrictions?

b What is the writer's attitude to alcohol abuse in the next sentence?

'If their abuse could be prevented, a large factor in producing crime would be eliminated.'

A He believes it could be prevented.
B He believes it produces crime.
C He believes crime would be eliminated.
D He believes it cannot be prevented.

In both examples, the writer assumes the reader will agree that alcohol abuse produces crime. This is his premise or starting point.

Now read the whole of Text 1. The author's reasoning can be shown in the form of a flow chart:

alcohol → crime → prohibition → enforcement → decrease in alcohol consumption → decrease in crime

We can infer that:

The writer believes that governments which do not restrict alcohol abuse are uncivilised.

We can see that the skill of **inferencing** involves detecting opinions and attitudes of the writer by understanding what he means but does not actually say.

D2 The best way to stop is never to start

Working in groups, read the following extracts and make appropriate inferences.

In 1920 the American government introduced a law which prohibited the sale and distribution of alcohol, known as 'Prohibition'

Text 1

The Liquor Problem and Crime Prevention. Alcoholic beverages and some narcotics have been so productive of antisocial conduct that practically all civilized governments have attempted some form of restriction of their use. If their abuse could be prevented, a large factor in producing crime would be eliminated. In the modern world, this movement began to rise in the eighteenth century after the use of distilled liquors as beverages had been popularized. The whole of the nineteenth century witnessed ineffectual attempts at the solution of the problem. Prohibitory laws were passed in a great number of American states, even before the Civil War, but they were never well enforced. Among English-speaking peoples, the prohibition movement gained great impetus during the early years of the twentieth century, and World War I resulted in an attempt to carry out prohibition of the supply of alcoholic beverages in the United States, Canada, and some other countries. The National Prohibition Law became effective in the

United States, January 5, 1920, and it was at first apparently fairly well enforced and observed, with great resulting benefits in decrease of the amount of alcohol consumed and of cases of public intoxication, and in increase in financial saving for the whole people, especially the working classes.

– What can you infer about the writer's attitude towards the National Prohibition Law?

Text 2

According to the writer, why has drunkenness decreased in these countries?

The Wickersham Commission in their second conclusion also condemned by implication the systems found in Great Britain, France, and Germany. In these countries, the licensing system of private dealers still obtains, with relatively stringent regulations as to the conditions under which liquor may be sold. While drunkenness has decreased in these countries, it seems probable that this decrease is due more to the increased cost of alcoholic beverages than to the restrictions which have been put upon their sale.

– What can you infer about the effectiveness of restricting the sale of alcohol in the writer's view?

Text 3

- *What is meant by 'drink fostered the bootleg trade'? Who was responsible for the increasing level of alcoholism and intoxication?*
- *What was fashionable among the privileged classes?*

Probably the gravest reason for the failure of prohibition in the United States, however, was that the law was tried at a time when there was a general decline in moral idealism among the American people. Obviously, an idealistic law will not be observed by a people who do not possess a great deal of social idealism. These statements are particularly true of our upper classes. It was the educated and privileged classes who in the main led the fashion, borrowed from the customs of European society, of using alcoholic beverages to promote sociability. The fashion of drink in these classes thus fostered the bootleg traffic and at the same time undermined respect for law among the young. Consequently, after 1920, the amount of alcohol consumed by the American people, and the number of arrests for intoxication, as we have already seen, slowly increased.

– What can you infer about the writer's attitude towards the American upper classes?

Text 4

- *Was the prohibition law successful?*
- *Can crime and vice be eliminated?*

The weakness of a prohibition law is like the weakness of any other law that fails to reach the evil which it seeks to remedy. No law will be obeyed until the great majority of the people *want* the law obeyed. It is the task of the school and the church to get the people to want just laws and to want to see them obeyed. The prohibition question and the crime question generally show that the deeper problems of social control fall in the field of morals, religion, and education. No law can be effective until it is backed by the convictions of the great mass of the people; and probably no law should be enacted until it has the intelligent support and will of the people behind it. The failure to eliminate crime and vice from civilized society is not evidence that these cannot be eliminated, but rather that the right way to eliminate them has not yet been followed.

– In the opinion of the author what was the attitude of the majority to the Prohibition Law?

Text 5

Summary. – This chapter may be summed up, then, by repeating that the problem of crime is in no way an insoluble problem in human society, though, perhaps, a certain amount of occasional and accidental crime will always exist. The solution of the problem, as we have seen, only demands that man should secure the same mastery over his social environment and over human nature that he has already practically achieved over physical nature; and the gradual development of the social sciences will certainly make this possible sometime in the future.

– What can you infer about the author's attitude towards the problem of law and order?

Texts from C.A. Ellwood, *Sociology Principles and Problems*, American Book Co., 1924

D3 Remaining in the same group:

a Choose **one** of the following texts and make any appropriate inferences you can.

b Be prepared to explain and justify the inferences you have made to the rest of the class.

c Critically discuss the inferences made by other groups.

Text 6

Drinking patterns are changing, but not always for the better. City lunches are now often as alcohol-free as on Wall Street: yuppies drink more bottled mineral water or low-alcohol lager. Heavy drinking, like smoking, is increasingly concentrated at the bottom of the social scale: in the north, particularly among working-class men, rather than in the south-east and south-west among white-collar workers. And, as with smoking, women persist after men give up. Drinking among women of all classes and in every part of the country is still increasing.

Most disturbing of all, more young people are taking to drink at an earlier age than ever before. A survey by the Royal College of Psychiatrists found that one-third of 13-year-olds drink alcohol every other day; and that half of all accidents involving teenagers can be linked to drink. Other surveys confirm that people are starting to drink at an earlier age than their parents did.

At a conference in Coventry this week, the junior health minister, Mrs Edwina Currie, confirmed that a new inter-ministerial group would co-ordinate a campaign against alcohol abuse. Since one of the government's first pieces of legislation this session will extend licensing hours through the afternoon, the anti-drink lobby remains sceptical.

From the Economist, Sept. '87

– What attitude does the writer of the article have to under-age drinking?
– What can you infer about the British Government's attitude to alcohol abuse?

Text 7

As time goes by, more and more crimes and accidents are caused by drink. In Britain the Government has long been aware of this problem. As far back as 1925 laws to control drinking and driving were introduced. In the 60's the powers of the police were considerably strengthened and far higher penalties and punishments for drunken driving were introduced. The new legislation gives the police virtually unlimited powers to stop and test any driver they suspect of being drunk.

The situation is much the same in America where it has been calculated that alcohol is responsible for more than half of road accidents. The authorities have devised various means of testing a driver's blood but none of them have proved effective as a deterrent.

The underlying reason for this failure of Western governments to solve the problem of alcohol abuse is the strategy they have adopted. Basically it is one of prevention rather than prohibition.

As long as a person remains within the bounds of man-made laws they can destroy their life through alcohol. In contrast Muslims have a divine law which guides them away from touching a single drop of alcohol.

– What can you infer about the writer's attitude towards the introduction of laws on drinking and driving?

Text 8

The statistics clearly demonstrate the problem. Britain with one of the highest levels of alcohol consumption in the world is in an advanced state of moral and spiritual decline. It is a great shame to see such a talented and resourceful people destroying themselves in this way.

Many educated people are aware that alcohol is one of the biggest problems facing their society. They have repeatedly warned society of the danger it is facing. You see we are not just talking about the death of a few thousand people due to alcohol related diseases but the impact on society as a whole.

– What is the writer's attitude towards the people he is describing?

Text 9

Muslims do not believe that a moderate consumption of alcohol is acceptable. Alcohol is habit forming. A person who drinks a glass of beer a day will sooner or later get into the habit of drinking two or more.

When the poison gets into a person's system they may do things that they will later regret. It is no coincidence that a large number of violent crimes are committed under the influence of alcohol.

When somebody regularly drinks to excess they become an alcoholic. One of the saddest sights in today's society is the heavy drinker who boasts. "I can stop whenever I like." The sad truth is that most of these people eventually destroy their careers, families and themselves.

It is plain common sense that alcohol is not suitable for people who claim to be intelligent. As a result all practising Muslims avoid alcohol completely.

Adapted from a recorded interview with Mohd. Ilham bin Abdullah, International Islamic University, West Malaysia

– What is the writer's attitude towards Muslims?

D4 *a* Look at Text 9 again.

– Why do you think the writer uses inverted commas in lines 10–11?
– Do you think the words are his own?
– Do you think he agrees with the view they express?

In academic writing you must distinguish between your own ideas and those obtained from other sources.

– Discuss with a partner the ways in which you can indicate clearly the use of outside sources in your writing.

b The causes and effects of 'Running amok'
The causes and effects of 'Alcohol abuse'

Work with a partner.

Choose **one** of the above for a short article of about half a page in which you will summarise your opinions on the topics.

– In order to decide which points to include re-read the appropriate passages and any relevant notes you have made.

– Make sure you indicate clearly in your article which views are not your own.

c Exchange articles with another pair who chose the same topic.
– Ensure that the opinions they express are accurately attributed.

SECTION 4

This activity takes the form of a company board meeting. It introduces the basic principles followed in formal meetings.

Let's briefly examine the main features of such a meeting:

I **The purpose of a meeting** is to enable those present to exchange information and ideas, to arrive at decisions about what is to be achieved, to agree on how to achieve this, to issue instructions, to solve problems. It is often necessary to **vote** on certain issues and in this case the majority vote wins; where 'for' and 'against' are equal the chairperson will cast the deciding vote.

II **The agenda**, prepared in advance, includes all the points of business for the meeting. It must be detailed and clear. People who will take part in the meeting should be consulted on what they wish to have included in the agenda. The order of the points on the agenda should be arranged logically with related items placed near one another and an overall order of importance of items observed.

AGENDA

O'Hanlon Board Meeting

29th February 10.00am

1. Minutes of last meeting
2. Matters arising
3. Fairchild case
4. Merger with IBM ?
5. Any other business

III **The chairperson** is responsible for preparing the agenda and for deciding whether the objective of the meeting is to **solve** the problems raised or merely to elicit opinions. He/She is also responsible for **leading** and **controlling** the meeting. He/She must introduce each agenda item for discussion and ensure that discussion is relevant. He/she must also ensure that every member of the meeting is allowed to participate. He/she must ensure that each item is concluded with a decision from the meeting on what action, if any, is to be taken.

The secretary does not normally take part in discussion in a formal meeting. His/her job is to assist the chairperson in preparing the agenda and to keep an accurate note of what was said during the meeting. These notes are later made available as **minutes** and are a record of the meeting. Particularly important is that minutes record decisions made and action to be taken.

Note: For the purpose of this activity notes should be taken by the secretary and these presented at the end of the meeting as an **oral summary** of decisions and recommended action. (You may decide that the secretary will also be allowed to take part in the discussion in this meeting.)

PROCEDURE FOR THIS ACTIVITY

- As there are seven roles in this activity, the class should divide into groups of seven where possible. (If this is not possible you may omit one or more roles and proceed with a smaller meeting. Scan all the role briefs first, however, and then decide amongst yourselves which 'character' to leave out.)
- Divide into your groups and read the introduction and the role briefs.
- Decide which role you wish to adopt.
- Meet and discuss your role with people who will be playing the same role in other groups.

INTRODUCTION

Supervisor accused in computer fraud case

Denis Fairchild, a supervisor of accounts employed by the multinational O'Hanlon Corporation, has been accused of embezzling more than $200,000,000 from the firm by putting false vouchers through the main computer, then programming it to issue cheques to fictitious companies he owned. The fraud was discovered when a clerk noticed that one of the cheques was for an unusually high amount.

An emergency meeting of six key company staff has been convened to discuss the embezzlement case and the implications that arise from it.

1 Decide on issues you wish to discuss at the meeting. Be thoroughly prepared with all the statistics, documents and any further information you wish to discuss.
2 Be attentive during the discussion and listen carefully. Do not be influenced by a speaker's personality, attitudes, opinions, status, or his speaking skills.
3 Contribute where necessary. Try to be brief and to the point.

Role briefs

1 COMPANY CHAIRPERSON

You have called a meeting in order to decide what to do about Fairchild and to discuss ways of avoiding repetition of this kind of incident in the future. Your main concern is that those present provide you with a clear overview of the situation so that you can deal with it at boardroom level. You should quickly read through all of the extracts in order to prepare and distribute an agenda for the forthcoming meeting.

2 COMPANY SECRETARY

As company secretary you do not have any voting rights and are not required to take part in the discussion. Your job is to assist the company chairperson in his preparation of the agenda and then to keep a full and accurate record of the matters raised during the meeting. At the end of the meeting you should read out the notes you have recorded in order to gain the consent of all present that they represent a full and accurate record of the proceedings that have taken place. If necessary, amend the notes to take account of comments received.

3 ACCOUNTS DEPARTMENT MANAGER

As an aspiring executive and the head of the department in which Fairchild is employed you strongly believe that firm action should be taken to ensure that others do not follow his example. Read **Extract A** in order to help you justify your stance.

4 PERSONNEL OFFICER

You are a very liberal person and you always see the best side of people. You are determined that Fairchild should be treated leniently and, if possible, allowed to continue working for the firm in some capacity. Under no circumstances do you want the case to be taken to court. Read **Extract B** and try to persuade the board to be sympathetic to Fairchild.

5 LEGAL ADVISER

Your job at O'Hanlon is your first as legal adviser. You therefore lack experience and don't want to commit yourself too strongly to a particular course of action. Although you feel legal proceedings should be instituted against Fairchild you are not sure if the prosecution's case is strong enough. Read **Extract C** and brief the board on the difficulties involved.

6 EXTERNAL CONSULTANT

You are a professor of industrial psychology who believes that most white collar crime could be prevented if an organisation such as O'Hanlon were more caring and sensitive to employees' needs. You are more concerned with outlining the proposals for a major review of policy than the specific details of the Fairchild case. Read **Extract D** and prepare a specific recommendation to put to the board.

7 CHIEF SECURITY OFFICER

You have little interest in why people commit crimes. You are more concerned that the culprits be caught and punished. Read **Extract E** and put forward a proposal to increase the level of security supervision in all areas of the company's computer operations.

When you have discussed your role fully, go back to your original groups and prepare to participate in the meeting.

CONDUCTING THE MEETING

The Chairperson should call the meeting to order (*i.e.* ask for silence and attention) and introduce the first item on the agenda. Do remember that he/she is in charge and must be obeyed. Discussion on the first item will follow, concluding with a decision of some sort and perhaps a recommendation for action to be taken. Point two on the agenda will then be introduced, and so on until all the business has been covered. Then the Secretary will summarise the main points, decisions and action to be taken.

When you have finished, compare your agenda and decisions reached with those of other groups.

– How similar were the agendas and the decisions reached?
– Meet with students who played the same role as yourselves and try to account for the success or failure of the strategy you agreed upon.

Extract A

For most white-collar criminals, crime pays. Embezzlers, pilferers, industrial spies, computer hackers, and other thieves who prey on corporations, government agencies, and nonprofit organizations in nonviolent ways can feel reasonably secure in thinking that the odds are in their favor. They'll probably never see the inside of a jail cell. Most of their crimes will go undetected for years – or forever. Those whose actions are uncovered usually are not prosecuted, and the conviction rate for most white-collar criminals is negligible.

Part of the problem lies in our current systems of legal enforcement and prosecution. Only 5 per cent of all white-collar crime cases end up in court, and less than 1 per cent of those convicted of these crimes serve more than one year in jail. But as least as much of the blame for today's epidemic levels of financial loss lies with organizations that have been lax in their security efforts, or refuse to admit that employee theft, vendor fraud, computer crime, and similar skulduggery might be cutting into their bottom lines.

Ignoring the problem won't make it go away. Because most white-collar crime goes undetected, estimates of its magnitude vary widely, from $40 billion to over $200 billion. One computer fraud alone cost investors $1 billion. Shoplifting and pilferage by employees account for 15 per cent of retail prices, according to the U.S. Chamber of Commerce. The National Office Products Association estimates American businesses lose at least $50 million a year to office supply scams. Insurance fraud is increasing, with annual losses to the industry of $4 billion – which increases both commercial and personal premiums. The average loss a bank suffers from embezzlement or fraud is $42,000, and 83.5 per cent of all bank losses are attributed to internal fraud. Significant increases in the costs of fuel, food, and housing have been blamed on corporate price-fixing. Bankruptcy frauds, tax swindles, and securities violations cost the U.S. economy billions of dollars each year. And in one American city, bribery and kickbacks for government contracts reportedly have increased local taxes by 40 per cent.

A National Priority

According to Special Agent Lane Bonner of the Federal Bureau of investigation, the agency is so concerned about this epidemic that white-collar crime investigation is now one of its four 'national priorities,' along with organized crime, counterintelligence, and terrorism. In fiscal year 1984 alone, FBI agents were involved in 19,800 investigations of government fraud, public corruption, union corruption, and financial crime. These investigations resulted in 3,490 felony convictions, 603 misdemeanor convictions, and 356 'pretrial diversions,' or alternative sentencing programs. Over $10 million in fines were collected; $450 million in missing funds and property were recovered; and an estimated $513 million in losses were prevented. And in 1983, 19 per cent of the bureau's agents were involved in white-collar crime investigations, and 44 per cent of all of its convictions were in these cases.

No organization is immune to criminal acts, whether they are committed by employees, vendors, contractors, or outsiders. The victims of white-collar crime, like their predators, are an incredibly diverse lot: multinational corporations, 'mom and pop' stores, charities, manufacturers, storage and warehousing operations, religious groups, and governmental bodies. A prominent lawyer embezzled millions from a major corporation. A payroll clerk in a charity for retarded children managed to rob the organization more than 70 times by falsifying business records. And a $10,000-a-year clerk in a federal agency stole $800,000 from payments to a city for building a subway system by altering vouchers. More than 50 banks and many savings and loans have gone under due to fraud. One surprising victim of stock fraud was the Vatican, which lost millions.

The criminals range from disgruntled shipping clerks to greedy executives to dishonest computer consultants. In a way, 'white-collar criminal' is a tag that refers more to *modus operandi* and financial impact than to actual job occupations or social class. White-collar crime almost always is nonviolent, committed in secret or by deceit or concealment, and usually involves much greater amounts than such traditional crimes as armed bank robbery or kidnapping. While the average bank robber takes only $15,000 per heist, a computer-wielding crook can expect to steal an average of $400,000 per crime. A bank robber may have to hide for months or years, pursued by the police and FBI, and finds his face on wanted posters across the country. The average computer crook faces only a one-in-one-hundred chance of even having the crime discovered.

The victims of these crimes are often unaware that they've occurred. But their impact can be incredibly widespread, sometimes affecting millions of shareholders, employees, and consumers. White-collar felons have the same kinds of goals as other criminals: money, property, tax-free income, unfair competitive advantage, or free services. Many of them have middle- and upper-class backgrounds and college educations; others are professionals or clerks with computer access to an organization's mainframe. The criminal may operate alone, in collusion with other employees or confederates, or may form a dishonest partnership or corporation for the sole purpose of defrauding and robbing others.

Pilferage and theft

According to a *Security Digest* report, employee-related thefts accounted for $13 billion in 1978, and as much as 40 per cent of all employees may be involved in theft of products, time, or services. (Again, all such figures are inexact, as they are extrapolated from *known* crimes.) In some industries, such as freight shipping and airport cargo handling, employee thefts are widely believed to account for 80 per cent of all losses. Retail stores also experience high shrinkage levels; when the Federals Department Stores chain went out of business in 1975, many blamed the collapse on internal losses. Not only goods and materials are stolen, however. Employees and vendors steal time and services by putting friends or relatives on company payrolls, padding overtime records, making false claims on travel expense forms, charging for services not rendered or goods never delivered, changing high-risk customers credit ratings for kickbacks, and creating false credit accounts. Simple pilferage – for example, when a sales clerk rings up a $200 sale as one for $100, or stealing from inventory and falsifying the records – is rampant in many industries. Many companies and organizations consider pilferage an insoluble problem, and write off shrinkage costs by boosting consumer prices as a matter of course.

Thus, the cost of employee theft is passed on to everyone who buys products or services in America.

Extract B

Why people steal

Because they need the money, right? Not always, but that's usually the right answer. Security expert Norman Jaspan says employees' motivations for theft and fraud are not limited to greed. Others include:

An urge toward punishment. Employees may commit blatant, senseless acts as a way of 'crying for help.' They continue to steal when they're under suspicion, or take money or property when others are watching them. They may be in deep trouble in their private lives and need a crisis to break out of an unbearable situation.

Spite and sabotage. Employees who feel frustrated or cheated by large, seemingly faceless bureaucracies often will commit crimes against them. A disgruntled employee may have been passed over for promotion, given additional responsibilities with no pay increase, or denied adequate resources to do the job. Malcontents are not always obvious; they are often smiling, 'loyal' employees seeking revenge on the sly. These workers have called in bomb threats to their workplaces, tampered with computers, set fires, and even dropped sleeping pills in their supervisors' coffee.

Threatened status. If an employee's status as a successful worker and family provider is threatened, as in a recession or a salary freeze, he or she may resort to theft or fraud to maintain his or her income and lifestyle. Corporate cultures sometimes enforce fraudulent behavior by emphasizing 'winning' and reaching unrealistic quotas and inventory figures over maintaining ethical behavior.

The self-effacing egotist. That generous employee who always helps coworkers, raises money for charities, and so on is probably on the level. But some go too far, using company funds to help those *they* see as needy. One New York City plant manager felt such paternal responsibility for his immigrant factory workers, he padded the payroll and used unclaimed paychecks to help 'his people.' The company didn't appreciate his generosity and gave him the boot. Self-effacing egotists often go to great lengths to cover crimes, sure they're motivated by 'higher causes.'

Love and sex. When employees have extramarital affairs, they usually need more money to finance their new flames. By breaking the taboo of cheating on a spouse, an employee may feel more willing to break other taboos. Affairs are especially dangerous when both lovers share an employer – one may act as the other's accomplice in theft, industrial espionage, or falsifying records. Security experts report that many criminal investigations expose these unhealthy relationships, often leading to disgrace, divorce, and sometimes suicide.

An equally dangerous spur to theft and fraud is an atmosphere of 'acceptable deception.' If company policies are so complex and unwieldy that they prohibit people from doing their jobs if followed to the letter, they add to the feeling that 'It's okay to bend the rules – just don't get caught.' If top management and supervisors wink at infractions of unreasonable regulations, the message is sent down the organizational chart that no one need be too concerned with playing by the rules. 'People are basically honest when they come to work for you – all too often the workplace becomes the school for dishonesty,' according to Jaspan. He sees dishonesty in a company as a 'barometer of the quality and integrity of supervision,' and credits lax attitudes and controls by management with encouraging dishonesty. In fact, he reports, supervisors and executives are the most dangerous class of employees: 'Of the more than $100 million in business dishonesty uncovered by our firm last year, these trusted employees accounted for more than 60 per cent.' Other major causes of losses are kickbacks, conflicts of interest, falsification of labor vouchers, improper disposal of scrap, and damaged materials.

Extract C

Selling the case to government prosecutors

If you can't sell the case, the thief will walk free. You can sue, or fire the culprit (if he/she is an employee), but there is little else you can do. In order to influence the prosecution to take your case, select an attorney willing and able to handle computer-related prosecutions. Outline the facts and evidence in simple, layman's terms. Prepare visual aids, such as graphs or charts which outline the specifics of your case, if possible. And ask for a personal meeting with the prosecutor – you will find it easier to answer questions and demonstrate commitment to the case in a face-to-face meeting.

The difficulties inherent in a civil suit are great. Although more and more states are enacting computer crime legislation, legal implications are still complicated and changing. The Better Business Bureau advises potential plaintiffs to determine damages *very specifically*, so that the suspect will be charged under the most appropriate local, state, or federal law.

Unwitting complicity

Security consultants report that many honest employees won't speak up about their coworkers' crimes. The culprits may be friends or acquaintances, and they may be afraid of off-the-job retribution for 'squealing.' Supervisors are often subject to the 'club ethic,' which prevents them from questioning or suspecting other high-ranking employees – although these are the levels most likely to be involved in major offenses. Others are hesitant to investigate theft thoroughly because they simply want to avoid an unpleasant duty. They know they'll have to fire someone if they find the thief, and perhaps will have to testify against the person. Dr. William Terris, director of psychological services for London House, a security consulting firm, reports, 'Most supervisors will admit, when asked anonymously, that they are sure one or two of their employees are stealing.' They also may be afraid that an employee they like or respect is dishonest, and people sometimes prefer to avoid unpleasant truths. Some dismiss theft by rationalizing that the company's insurance will cover it – forgetting that each theft contributes to higher corporate premiums. 'We'll just pass the cost on to the consumer' is another standard line; this makes the company's products and services less competitive and cuts into the bottom line.

Family owned businesses, especially small ones with ingrown managements and 'all in the family' atmospheres, often have casual attitudes toward parts and product theft. In one case, a trusted employee of a pipe organ company managed to steal enough parts over several decades to build and sell 130 organs to customers and pocket the money. Unless top managers seem concerned about materials and inventory leaving the business illegally, the other employees won't consider it a high priority. Small firms are in a sense at greater risk because one big theft could bankrupt them, but it's easier to track down and catch a thief (or thieves) if the number of suspects are limited. Mergers and acquisitions are also a pressure point for losses to employees. Frustrated or angry employees of a company taken over by another may decide their loyalty doesn't extend to the new management.

Today's corporate and governmental managers and supervisors can't afford to ignore employee theft and fraud. They are under constant scrutiny by the public, the press, other executives, stockholders, boards of trustees, and others. Emphasis on streamlining costs and increasing productivity means that employee theft is no longer a reasonable 'cost of doing business.' Laventhol & Horwath's Rockhill notes that more internal crimes were exposed during the recession of 1981–1983 because of the rigorous financial controls necessitated by cost-cutting. Today most companies and organizations have tighter controls, but the *amount* of the average theft is higher. He cites a typical case in which an employee embezzled $100,000 to $200,000 per month for 18 months.

There are many problems with bringing criminals to justice in data-related cases. First, prosecutions are still relatively rare, though increasing, and evidence is often circumstantial at best. If the theft is carried out electronically, there may be no physical evidence at all. Second, enforcement of laws concerning theft of confidential information is lax, and laws vary from state to state, nation to nation. (Often, a company has only civil recourse to regain the value of the stolen information, as the employee or industrial spy may be only criminally liable for the theft of a sheet of paper on which the information was written. If the thief used a camera, he may only be liable for illegal entry.) American law is starting to catch up with industrial spies, but it will be years until it has the teeth necessary to make the punishment fit the crime. Companies often shy away from taking legal action against thefts of confidential information, for fear of adverse publicity and possible loss of confidence in the management by shareholders.

Extract D

One effective way to keep criminals out of the workplace is carefully to screen all job applicants. Simply checking references is a start; thorough interviews and the use of psychological 'integrity tests' approved by the American Psychological Association is another wise step. London House's Personnel Selection Inventory, for example, has been found statistically valid in predicting dishonest behavior by applicants, according to Dr. Terris. (He points out that 'more and more jobs don't require great skills, but do require integrity.' Young, relatively unskilled workers now have access to and responsibility for expensive merchandise and large amounts of cash, but are paid low or minimum wages.)

The roots of crime

Getting at the roots of crime is a tough job. But only by creating a corporate culture that values integrity and enforces security can losses to internal theft and fraud be brought under control. Jaspan recommends five ways to create and maintain a healthy, honest organizational climate:

Estimate employee cabablities and set reatistic performance standards. Setting unrealistic performance goals leaves employees with a choice between failing and resorting to dishonest measures. Many employees have been forced to manipulate sales figures to satisfy top management. This only ends up costing the organization money, as the company then pays taxes on nonexistent profits.

Don't just announce operating rules for security; communicate them. Enforce the rules, make sure all levels obey them, and make sure they are properly understood by everyone.

Be unpredictable in establishing and enforcing controls. Spot checks are very effective in uncovering theft, as is introducing occasional deliberate errors to test the system's controls. Let employees know that such tests can occur any time, without warning.

Maintain uniform policies. Don't show favoritism or use double standards in judging or supervising favored employees. (This is especially true in family-owned businesses.) Favoritism ruins morale and lessens respect for management procedures.

Measure work output and evaluate employee performance regularly. Employees need and want to know how they're doing and what management thinks of their productivity. Supervisors have the responsibility to let them know.

Jaspan adds, 'responsibility for the integrity of a company and its employees begins and ends with the chief executive . . . No one else can play a greater role in setting the moral tone in which business is conducted.'

In the end, the most effective solutions to the epidemic of employee theft and fraud will not come from state-of-the-art technological advances and leading-edge management theories, but from the application of common-sense security policies and a work environment that supports and rewards honest behavior.

What Managers can do

Managers need to take strong, aggressive steps to coordinate security policies and procedures, and top officials need to realize that security should be considered as important a function as strategic planning or financial controls. It is imperative that managers study white-collar crime and criminals and understand the many ways an organization can be victimized. Yale's Wheeler points out: 'We have tended to treat white-collar crime as a homogenous category; it actually has the complexity of all other forms of crime. We have to look at the specific dynamics in each area.' He also cautions that, with the growth of large bureaucracies, mid-level managers have control over huge amounts of money and inventories – and are often tempted to steal because of the tremendous disparity between their salaries and the amounts they're handling at work.

The golden rule of security is separation on duties: Never let one person have responsibility for a whole function such as approving payments, inventory, or accounts receivable. No matter how long the person has worked for the organization, no matter how 'nice' he or she is, if the opportunity for theft is present and the employee has a strong enough motive, a theft is likely. It is essential to have outside accountants thoroughly audit the company's financial records at least quarterly – many frauds and thefts are committed with the aid of staff accountants or bookkeepers. If a loss is discovered, insist on an 'inventory of exposure' to uncover the full extent of the theft, document how it was committed, recover the maximum amount possible from the thief's fidelity bond, and establish controls that will close up the security gap in the future.

In his book *Mind Your Own Business* (Prentice-Hall, 1974), security consultant Norman Jaspan warns of five false assurances of safety that managers should *not* trust:

1. Don't try to justify *some* employee theft as a 'cost of doing business.'
2. Don't believe in 'foolproof' security methods.
3. Don't assume that your company's team spirit will ensure the loyalty of all your employees.
4. Don't assume that a long-time friend or employee would never steal from the company.
5. Don't assume uniformed guards are uniformly trustworthy. (Many outside security guard services hire employees at minimum wages with no background checks, no real experience.)

Jaspan reports finding cases of employee dishonesty in 50 per cent of the systems surveys and inventory control projects his firm conducts.

Extract E

Taking a byte out of crime: some guidelines on computer theft prevention

BY SALLY J. BLANK

Business computers have lent a pernicious sophistication – even a glamor – to white-collar crime in its myriad forms. We hear awe-in spiring stories of slick data processing bandits who embezzle fortunes at the touch of a button, and then publish spectacular memoirs from their minimum-security cells – or their Swiss retreats – to the shock of the business world.

But when you look at the hard figures of computer crime, they are anything but glamorous. The theft of information – committed more often than not through a computer – costs us as much as $20 billion a year, reports the National Institute of Justice. And where the average bank robbery pulls in a mere $15,000, the average computer theft nets a neat $400,000, and can be committed in less than three milliseconds.

Such efficiency is enhanced by incredible post-crime odds. According to August Bequai, white-collar crime expert and author of *How to Prevent Computer Crime* (Wiley, 1983), the likelihood of a computer crime being discovered by the authorities is one in a hundred. Technological advances grow at a rate leaps and bounds ahead of law enforcement's ability to keep up, says Bequai. And hard evidence is a scarce commodity in computer capers, where a thief can cover his or her tracks with the touch of a button, making prosecution very difficult for victimized companies.

What, then, can management do to protect itself against such costly rip-offs? Data security experts all cite four main activities for employers and managers: keep your eyes open and know the danger signals; install and maintain strict prevention measures; know how to effectively investigate possible crimes in-house; and know what laws might apply, if worse comes to worst and you must 'sell' your case to government prosecutors.

Warning signals

'Several red flags can signal alert managers that a fellow employee could be a "wolf in sheep's clothing,"' says Louis Scoma, founder and CEO of Houston-based Data Processing Security, Inc., which has aided over 650 companies with their computer security systems since 1970. Consider the following:

Does one of your employees consistently come in early and stay after hours – with no visible results from the extra hours of work?

Have you recently fired an employee who had access to sensitive information? Do you have any such workers on staff who are disgruntled with the company for any reason?

Do any of your employees with access to sensitive data tote personal microcomputers to and from the office in order to do 'extra work'?

Did an employee you transferred from headquarters to a branch office come back to 'clean out his desk' or 'visit old friends' even though he knew the security codes had been changed?

Has your company experienced a recent increase in data processing needs, while you have not upgraded your security system to accommodate the change?

'If you have answered yes to two or more of these questions,' says Scoma, 'double-check your security system and the people responsible for keeping it intact. If you don't, you could be headed for high-tech trouble.'

An ounce of prevention

According to the Better Business Bureau, the vast majority of computer crimes are preventable. Managers must be aware that technology creates myriad opportunities for crime, and that installation of computer equipment and installation of security measures should go hand in hand. Although the following measures may seem like common sense, consider them in light of your company's own practices. How many are fully followed?

Employee hiring. Conduct thorough background checks on all potential EDP employees. Check with former employers; get references – both professional and personal. Verify technical skills, and check credit histories.

Controlling access to facilities. Maintain a log book with times and names of all who have access to the computer facilities. Allow only employees who work with the computer to sign in. Confirm and verify any service calls, and have a company employee accompany any technician to the worksite.

Physical security. Separate computer facilities from other departments, in a secure, isolated area with few windows or doors, adequate lighting, secure locks, and, if possible, a security guard at each entrance. Provide the appropriate personnel with proper identification that can be verified at the entrance, such as photo or fingerprint IDs.

Protective devices. Take advantage of all the security devices built into the computer system. Have the company that sold or leased you the equipment explain how password rotation, security codes, and code scrambling de-

The average computer theft nets $400,000, but most computer crimes are preventable.

vices can control access. Electronic security, such as closed-circuit television and sound-sensitive listening devices, might also be worthwhile investments.

Computers can 'stall' after wrong passwords are entered, disconnect after a certain number of wrong guesses, record attempts to penetrate, and even trace phone calls. Take advantage of these features.

Storage procedures. It is essential to have a duplicate set of all vital tapes, software, and company data stored in a secure, isolated storage space accessible to only a few top EDP executives.

Audits. Conduct periodic security checks both internally and independently. Many auditing firms now will attempt to defraud your company's system, to determine whether security is sufficient.

'Keeping in mind that some computer crimes are so sophisticated that they may take months, even years, to detect and unravel, management should be constantly on the alert for possible indications of wrongdoing,' warns the Better Business Bureau.

Investigating in-house

Your suspicions are aroused. What now? Management should consider several preliminary investigative issues. 'By simply learning how to identify and analyze these criminal acts,' asserts August Bequai, 'management can assist in the investigation and prosecution of the computer criminal.' Bequai's basic investigatory steps require managers to:

Ascertain, before anything else, whether a crime has indeed been committed. This is not always easy to do, and you should consult your legal department.

Attempt to identify the nature and type of the illegal act (or acts) you are dealing with. Did it involve theft of property, data, or money? If it involves physical damage to the system, determine if it is sabotage, vandalism, or merely an 'act of God' (a natural phenomenon).

Determine the degree of technical know-how needed to pull off the caper. This limits your pool of suspects: The more sophisticated the crime, the smaller the suspect pool.

Determine possible motives for the crime. These can include revenge, industrial espionage or sabotage, simple (or not so simple) pranks, and financial need, among others.

Identify, record, and safeguard all evidence. Do not misplace, damage, or destroy it.

Always record any initial interviews you may have with potential witnesses or suspects. If you can, make transcripts of all statements and have the witnesses/suspects sign them in front of impartial witnesses. Keep these in a very safe place.

Review past personnel records of suspects to determine if they have a history of such problems. Also review all prior instances of crime at the workplace. Determine and detail any similarity between the criminal acts.

'Determine the impact of the illegal act on your organization's viability, financial health, and share of the marketplace,' Bequai advises. The assessment of the situation 'should be meticulous, factual, and in line with the above basic investigatory principles. If it is, it will prove of great value to the police.'

From *White Collar Crime* by Rod Willis, Management Review, Jan. 1986. Adapted.

SECTION 5 *TAKING THE LAW INTO YOUR OWN HANDS*

In this unit, you have been practising the skills shown in capitals below. It is possible to use these skills every time we open a newspaper or listen to a discussion. However, these skills can be made more useful to you by extending them into your own subject area.

Skills and techniques	Task
1 Collect and analyse information – draft a questionnaire – collect and analyse results – present results in a tabular diagrammatic form	Think of a problem about which there has been some disagreement among experts in your subject area. – Conduct a survey of the causes. – Evaluate the solution the experts propose. – Prepare a short report outlining the causes of the problem and justifying the solution you agree with.
2 Expressing opinions – presenting your opinions in a clear and reasoned way – avoiding pitfalls – avoiding manipulation of statistics – avoiding undue bias	– Deliver your report to the rest of the class. – List the various sources you used to compile the report and make them available to the other students.
3 Identifying bias – subjectivity/objectivity – mixing opinion with fact – questionning premises and basis of arguments **4 Inference** – what is implied, but not stated in the writer's attitude the writer's perspective	– Listen to the other presentations, make notes of any points where you feel the presenter is biased or where he uses statistics to his own ends. – Reread the notes you have made. What can you infer about the writer's attitude which may account for the bias? – Examine the sources the presenter used and decide which ones influenced him most.

UNIT 3 · *A question of power*

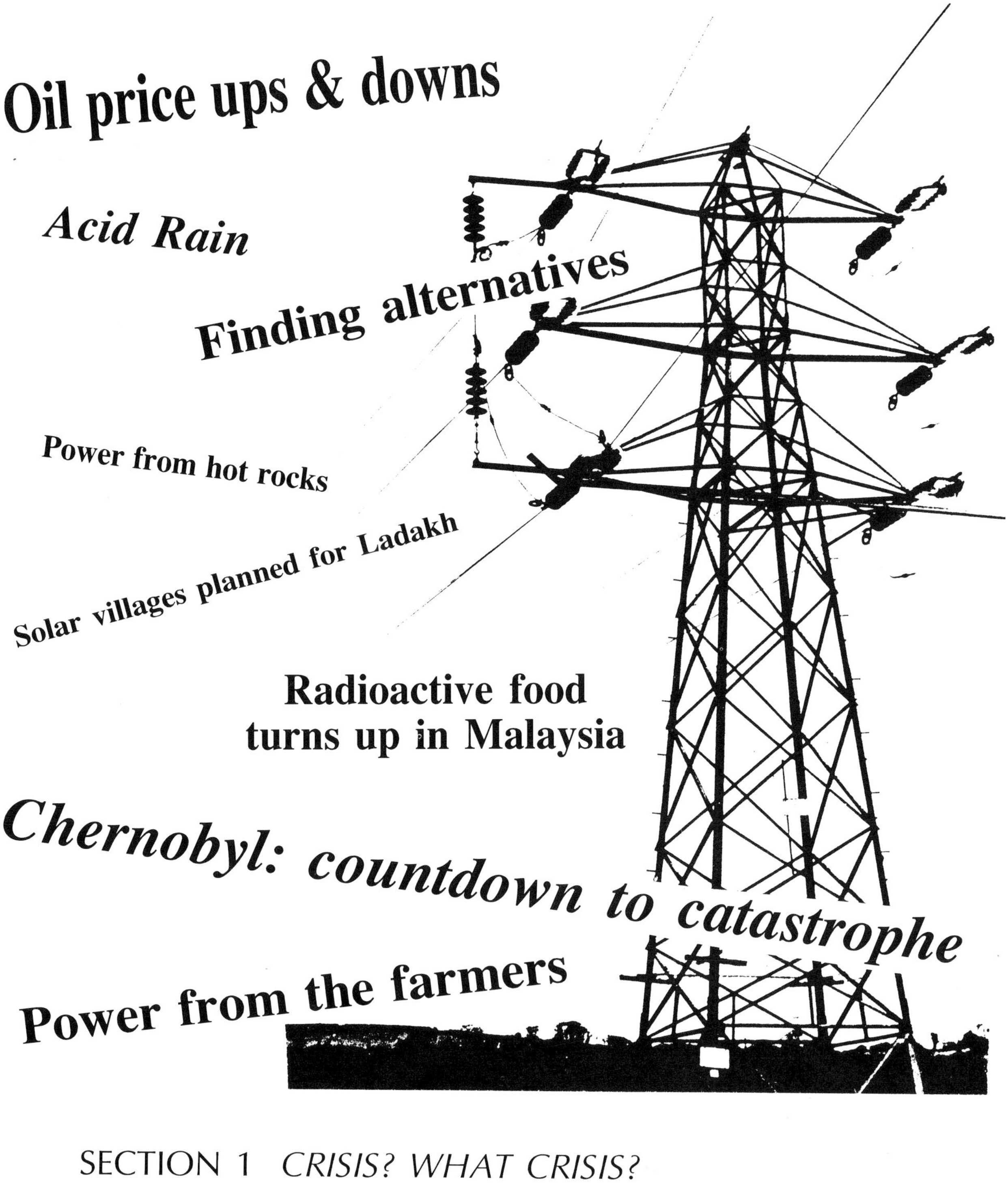

SECTION 1 *CRISIS? WHAT CRISIS?*

A How much do you know about energy?

Discuss these questions and note down your answers.

1 What sources of power are used in your country in order to generate electricity?

2 Choose the three main sources and decide on their advantages and disadvantages.
3 What do you think will be the most common sources of power in the future?
4 If these sources are different from the present most common sources, explain why.
5 Do you foresee an energy problem in the future?

B An expert's opinion

B1 You are going to listen to an expert talking about the world energy situation. As you listen mark on your notes any points which you have already listed.

B2 How does the speaker's assessment of the world situation compare with the position in your own country?
Discuss this question with other students, referring to your notes.

B3 The speaker mentions some very important background information concerning the energy question. In this unit you are going to be considering this question, so this information may be useful to you. Therefore you might like an opportunity to make notes on what is said.

A talk or discussion can usually be divided up into a number of main areas. Identifying these areas may be difficult sometimes. However, when you come to use your notes again, it certainly helps if you have organised the information under a series of headings.

a What do you think the main headings of this talk could be? Compare your answers with other students.

b Listen again and check that you are satisfied with your list.

C Taking notes – Two approaches

How you take notes is a personal decision. Below are examples of two possible approaches.

Which one is closest to your style of note-taking?

What differences are there between the two styles below?

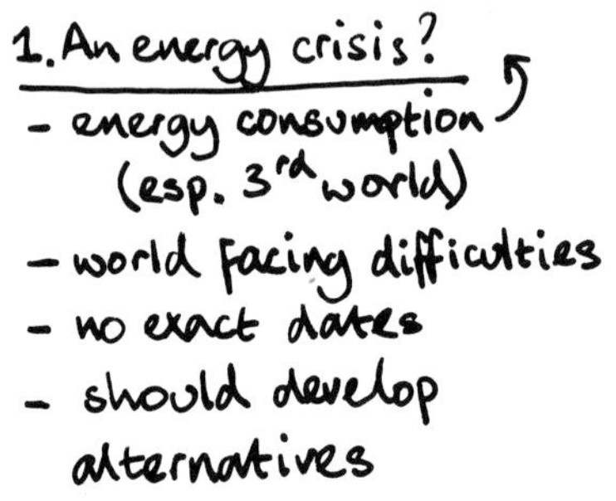

Outlining
This approach shows the importance of the main areas by using underlining, numbering and indentation.

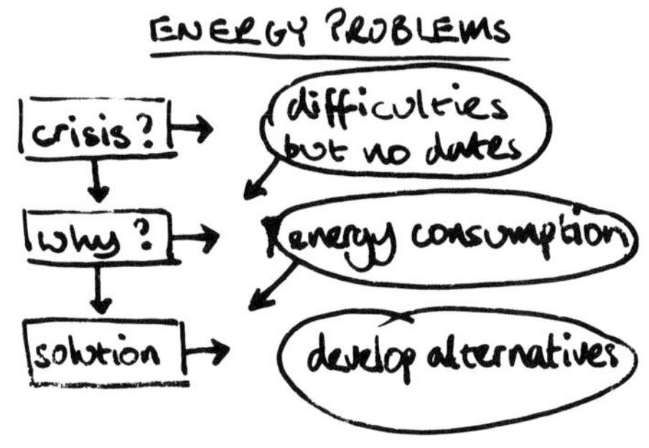

Using key words
This presentation of notes can help you to memorise, especially if you have a better memory for pictures than for words.

C1 Listen to the first part of the talk, studying these notes at the same time. Do you agree that all the important information has been included?

C2 Which style of note-taking do you prefer?

Listen to the rest of the discussion and continue the notes using that style.

C3 Compare your notes with a student who used a different system. Is it clear in both sets of notes:
- what the main headings are?
- what the sub-headings are?
- which points are inter-linked?

If not, how can this be made clearer?

SECTION 2 *SOURCES OF RENEWABLE ENERGY*

Whether or not our conventional sources of energy are running low is a matter of controversy. In any case, for a number of reasons there has been an increase in research into renewable forms of energy in recent years. In this section we are going to take a closer look at four of these: **tidal, geothermal, hydro** and **solar** energy.

A

B

C

D

E

F

G

A1 The power of water

From the pictures on page 47, can you identify the sources of power represented?

The title on page 47 indicates that these are all renewable sources. Can you imagine what this means?

A2 Pictures E and F on page 47 show a hydro-electric power station and a tidal barrage respectively.

How is electricity generated in each case?

Does one have any advantages over the other?

A3 Read through the text below and check your conclusions.

A comparison of hydro-electric and tidal power

In addition to the established energy sources such as gas, coal, oil and nuclear, there are a number of other sources that we ought to consider. Two of these are hydro-electric and tidal power.

These two sources are similar in that they are both renewable. However, hydro-power is more widely used then tidal. In fact, a substantial amount of electricity is already produced in HEP stations world-wide, whereas tidal stations are still in the very early stages of development.

As far as geographical location is concerned, HEP schemes are to be found on lakes and rivers, while tidal schemes are constructed only in estuaries where tidal variation is great. Unfortunately these are few in number. At present HEP stations are found mainly in Norway, Canada, Sweden and Brazil, whereas tidal plants are in operation in France, USSR and China.

As regards capital outlay, both require very high investment. On the other hand, generating costs are quite low in both cases. In fact, a large-scale HEP plant is capable of ¦ roducing power more cheaply than conventional sources, such as coal, oil and nuclear plants. Tidal power also compares favourably with nuclear and oil generated electricity, in terms of production costs. Like HEP stations, tidal barrages have a long life-expectancy. It is estimated that they can operate for over 100 years. With respect to continuity of supply, tidal stations differ from HEP schemes in that they often can only supply power intermittently. HEP stations, however, provide a constant supply of electricity.

Turning now to environmental impact, tidal plants do not seem to create too many problems. In contrast, HEP stations often involve the flooding of large amounts of agricultural land, the destruction of ecological habitats, and may even cause a change in the climate of the area.

Both tidal power and HEP have one big disadvantage, in that if the demand for power exists at any distance from the generating plant, transmitting the electricity is expensive.

B Constructing a grid

In order to summarise the relative usefulness of these two energy sources, the main points of similarity and difference can be recorded on a grid or table.

1 In groups, draw up a list of headings for such a grid.

Note: Your grid should focus on **main** points only.

B2 Compare your list of headings with other students and reach a consensus.

B3 Now look at the grid opposite.

a How many of these points have you included?
b Would you add any of these points to your list?

A grid to compare energy sources

	Hydro-electric power
Importance on world scale	V. important 7% electricity 7% electricity (world)
Suitable location	- rivers and lakes
Where currently exploited	many countries: eg Norway, Brazil, Canada, Sri Lanka, Ireland.....
Capital outlay	- high - (no figures) - expensive to construct plant
Generating costs	- low (no figures) - cheaper than coal/oil/nuke
Life expectancy of plant	100 Yrs (approx)
Advantages	- no risk to life - feasible on large + small scale - also provides: irrigation/flood control/ water supply
Disadvantages	- expensive to transmit - may flood ag. land/change climate/ destroy natural habitats.

B4 Now draw up a similar grid, using your own list of headings, and complete it for tidal power. Refer to the text on page 48 for your information.

Leave enough room to extend your grid to include similar information on two more sources, in addition to tidal power.

Note: The information on a grid must be brief. Try to use key words where possible.

C **Power from heat**

Two other renewable energy sources, which are currently being developed, are geothermal and solar energy.

1 Scan the two sets of texts which follow, and decide if these two sources would be suitable for the countries listed below.

You should spend no more than 5 minutes doing this.

Iceland	Uganda	Australia
Saudi Arabia	Britain	Italy
China	The Philippines	Your own country

C2 Compare your conclusions with other students.

C3 Form two groups. Each group will read about **one** of these sources in more detail.

As you read, fill in the second column of the grid you drew up in B4.

Check your results with other students in your group.

C4 Working with a student from the other group, complete your grid by swapping information.

Solar Energy

By solar energy we mean the direct capture of either the sun's heat or its light. This energy is put to use for a wide variety of purposes and through a great number of methods.

It can involve: 1. *Direct solar technologies* e.g. solar architecture, solar cookers, desalination, solar ponds, solar water pumps, solar furnaces and photovoltaics.

2. *Biomass energy* by allowing plants to capture sunlight through photosynthesis and then burning or otherwise using these plant products. e.g. firewood, charcoal, biogas, pyrolysis, oil plants and animal power.

Here we are concerned with direct solar technologies, and in particular *solar furnaces* and *photovoltaics*, since these are established means of supplying high quality energy in larger schemes.

SOLAR FURNACES

(Solar Thermal Electric Conversion)

How it works
A set of mirrors (heleostats) connected to a computer follow the sun. They focus the light on a receiver, which is placed at a considerable height above the ground (solar power tower). This receiver transmits the heat to a boiler, which produces high pressure steam at a high temperature. This steam in turn drives a turbine generator.

Power Tower

Present schemes
Extensive research has been done into STEC in Japan, France, Italy, US, Spain and Germany in recent years. In some projects vast areas of mirrors are used to trap and direct the sun's rays. For example, in France a plant with a 4kW peak output uses a total mirror area of 4.3 acres (1.8 hectares).

Sicily. The Adrano solar power station

Costs
Consequently costs of STEC prototypes are very high – estimated at \$20–30,000 per kilowatt produced. Only with mass production of these devices could costs come down. This represents a capital cost at least twice as high as for any fossil fuel or nuclear plant. As a result the electricity produced would cost in the range of 10 cents per kWh – high compared to conventional sources.

Prospects
Nearly all the research and development work being done on STEC is directed towards large plants (100 kW) upwards). This technology, still in its infancy, will only survive if costs are kept down.

PHOTOVOLTAICS

The principles When light hits certain types of material, it dislodges electrons which flow as an electric current. Most solar cells are made from semi-conducting materials, which are composed of two layers one or both of which are pregnated with a photo-active chemical. The cell is small and a photovoltaic panel is made by assembling a large number of cells together. A number of panels, plus voltage controllers and DC/AC converters, can produce usable electricity.

Present schemes
An estimated 3000 photovoltaic systems are at present in operation in the US. The largest single system is located in Utah and it produces 100 kW. In 1978 Papago in Arizona, USA, became the world's first photovoltaic village. The village's 97 inhabitants are entirely dependent on this source for their energy. In Australia, photovoltaic systems are in use to provide power for communications relay stations. In Colombia a radio telephone network is powered with 2550 solar units with an output of 100kW. Saudi Arabia, Algeria and Oman have built villages which are largely fuelled by photovoltaic systems. Similar projects are being planned and carried out in a number of West African countries.

Future prospects Since the 1950's the cost of producing solar cells has fallen rapidly.

The dramatic reduction in the size and price of pocket calculators over the past decade indicates the achievements of semi-conductor technology.

This is the reason why many people feel that photovoltaics will have a strong effect on the pattern of electricity generation in the future. Some forecasts predict that solar cells may provide up to 30% of all electricity for the US by the year 2025. The European Community has announced an ambitious programme of photovoltaic demonstration projects with a total capacity of 1334 kW, predicting that 7% of all EC electricity will be produced by photovoltaics by the end of the century.

Costs and investment NASA, USA, claims that the needs of small rural communities requiring less than 500 kWh of electricity per year, can be met more cheaply by solar cells than by any other system. If costs continue to fall, then solar voltaics could be the cheapest source of electricity available to isolated communities worldwide. Although running costs are low compared to other energy sources, capital costs remain high. A series of solar panels producing 1kW costs between \$20–30,000. A diesel generator with the same output costs \$1500.

Yet researchers in the US remain optimistic and expect solar cells to continue to fall in cost. If their projections are correct, then by the end of the century solar plants will be as cheap as nuclear plants.

Pros and cons
One major advantage that photovoltaic energy has over most other energy sources is the relative simplicity in operating it. Once such a device is installed, maintenance is simple, problem free and cheap. A further advantage of all solar energy plants is that they are functional on a small scale as well as on a large scale. They do not need to be linked to the national grid and can be established where there is a need for energy.

Contrary to popular belief the variation in solar irradiance between temperate and tropical regions of the earth is not very great. In summer in high latitudes the length of the day helps to compensate for the more intense sunlight of the shorter tropical day. Solar energy is therefore exploitable on a worldwide basis.

The main disadvantage of any solar system is of course that they are dependent on direct sunlight. So some storage or back up power is normally needed.

Solar and Wind Systems

The solar (photovoltaic) cell could make a substantial contribution to electricity production if it proves possible to overcome certain technological and economic barriers and after enough time (several decades) has passed to bring the technology into large-scale commercial use.

The relatively small amount of energy received from the sun's rays by each square meter of the earth's surface, even in the sunniest climates, and the relatively low efficiency that could, at best, be achieved in converting the suns's rays into electricity (the maximum is about 20%) means that large areas of land would have to be covered by solar cells in order to generate a significant amount of power. For instance, thirty to fifty square kilometers of solar cells would be needed to generate the amount of electricity generated by a single large power station (1000 Megawatts electric). Moreover, these thirty to fifty square kilometres of cells would produce 1000 MWe only when they were receiving the highest level of radiation. The cells themselves, which represent the largest but by no means the only cost of such a plant, are still very expensive although their price is falling quite rapidly.

The chief problem, however, with solar cell installations and with most other renewable sources of energy such as solar-heated boilers and wind generators is that the energy supply is intermittent and varies according to the weather, the time of the day and the season of the year. In some places this problem can be partly overcome by using some of the electricity which such plants generate at peak output to pump water into dams (pumped storage) and by using the dams to generate hydropower when the output of the solar or wind generator falls or stops.

Generally speaking, however, solar and wind systems must be backed by a central coal or oil burning or nuclear system to ensure continuity of supply. No renewable system, except hydropower, offers a dependable energy source to meet the large needs of modern urbanized societies.

Geothermal power

Geothermal energy has been exploited for centuries. The Romans, for example, used hot springs for baths. More recently, it has been used to heat buildings such as greenhouses, and to generate electricity.

How it works Radioactive elements in the earth's interior are continually decaying. The heat they release maintains the earth's core in a white hot molten state. This heat seeps upwards towards the earth's surface. In most areas the heat flow is tiny; the heat hitting the surface from the sun is a thousand times greater. But in some zones, known as seismic zones, geothermal heat is more concentrated. These are situated near volcanoes, magma flows, geysers and hot springs, and in areas where earthquakes most often occur.

The resource The average temperature increase as one drills downwards through the earth's crust is 25–30°C/km. However in seismic zones the gradient may reach 80°C/km.

Such seismic zones are estimated to cover 10% of the earth's surface. They include:

a. The Pacific coast of the Americas
b. The western Pacific rim, including New Zealand, the Philippines, Indonesia, southern China and Japan
c. The Rift Valley in Kenya, Uganda, Zaire and Ethiopia
d. Around the Mediterranean

Tapping the energy There are two main ways of tapping geothermal energy:

1 **Groundwater** Using hot water that occurs naturally
2 **Hot dry rocks** Extracting heat from hot rocks by injecting and then recovering water

1 **Groundwater** For naturally occuring hot water to be a usable energy source, certain geological conditions must exist. There must be a geothermal reservoir. This is similar to the rock-trap in which oil or natural gas accumulates, where a permeable rock, such as sandstone or limestone, is capped by an impermeable stratum, such as clay.

Hot ground water percolates upwards into the reservoir, where it is trapped below the cap-rock. If there are cracks in the cap-rock water or steam may escape to the surface as hot springs or geysers. This water is replenished continually and natural geyser basins can have a life-span of up to 10,000 years.

However if man deliberately increases the escape of hot water from the reservoir in an effort to increase energy output the lifetime of the basin will be much less.

Since this groundwater rarely circulates naturally below 4 km deep, its temperature is usually below 300°C, and is usually much less.

In fact most geothermal water is below 150°C and has not been hot enough to generate electricity. It could only be used for bathing, to heat buildings, to warm greenhouses or as pre-heated water for boilers.

However, recently a US company has produced a turbine designed to use geothermal water and steam, as cool as 100°C for electricity production.

2 **Hot dry rocks** The potential of geothermal energy would be far greater if heat could be extracted from hot dry rocks, which do not naturally contain water. Such rocks occur almost all over the earth, and not just in seismic zones.

The technology to exploit the heat in hot dry rocks is still at an early stage of development, but the principle is simple. Two holes are drilled down to the required depth. The space between them is shattered by explosives and/or water pressure (hydrofracturing).

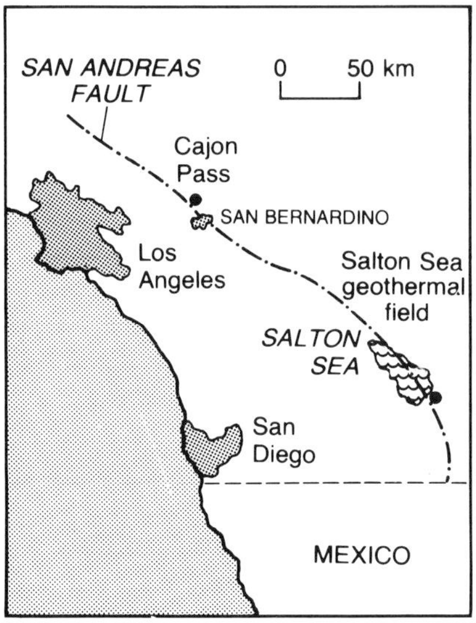

Tapping hot rocks beneath the Salton Sea now it may prove economic

Then cold surface water is pumped down one hole, allowed to percolate through the hot rock, and pumped up the second hole.

As with groundwater, the problem with hot rocks is lifespan. The original crack surfaces would cool rapidly, and power output could in practice decline sharply after a relatively short period of operation.

Pros and cons

Geothermal heat cannot be effectively transmitted over long distances. Therefore the hot water or steam must be used near the source before it cools. If it is used to generate electricity, and the plant is not situated conveniently close to an electricity user, the extra cost of transmitting the electricity must be considered.

Geothermal energy use does pose some environmental problems, chiefly the release of sulphurous gases into the atmosphere and the discharge of warm water into rivers, often containing a high level of undissolved solids. In practice, however, pollution has not proved to be a great problem. Waste water can normally be re-injected into the ground, in some cases after the removal of commercially valuable potassium salts.

Costs and investment

At the moment geothermal energy is technically and economically feasible in areas where hot water and steam exist near the surface and where there is a demand for heat or electricity. Development will normally be on a large scale and capital intensive.

Initial UK research indicates that electricity from hot rocks would cost around 2–3 pence/Kwh. The British government put £6 million into large scale tests in the south-west of England in 1983. If successful this technology could make geothermal energy practical amost anywhere in the world. But investment costs would still be high. Forecasts show that 600 MW of electricity produced from hot rocks would need 120 pairs of 6000 metre wells. The drilling costs for such a project would be enormous and such work would take several years to complete. Capital investment in one such station would therefore be very high. According to figures from Britain's Camborne School of Mines, costs could be in excess of £1000 million. World Bank estimates indicate that a single geothermal well would cost between \$200,000–\$600,000. It would produce between 5–10 MW and work for between 5–20 years.

However these figures still compare favourably with other energy sources. World Bank figures show geothermal energy to be cheaper than electricity from wind or solar power, cheaper than nuclear power (except large multiple units), cheaper than small scale hydro-electric power, and than most oil generated electricity. But large scale hydropower and gas generated electricity work out cheaper than geothermal power.

Power from hot rocks and warm water

SCIENTISTS in New Mexico and California are pushing known technologies to their limits in attempts to extract energy from the Earth.

In New Mexico, scientists from Los Alamos National Laboratory are working on ways to heat water by pumping it through hot dry rocks. The scheme is similar to the long-running project at the Camborne School of Mines in Cornwall, but the tempertures achieved in New Mexico are much higher.

To exploit hot-dry rocks at least two wells are drilled. They are separated by a reservoir of fractured rock, which provides a source of natural heat. Water is pumped into one well, heated in the rock, and then forced under high pressure back through the second well.

During a recent test in northern New Mexico, 40 million litres of water were heated under pressure to 190°C. Fifty million litres of water were pumped into the first well – 10 million litres were lost during the conversion process. However, enough energy was produced to have provided electricity to a town of 2000 people. The test lasted one month. The amount of water recovered increased as the test progressed.

The technology could be used on a small scale to heat homes, greenhouses, and factories. Los Alamos is now planning to run a year-long test to demonstrate commercial feasibility. Japan has partly funded the work.

At Heber in California's Imperial Valley, a geothermal power plant has been developed that could make use of brines at lower tempertures than are normally required for geothermal energy. The plant is already producing 24 megawatts of electricity. It will be tested over the next two years.

Hot underground water is pumped up from 13 different wells and piped to the plant. The brine flows through pipes and gives off heat to a second fluid (90 per cent isobutane and 10 per cent isopentane). The two fluids never contact each other. The second fluid vaporises and the vapour spins a turbine to generate electricity. It is called 'binary' technology.

In conventional geothermal technology, the steam from extremely hot water is harnessed – a second fluid is not involved. But most geothermal resources around the world are not hot enough to 'flash' into steam after being extracted.

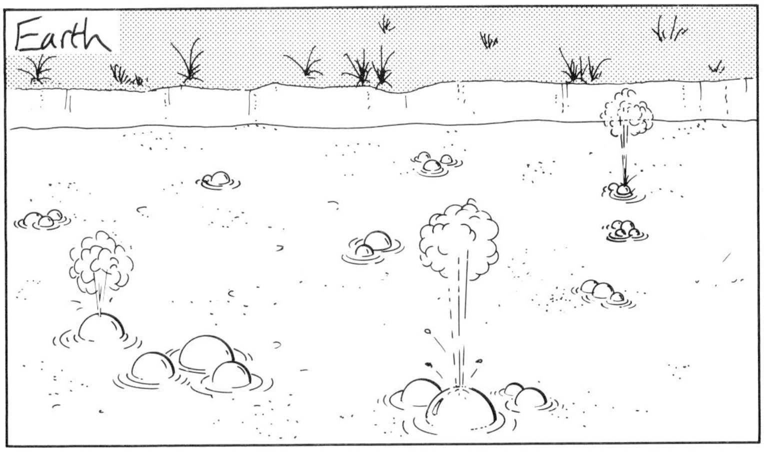

Geothermal energy comes from nature's own nuclear reactor. It arises from the radioactive decay of an isotope of potassium and other elements which are spread about in the earth's crust.

For every kilometre down this generalized heating raises the temperature 30°C. In some areas geological activity accentuates this effect and temperatures may rise by 80°C per kilometre. Where sandstone and other porous rocks allow groundwater to circulate, heat is transferred to the water which may come to the surface naturally at springs or geysers, or may be obtained by drilling. However, since the weight of the rocks makes the crust impermeable deeper than four kilometres, geothermal steam is rarely hotter than 300°C, limiting efficiency. The water and steam are often corrosive and are difficult to use in conventional turbines. New designs may overcome this difficulty.

When geothermal energy provides merely hot water it is used for space heating and agriculture, or to preheat water in conventional steam-generating power plants. Italy pioneered geothermal exploitation for its electrified rail system. New Zealand, Iceland, France and Japan apply geothermal energy to space heating. The African Rift and Pacific Basin rim are other favoured areas.

There are great hopes for hydrofracturing hot dry rocks which are far more widely distributed than porous rock geothermal fields. Water is pumped down one hole, through the fractured rock and back up another hole. The main problem is how long before the hot rocks cool (they take a very long time to heat up again). Current geothermal electricity costs are competitive with nuclear and oil powered stations.

D Assessing the grid

A grid can present a lot of information in a succinct way. However, it is sometimes necessary to expand on this information. For example a report generally requires written explanation of a grid or a table.

1 Look at the text on page 48 comparing and contrasting hydro and tidal power.

a Note down all the phrases which express the similarities and differences between the two sources.

b Note down the phrases that are used to introduce a new topic.

D2 Which of the sources described in this section would be most appropriate to your country?

Discuss your ideas with other students.

D3 Using information you have gathered in this section, write a report justifying your choice by comparing and contrasting it with other renewable sources.

SECTION 3 *ENERGY FROM THE NUCLEUS*

Nuclear power is assuming greater importance in a number of countries. Examples are Belgium, Bulgaria, West Germany, Korea and Sweden, where nearly half of the electricity demand is met by the nuclear industry.

Most people would agree that as informed members of the general public, we should be aware of what this sort of energy entails.

A1 Facts and Figures

a What questions should we be asking about nuclear power? Draw up a list with a partner.

b Look briefly at the texts which follow. Do they answer any of the questions which you asked?

A2 Test your nuclear vocabulary.

a Go through the following list of terms and explain as many as you can. Compare your explanations with a partner.

nuclear reactor	moderator
uranium	control rods
fission	coolant
chain reaction	turbine

b Scan the texts below and locate as many of these words as possible. Can you improve your original explanations?

Text 1

Environmental impacts of energy production

All primary energy sources that are economic will be required if the world is to avoid energy starvation. The world's needs for energy have been met successively by wood, coal and oil. As these sources decline in importance or approach depletion, natural gas, nuclear power, solar and other 'alternative' energy sources are expected to meet an increasing fraction of total demand.

The production and use of energy can have a significant effect on the environment. The environmental consequences of the use of some energy sources could conceivably become so great that they could limit growth in energy consumption. On the other hand, meeting energy needs for economic development and social well-being may require that some environmental impacts be accepted.

Environmental impact assessments are being used increasingly in decision-making by national authorities responsible for selecting appropriate energy options or energy mixes. The impacts of energy production may be of short duration, long lasting, or irreversible. They may be of local or global concern, and may involve trans-boundary issues of international significance; they may affect different communities, population groups and countries in different ways. They may be detrimental or beneficial. The nuclear industry has taken a leading role in addressing systematically both short- and long-term issues.

Nuclear energy

Uranium-235 is a naturally occurring radioactive isotope with a long half-life of 7.1×10^8 years. In nature it occurs in the proportion of 1 part in 140 with uranium-238 which is also radioactive but with a much longer half-life of 4½ billion years. (The third natural uranium isotope, uranium-234, occurs in negligible amounts.) Uranium-235 normally decays by emitting an alpha-particle. If this were all, there would be no nuclear bombs and no nuclear power industry. The unique property of uranium-235, among naturally occurring materials, is that its atoms occasionally split spontaneously into two approximately equal portions and emit two or three neutrons, as well as releasing a considerable amount of energy. This is nuclear fission. It does not, however, occur sufficiently frequently to give useful amounts of energy.

The nuclear industry is possible because uranium-235 can be made to split by hitting its nucleus with a slowly moving neutron. Thus, if the neutrons emitted in a spontaneous fission can be controlled in speed and directed into the nucleus of other uranium-235 atoms these will in turn split and release neutrons to keep the process going. Since each fission absorbs one neutron and releases two or three, if all the released neutrons are used to cause further fissions, the process will rapidly accelerate. This is the chain reaction which is the source of power for the atomic bomb.

The requirements of a reactor are obviously different from those of a bomb. A reactor is designed to use a steady chain reaction to produce heat, which is then used to produce steam which in turn drives electricity-generating plant. In a nuclear power station the reactor plays the part of the coal- or oil-fired boiler in a conventional power station. (See Figure 9.)

Neutrons emitted from the fission of uranium-235 have different speeds but only those travelling slowly will cause other uranium-235 atoms to split. In a nuclear reactor a substance called a moderator, which slows neutrons without absorbing them, is used to bring some of the faster moving neutrons down to a speed at which they can cause a fission. In this way neutrons which would otherwise have been wasted become 'productive'. When each fission produces, on average, one productive neutron the rate at which nuclear fission is occurring is neither increasing nor decreasing. This steady chain reaction will continue as long as sufficient uranium-235 remains. The moderator, because its action brings the use of neutrons up to the required efficiency, is an essential ingredient of the system. Water is a reasonably good moderator and so is carbon.

Fine regulation of reactor operation is obtained by the use of control rods. These are made of a good neutron absorber such as cadmium or boron. When inserted into a reactor core they absorb neutrons and thus slow down the rate at which induced fission occurs. They can therefore be used to bring a reactor off power. In some reactor designs they are suspended by electromagnets above the core. In the event of any malfunctioning which cuts off the power supply to the electromagnets the control rods automatically drop into position and shut down the reactor.

When a nuclear reactor is operating it produces heat. Whether it is usefully used or not, this heat must be removed otherwise the reactor would melt. This is done by a 'coolant' circulating through the reactor core. A coolant should have a high heat-absorbing capacity; it should not, on the other hand, absorb too many neutrons, it should be non-corrosive, and it should be stable within the operating temperature range of the reactor. There is a variety of coolants. Gas-cooled reactors use air, carbon dioxide or helium. Liquid-cooled reactors use water, heavy water, liquid sodium or a molten alloy of sodium and potassium. In some present reactor designs the coolant is circulated

Figure 9. Operation of conventional and nuclear power stations – schematic

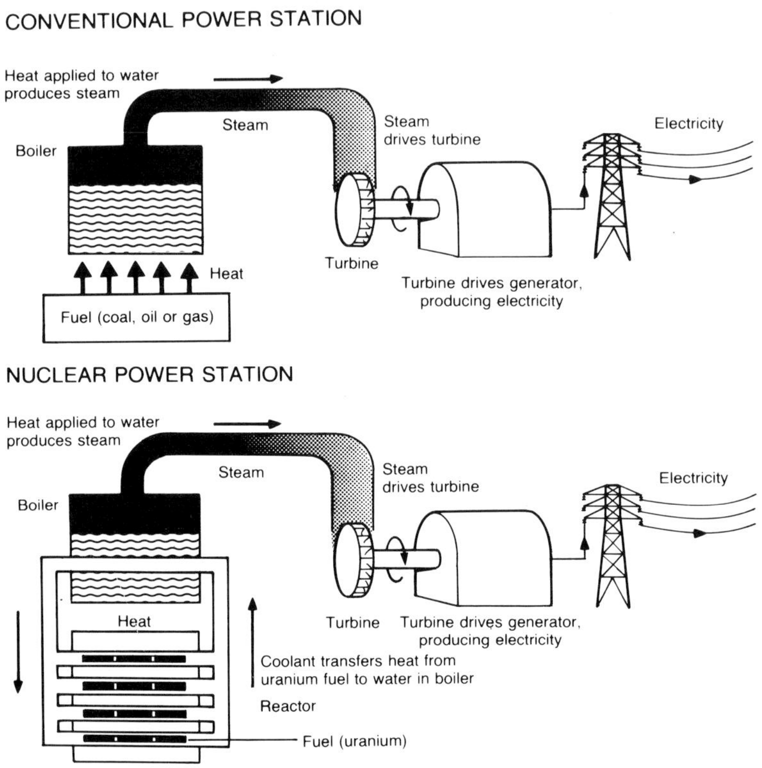

directly through the electricity-generating turbines. In most cases, however, an indirect system is used and the coolant passes through a heat exchanger where it gives up its heat to produce the steam which then drives the turbines as shown in Figure 9. There is a bewildering variety of reactor types using different combinations of coolant, moderator and fuel type. They are usually referred to by sets of initials or technical nicknames.

Text 3

Area of contamination resulting from the Chernobyl nuclear accident, May 1986

Theoretical risk

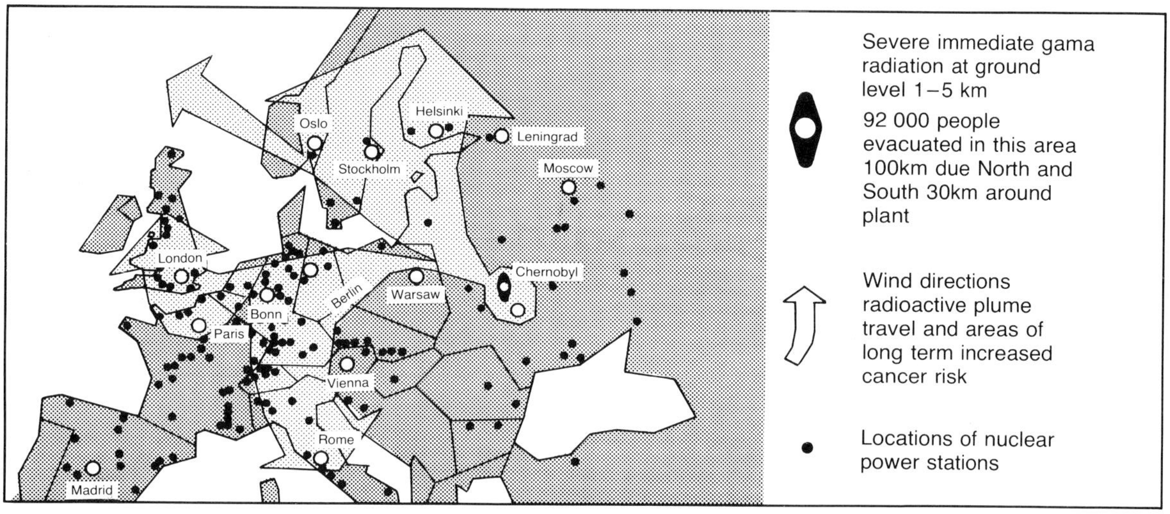

There are 211 reactors operating within Europe. Each, like the Russian reactors, has a theoretical risk of one major accident per 10,000 years of operating life. It should be borne in mind that no reactor operates for 10,000 years. The design lives vary between twenty and forty years so that the theoretical risk of an accident at any one reactor is remote. The theoretical risk of a 'second Chernobyl' occurring within Western Europe is one in $\frac{10,000}{211}$, i.e. once every 47.4 years. The theoretical risk is vastly increased by the number of reactors working simultaneously.

The notion of theoretical risk is an important decision-making and public relations tool widely used within industry. Actual as opposed to theoretical risk cannot be calculated. The risk, which in theory can only happen once in ten thousand years, could in practice happen as easily tomorrow or the next day, or the next day after that, as in ten thousand years time. It is a gamble. But gambles don't always pay off. It is the job of the nuclear industry's public relations department to make sure the public's 'gut' feeling that nuclear power is just not worth the risk, is adequately balanced by their rationale of theoretical risk.

B Different perspectives

The three texts deal with the same topic, but look at it from different points of view. It is helpful to be able to identify the perspective of a writer, as this can aid our assessment of the information presented.

The sources used in this section were:

Foley, G., *Energy*. Penguin 1976 – reprinted 1982

Greenpeace Environmental Trust, *Facts You Should Know About Nuclear Power*. (Leaflet) London, 1986

International Atomic Energy Agency, *Nuclear Power, The Environment and Man – A Layman's Guide*. Vienna, IAEA, 1984

B1 What do you think these authors attitudes to nuclear power might be? Discuss this with other students.

B2 In the light of your discussion, match the authors with the texts.

C A closer look

1 Look through the texts again briefly and decide what the main point of each one is. Use the list below to help you.

a The difference between a nuclear power station and a nuclear bomb.
b The nuclear risk calculated by experts gives us a false idea of the real situation.
c The environment must suffer if we are to continue to have an energy supply.
d How a nuclear power station produces electricity.
e The risk of nuclear accidents is very low.
f We must consider the environment when developing new energy sources.

C2 You will later be required to look more closely at nuclear reactor types. It will therefore be helpful to you if you understand the **basic working** of the reactor.

a Locate the appropriate text and paragraphs and make brief notes. You might consider using a flowchart for this.

b Compare your notes with other students. Whatever form of notes you have used, make sure that:
– the key points are clear.
– the relationship between the points is shown.

D The AGR *vs* the PWR

Having looked at the workings of nuclear reactors in general, we turn now to two particular types, the Advanced Gas-cooled Reactor and the Pressurised Water Reactor.

The relative merits of these two reactor types have been very much under discussion recently. For example, the British Central Electricity Generating Board proposes to build a PWR at Sizewell on the Suffolk coast. This has provoked a lot of public debate and a report has been completed by the planning inspector.

1 Listen to the interview and decide what are the two major areas that are considered in the report.

D2 What do you think the speaker's opinions on this subject are? Decide which of the following are true.

a He is against nuclear power.
b He prefers the AGR to the PWR.
c He feels that nuclear power is a very acceptable source of energy.
d He thinks that Britain should return to coal and oil generated electricity only.
e He thinks that the dangers of nuclear power are far greater than those of the chemical industry.
f He is strongly in favour of the PWR.

D3 Listen to the interview again and make notes on the differences and similarities between the AGR and the PWR under the following headings.

a Means of heat transfer
b Size
c Safety Question
d cost

D4 Write a short passage based on your notes comparing and contrasting the AGR and the PWR.

SECTION 4 *MARCH ISLAND – A CASE STUDY*

March Island – Ever heard of it?
Where do you think it might be situated?
What kind of climate would you expect to find there?
What would you imagine the standard of living is like?
Would you like to live there?

A Read through the information on pages 59 and 60 and answer the questions above.

March Island – A government information sheet

Though March Island covers a considerable area – 1500 square km – its population is low, and is concentrated mostly in the two major towns, Prizewell and Dunmore.

In terms of development, March Island has recently been classed as an MIC – Middle Income Country. The upgrading of its status from a 'developing country' has come about mainly due to a surge in industrialisation in recent years.

The traditional main products of the island include fresh and preserved fish, fruit and mineral water. In recent times this list has been extended to include the manufacture of bicycles (the most popular model is the high quality 'March Hare'), and the production of aluminium pots.

Lately the demand for energy on the island has grown with increased industrialisation. This continues to be the source of much debate, and the government is eager to find a solution soon.

Energy demands on March Island are due to increase dramatically over the next 10 years. This is forecasted to happen for a variety of reasons.

- Many parts of the island which have hitherto been uninhabited, are now being developed for agricultural purposes.
- A large number of fish processing plants around the coast are being modernised.
- The telecommunications systems on the island, and from the island to the continent, is to be modernised.

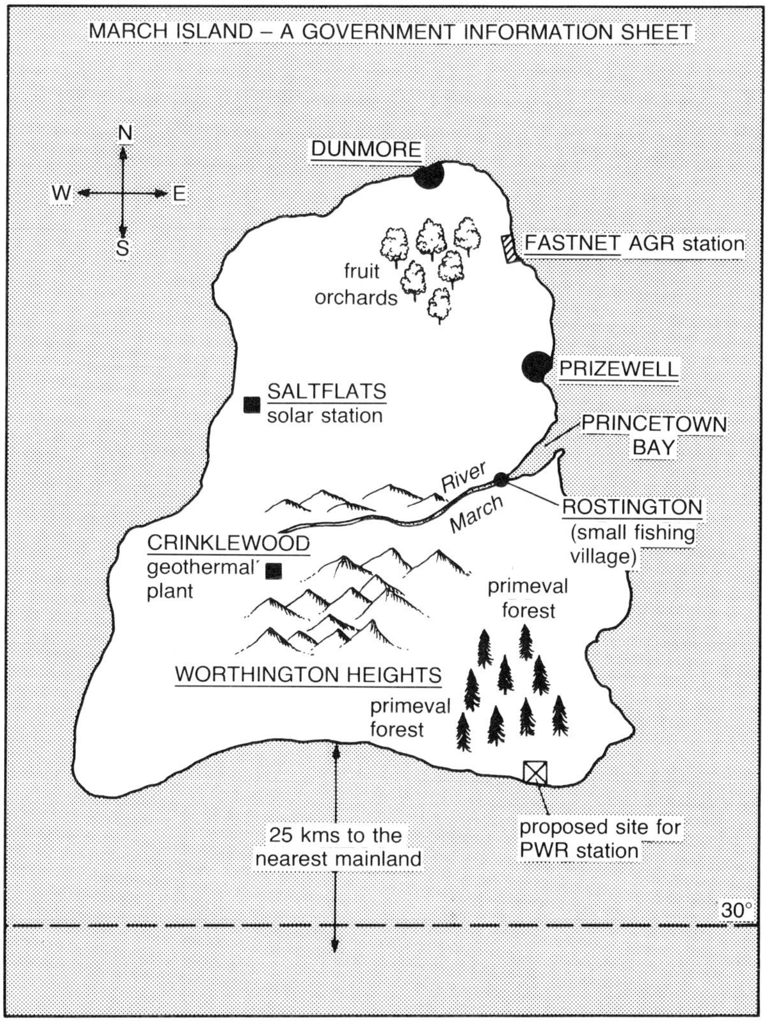

- Recent offers by the government of favourable tax benefits have attracted a large number of foreign industries to the island. A total of 400 new factories are due to be built over the next 5 years.
- It has been decided to begin work on a new communications system. An electric rail

network is to be constructed within the next 10 years and will connect the capital with most coastal villages. This is intended to facilitate the tourist industry.

As a result of these plans the government is looking for a source of power which

a will not cost much in excess of the annual energy budget;

b can be completed relatively quickly and be in operation within 3–5 years.

So far the PWR system seems to be the most acceptable suggestion, but no final decisions have been made.

Facts and figures

POPULATION:		500,000
ELECTRICITY CONSUMPTION:		
	1950	1000 MW
	1970	1500 MW
	1990	2500 MW
PRESENT ELECTRICITY SOURCES:		
	AGR	50%
	Imported OIL	40%
	SOLAR	5%
	GEOTHERMAL	5%
ANNUAL ENERGY BUDGET		US$2000 million

You are now being asked to take an active part in the discussion of March Island's energy problems.

B First of all . . .

- Depending on the number of students taking part in this exercise, you should decide on the allocation of the roles listed below.
- It is not necessary to have representatives for all the roles, so you should decide whether you will drop one (or more) and if so, which one(s).
- Though each role can be played by one person it is also fun if two or more students work together.
- You should also elect a co-ordinator, who will be responsible for the smooth running of your discussions.

Alternatively, you may decide that your teacher could best play this role.

C List of roles

1 Representative from Ministry of Energy
2 PWR representative
3 AGR board member
4 Tidal energy expert
5 Member of Solar Energy Commission
6 Representative of Geothermal Energy Board
7 Spokesperson for Greenwatch, environmental group
8 Co-ordinator

D You are asked to observe the following principles:

1 When you have chosen your role your task will be to prepare your case as thoroughly as possible.
2 In order to do this, you may:
   a look back over any relevant material to support your point of view and help you argue against other cases:
   b request meetings with other groups in order to compare cases and seek common ground.
3 Meetings with other groups may only be organised through the co-ordinator. If you desire a meeting you should make a written request to the other group, and hand it to the co-ordinator.
4 The co-ordinator will set a limited time for each meeting, which you should observe. (We suggest 5–10 minutes)
5 A final general discussion will then be held to try to reach a consensus.

Role 1
You represent the Ministry for Energy. You are responsible for the island's power needs.
- Make sure that you interview all the interested parties.
- Find out as much information as possible about each, in particular:
  Future proposals for expansion
  Potential costs
  Jobs created
  Geographic position
  Proximity to major towns
  Environmental impact
- Consider these details carefully and try to find a solution for bridging the energy gap.
- Don't forget how important public opinion is on environmental issues.

You will play an important part in the final discussion. You might like to suggest to the co-ordinator that you chair it.

Role 2
Your company has decided to promote the building of a PWR at a site in the south east of the island.

So far the reaction of the Ministry for Energy has been favourable, and you are confident that you will receive the £850 million capital necessary.

When putting your case to the ministry, a number of points might be worth keeping in mind:
- The safe distance of the PWR site from the cities in case of accident.
- The deep seabed near the site, useful for the disposal of waste.
- The large number of jobs that the construction and maintenance of the plant would create. (approx 3,500)
- The high rate of unemployment in the country at the moment, particularly in rural areas.
- The relatively short construction time (7 years).

Role 3
You are on the board of directors of the AGR, presently operating at Fastnet, just over 50 miles from the capital.

You have the following points to make:
- You have been operating the AGR plant for 6 years now.
- So far, your record has been good. – No accidents.
- You have a project for the extension of your plant, with a planned increase in output of 500 MW per year.
- Extension costs would be $1,200 million, approximately.
- This would create an extra 800 jobs for the population of the two main cities.
- Point out your advantageous position for the transmitting of power to these cities.
- The PWR would not enjoy the same advantage.

Role 4
You have just returned after spending some time studying a tidal energy station in the north of France.

You feel that this source of energy has been ignored on the island, and deserves some consideration.

Here are some useful facts to support your case:
- You've carried out some research around the island and found Princetown Bay to be a suitable site for a tidal barrage.
- The variation in water level there between high and low tide is 10 metres.
- The estuary of the river March is 2 miles wide, and therefore suited to barrage construction.
- You estimate that a tidal barrage costing US$3500 million could be built within 5 years, and would produce over 1000 MW.

Role 5
You represent the new solar energy commission. You are at present involved in a solar scheme at Saltflats. This is a small project but you have hopes for its expansion.

Your next step is to get the support of the Energy Ministry. When putting your case for further investment in Saltflats, keep these points in mind:
- You are at present relying on a simple and inexpensive solar furnace system for power supply.
- To date the government has invested very little capital in this energy sector.
- You propose the setting up of a photovoltaic system to back up existing output.
- You have done some research and come up with the following facts:

Proposed Photovoltaic System

Potential output	100 MW
Estimated cost	$500 million
Jobs created	1700

Role 6
You represent the Geothermal Energy Board and are at present involved in a large and expanding scheme on the Worthington Heights.

You feel that this scheme has great potential and hope for continued investment in it.

With this aim in mind you would like to make the following points:
- A large number of natural geysers, all within a 50 mile radius of Crinklewood, are as yet untapped.
- Further hot dry rock beds exist throughout the heights.
- More money is needed for research into these possibilities. You have estimated that for this research an added $130 million is necessary.
- If these sources prove financially viable, they could provide a further 15% of the island's power.

Role 7
As spokesperson(s) for the environmental group Greenwatch you are concerned about protecting the ecology of the island.

New plans for developing the island and introducing new power sources could pose serious threats to the vegetation and wildlife.

The following facts could be important in your enquiries into future government plans.

- A sanctuary of rare birds exists in the south-east region of the island.
- Princetown Bay is a well-known habitat for some unusual marine life, and should be protected.
- The thermal springs of Worthington Heights have been used for centuries by the people of that region for domestic purposes. They should not be disturbed.
- The primeval forests of the south and south-eastern regions are among the few remaining virgin forests in the world, and attract nature lovers from all corners of the Earth.
- There have been recent reports of pollution by radioactive waste off the north-east coast of the island.

Role 8 Co-ordinator
As co-ordinator you will be responsible for bringing the parties together in small groups to iron out their differences, to create lobbies, to put forward new proposals, and hopefully, to eventually reach a general concensus.

In order to do this a number of preliminary meetings are necessary. For example, you should ensure that there is a meeting between representatives of alternative energy sources.

A meeting between the nuclear energy groups would also be desirable. The environmental group should have an opportunity to talk to everybody.

Don't forget to inform each meeting of the time limit you are imposing (between 5 and 10 minutes). You may vary the time depending on how the group is getting on.

The final activity should take the form of a formal discussion where all cases can be put. This meeting could be chaired by the government representative, or by the co-ordinator.

If class numbers are low, the number of roles can be reduced by putting the AGR and PWR reps together and/or suggesting that all the renewable energy reps work together.

Adding fuel to the fire
At your discretion a number of important revelations can be introduced at various stages.

This can be done by passing the information to the people involved on a piece of paper.

The following are some suggested news items.

1 **Message to all groups** – The Ministry for Energy of a nearby country has just offered considerable financial support for the construction of further energy supply plants. In return your neighbours would receive some of the supplementary power, transmitted by way of an underwater cable system.
2 **Message to tidal power/environmental groups** Members of the Rostington Fishermen's Association have just lodged a complaint. If the proposed plans for a tidal scheme go through, the exit of their boats to the open seas will be hindered.
3 **Message to Environmentalists/AGR/PWR reps** A meltdown has just

been reported at an AGR station in Italy, which is of a similar design to the one at Fastnet.

4 **To Geothermal/Environmentalist reps** Residents of the Crinklewood area are complaining that fishing in the River March has been greatly affected by discharge from the geothermal plant.

5 **To Solar rep/Energy Ministry** A discovery has been made on the island which is very important for the development of solar technology here. Very high quality silicon has been discovered on some of the islands eastern beaches. This should have a dramatic effect on the costs of installing photovoltaic systems.

SECTION 5 *OVER TO YOU*

While making your way through this unit, you have had practice in a wide range of skills. Below, we have isolated some of the individual skills. All of them are vital in effective study, whatever your subject is.

Ideally, you should be able to apply these to your own studies. For each area of skills we have made suggestions as to how you can do this.

A Writing notes

- listening and taking notes on main points.
- reading and making notes on specific information.
- writing notes in different forms, using outlines and key words.
- presenting notes in grid form.

Application
Look at some notes that you have already taken in class or from your reading.

1 Examine the system you use. Is it clear?
2 Does the visual presentation please you?
3 Have you included unnecessary detail?
4 Have you high-lighted main points?
5 Have you made use of key words?

In a forthcoming lesson, try out a different note-taking technique to the one you usually use, and assess its effectiveness.

B Coping with texts

- finding the main point of a text quickly.
- assessing the bias of a text.
- scanning a text for specific information.
- guessing the meaning of unknown words from context.

Application
When you read, do you employ any of the strategies listed here? Take a text which you have recently read and found difficult.

1 Read it through quickly to find the main point of the whole text.
2 Are **all** sections of the text equally important for your study purposes? If not, concentrate only on the important parts.
3 Now note down the main points of the sections that are important.
4 Present them in a concise way. Is it possible to use a grid?
5 List any words which you don't know and which are vital for your understanding of the text.
Try and guess their meaning.
Check your answers in a dictionary.

C Understanding talks

- identifying the main points of a talk.
- identifying the bias of a speaker.
- picking out expressions of comparison and contrast in speech.

Application
The next time you are taking notes in a talk, discussion or lesson:

1 afterwards check that you have picked out the main areas.
2 cross check by looking at another student's notes.
3 if you have not divided your notes up into main areas, do so now.
4 if the speaker makes any comparison or contrast, pay special attention to the language he/she uses.

D Writing passages

- synthesising information from a number of sources for a particular purpose.
- writing a report to compare and contrast two (or more) factors/aspects/objects.

Application
The next time that you have a written assignment to do, try the following procedure.

1 Make a list of all possible sources of information.
2 Check through contents lists and indexes for relevant chapters or sections. Note them down.
3 Read **quickly** through chapters/sections for relevant paragraphs, and note down their position.
4 Now read through the information you have collected **in more detail** and note down the main points, keeping in mind the assignment you have.
5 Organise your list of main points before writing.

UNIT 4 · *Ringing the changes*

SECTION 1 *A HISTORY OF CHANGE*

A Do you think that your world is changing? Discuss these questions with a partner.

1 *a* During your lifetime, in which of the following areas have you observed changes?

fashion	the role of the sexes
technology	the human body
morals	the landscape
behaviour	plants and animals
education	buildings

b How have these things changed?

c Of the things that have changed, which have done so as a result of man's activities?

d Have all of these changes been good ones in your opinion?

e Do you feel that over the last 50 years the speed of change has
- increased?
- decreased?
- remained constant?

A2 When you have considered these questions, try to find out what the general attitude of the class is towards change.

A3 Read the short quote which follows to see if your opinions are the same as those of the author.

> 'Change and development are an integral part of our lives. Our past is governed by them. History **is** development.
>
> There are certain changes that man has no influence over. There are other changes that man has brought about.
>
> There are changes that man observes as they take place. There are others that he is oblivious to, because of their gradual nature or their place in the past.
>
> It is generally agreed that this phenomenon of change has picked up momentum in recent time.' – M. Gaynor

B Close to home

Let us now consider changes which are closer to home.

1 Think of a town, village, place, building or view you know which has undergone change in recent years.

a Note down details of how it used to be.
b Note down details of how it has changed.
c Can you explain why this has happened?
d Was this change necessary?
e Was this change advantageous?
f How do you imagine this place will look in 10 years time?

B2 Report on these changes and your predictions to another student.

C The rise and fall of Malacca

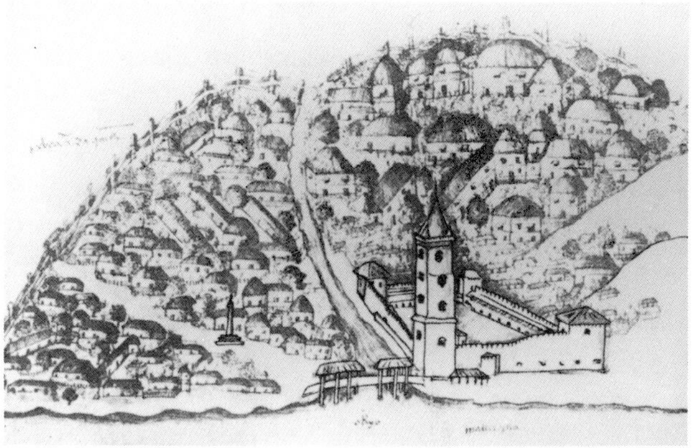

Malacca is situated on the west coast of Peninsular Malaysia, about 150 km north-west of Singapore. In the 15th century this town was the most important political and economic centre in south-east Asia. Because of its geographic location, trading ships from both east and west frequented the port in great numbers. For a long period of its history Malacca prospered. However, this prosperity was not to last forever.

C1 You are now going to hear two Malaccan residents talking about what their town is like today. Before you listen look at the pictures of old and modern Malacca and consider these questions.

a Is Malacca experiencing a 'rise' or a 'fall' at the moment.

b Listen to the recording and note down what the speakers feel have been the greatest changes in their lifetimes. Compare your notes with those of other students.

C2 Listen again and note down exactly what the speakers say about the following:

a the port
b shipping
c warehouses
d trade
e old buildings
f the skyline
g industry
h tourism

C3 The two speakers' attitudes to Malacca are clearly different. Listen again and note down the phrases which *a* show optimism and *b* show pessimism.

D Back home

Consider again the place that you described earlier.

Write a short passage about it and, where possible, use some of the language you have just noted down.

Find out what other students have written about and read some of their passages about places that you don't know.

SECTION 2 *BETTERING NATURE!*

A The ecosystem

The ecosystem is the complex web linking animals, plants, air, water and every other lifeform in the biosphere. It all hangs together. The system is in a 'steady state' of dynamic balance, which means that by altering any one part you affect all the others. Humans are only one factor in the ecosystem. But we don't quite see it that way. We set ourselves apart and call all the other factors or species natural resources – or simply *nature*.

A1 The cartoon suggests that humans are chauvinistic in their attitude to nature.

What does this mean?

Do you agree?

A2 The definition suggests that the individual parts of the ecosystem depend on each other.

Can you think of any examples that demonstrate this?

A3 *a* Can you think of any factors that threaten this state of balance?
b Do you know any examples close to your home where this balance has been upset?

Discuss your ideas on these three questions with other students.

A4 Look very briefly at the following page and extend your list of 'threats'.

Arable land is currently under threat from many different sources. Every year between 5 and 7 million hectares of good land are built on. Between 1960 and 1970 Japan lost no less than 7.3 per cent of its agricultural land to buildings and roads.

Soil erosion is also on the increase. In India, more than half of all agricultural land is subject to degradation. Some 6,000 million tonnes of soil are lost every year from just 800,000 square kilometres of land. They carry with them more than 6 million tonnes of nutrients, more than the amount that is applied in the form of fertilizer.

The use of intensive methods of farming is also leading to loss of organic matter in the topsoil and the buildup of both toxic chemicals and salts in the soil. At the current rate of land degradation, it is estimated, as much as one-third of all good agricultural land could be lost within the next two decades. The problem is aggravated by the fact that so much natural organic fertilizer, instead of being returned to the soil where it is badly needed, has to be burnt for fuel. Currently, an estimated 400 million tonnes of dung and crop residues are used as fuel, almost entirely in the developing countries.

The UN Food and Agriculture Organization claims that food production needs to be increased by 60 per cent over the next twenty to thirty years. This could be achieved by intensifying production and bringing another 200 million hectares of arable land – an increase of 1.3 per cent – into production by the end of the century. But according to FAO this would only just compensate for the amount of land lost by degradation if current rates continue unchecked.

Desertification is one of the major problems. Aridity affects nearly one-third of the land surface. It is currently threatening the lives of the 80 million people who survive on the 19 per cent of the land under attack from desertification. Some 20 million hectares now deteriorate annually to the point where they stop yielding an economic agricultural return. The cost of lost production has been estimated at $26,000m. a year.

Desertification is not being produced by climatic change but by overcropping, overgrazing, and salinization. It can also be produced by deforestation, which exposes soil to wind and rain, resulting in sudden soil erosion and flooding. But as the soil disappears so does the ability of the land to trap and retain moisture. The desert begins to get the upper hand.

In the late 1970s work by FAO and the United Nations Environment Programme revealed that rates of deforestation were not quite as bad as had been feared. Nevertheless, it is thought that for the period up to 1985 the open forests will disappear at a rate of 3.8 million hectares a year and the closed forests at 7.5 million hectares a year. On present trends 9 countries will have destroyed all their closed forest within 30 years, and a further 13 nations within 55 years.

The implications are serious. For one thing, deforestation inevitably adds to the carbon dioxide burden in the atmosphere, increasing the chance of climatic change as a result of the greenhouse effect. For another, exposing thin tropical soils to the elements often leads to their eventual disappearance. The land which supports tropical forests is often unsuitable for agriculture, even though this is still the commonest reason for felling in the tropics. Thirdly, the increasing scarcity of timber in tropical regions is leading to fuel-wood problems for hundreds of millions of people. And, finally, the forests contain most of the world's genetic resources, which are now under increasing threat.

From R. Clarke 'Science and Technology in World Development' OUP. 1985

B Mapping your thoughts

1 The text above does not have a title.

a From the list below, which do you think would be the most suitable?

Means of Increasing Food Production
Arable Land Management
Threats to Arable Land
Arable Land
The Effect of Human Activity on the Earth

Remember that the title should give an indication of the contents of the **whole** text, and not just a part.

b Once you have decided on your answer, check it in the key. If you chose a different title, discuss with other students why the answer in the key is the most suitable.

B2 Five major areas of concern can be identified in this text. Decide what you think they are from the list below.

Soil erosion	Intensive methods of farming
Degradation	UN Food and Agriculture Organisation
Loss of natural organic fertilizer	Desertification
Food production	Aridity
Over-grazing	The greenhouse effect
Deforestation	Over-cropping
	Building

Compare your answers with those of other students, and then check them in the key before you continue.

B3 One way of summarising the information in a text is to use a **mind map**. This system of note-making is also known as 'pattern notes', since what you produce resembles a pattern more than it does conventional notes.

One of the main features of mind maps is that the heading appears in the centre of the page, and the sub-headings are placed around it, beginning above and to the right of the central heading.

Another feature is that the main heading should stand out from the sub-headings, and that the sub-headings should stand out from the detail and supporting examples.

Below is an example of a mind map, but it is incomplete.

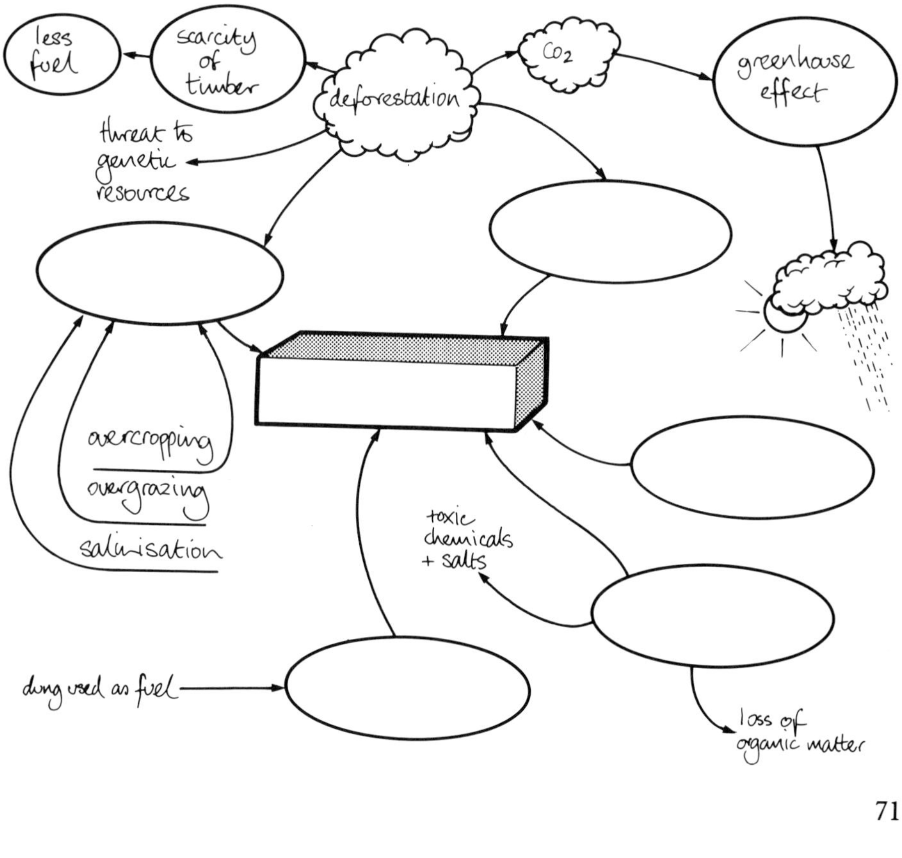

a Copy down the blank sections of the mind map above, and by referring to the text on page 70, fill in the gaps appropriately.

b Compare your work with that of other students and note the various ways of distinguishing the different headings.

c Compare your work with the key.

B4 One major advantage of using mind maps is that the relationship between different points can easily be seen.

This is commonly indicated with **arrows**. Care must be taken in drawing these arrows as you can change the meaning of notes by putting an arrow in the wrong direction.

a Look at the completed mind map and decide if the following statements are true or false. The arrows should help you.

(i) Deforestation occurs as a result of desertification.
(ii) Deforestation leads to an increase in the amount of carbon dioxide in the atmosphere.
(iii) Because of threats to arable land, intensive farming takes place.
(iv) Because dung and crop residues are needed as fuel, less organic fertiliser is available to farmers.
(v) Due to continued building, the area of arable land is constantly being reduced.
(vi) The world's genetic resources are increasingly threatened. Consequently deforestation occurs.
(vii) Increased building results in higher rates of erosion.

b Check your answers in the key and rewrite the false statements so that they conform with the mind map.

C Eco trends

1 Whatever your field of study you often have to identify, describe and interpret trends. The exercises that follow offer some guidance in this.

a What does the graph below predict about the future situation?

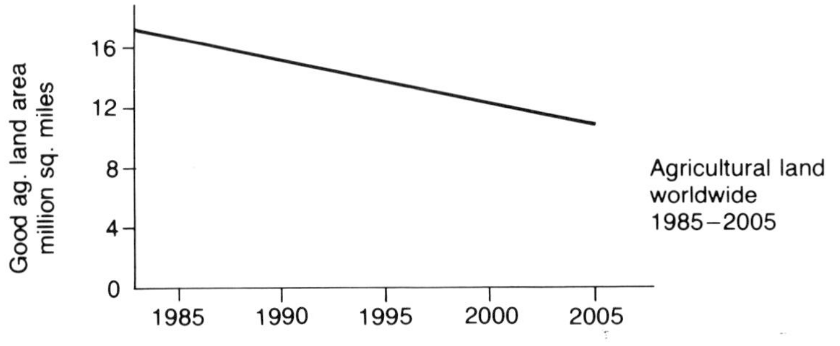

Agricultural land worldwide 1985–2005

b Locate and note down the sentence in the text which forecasts this trend.

c From this sentence, pick out two indicators that this is a **prediction** and not a certainty.

How does the author indicate the time span?

How was the calculation made?

C2 Deforestation is a further major contributor to land degradation.

Locate the section of the text on deforestation and with other students find answers to the following questions.

a What are the predictions for the future of world forests?

b Is the fate of the forests certain?

Pick out the phrases which express the prediction and note them down.

c How does the author indicate the time span here? Note down the two different phrases he uses.

C3 *a* Look at the graph below and decide which of the following captions best matches it.

(*i*) The rate of construction in a particular area over 200 years.
(*ii*) The increase in soil erosion around the world.
(*iii*) Various uses of land over a period from 1800–2000.
(*iv*) The rate of soil erosion resulting from different types of land use.

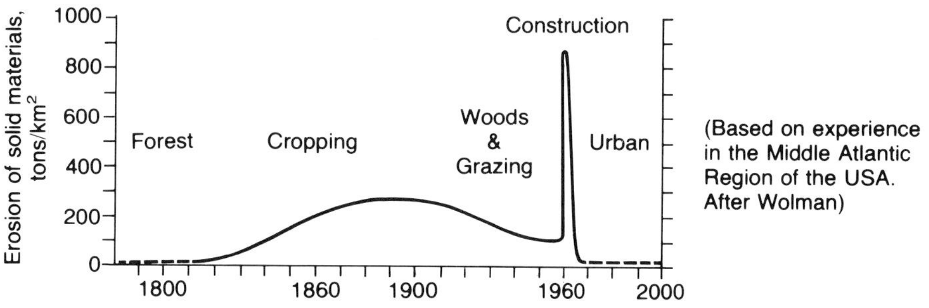

Based on experience in the Middle Atlantic region of the USA. After Wolman

b What is the overall trend of the graph?

(*i*) A steady increase in soil erosion.
(*ii*) No single trend.
(*iii*) A dramatic decrease in soil erosion.
(*iv*) A levelling off in the rate of soil erosion.

c What does the graph predict for the immediate future?

(*i*) The rate will level off.
(*ii*) The rate will rise sharply.
(*iii*) The rate will continue to decrease.
(*iv*) The rate will follow the previous trend.

d Complete the following passage about the graph, using words and phrases from the box below.

reached a peak	proceeded	expected
levelled off	rate	increase fell
steadily	was reduced	dramatic rise

The graph shows variation in rates of land erosion in the Middle Atlantic Region of the USA as a result of different types of land use.

It demonstrates that, under original forest conditions in the early part of the 19th century, erosion (*i*) at a low rate. With the rapid (*ii*) in cultivation in the mid-19th century, the rate increased (*iii*). The rate (*iv*) towards the end of the century. Due to the return of some of this land to grazing and woodland in the 1940's and 50's, the relatively high rate of erosion (*v*) by half.

However, in the late fifties there was a (*vi*) in the rate of erosion, and it (*vii*) in the early sixties. This came at a time of widespread building in the area.

Once this construction was completed and areas were urbanised, the erosion rates *(viii)* as quickly as they had risen. The level dropped to a *(ix)* almost as low as it had been 160 years previously.

It is *(x)* that these rates will remain low from now on.

In conclusion, we can see that the greatest causes of soil erosion are cultivation and, in particular, construction. The lowest rates are achieved when the land is covered by either vegetation or buildings.

e Identify the paragraphs of this passage which:
(i) describe
(ii) interpret
(iii) predict

D Choose a trend

The following three exercises deal with:
- the emission of CO_2
- food production in Africa and S. Asia
- energy consumption and population increase

Choose **one** of these and follow the instructions to produce a written passage which includes:

a a description of the trends

b your interpretation of those trends

c where possible, a prediction of future trends

D1 *a* Which of the following predictions best matches these two pie charts?
(i) The emission of CO_2 will increase significantly by 2025.
(ii) The Third World and China will be emitting a higher proportion of the world's CO_2 by 2025 than they were in 1974.
(iii) The US will be emitting less CO_2 in 2025 than it did in 1974.
(iv) The proportion of CO_2 emitted by the developed world will rise significantly by the year 2025.

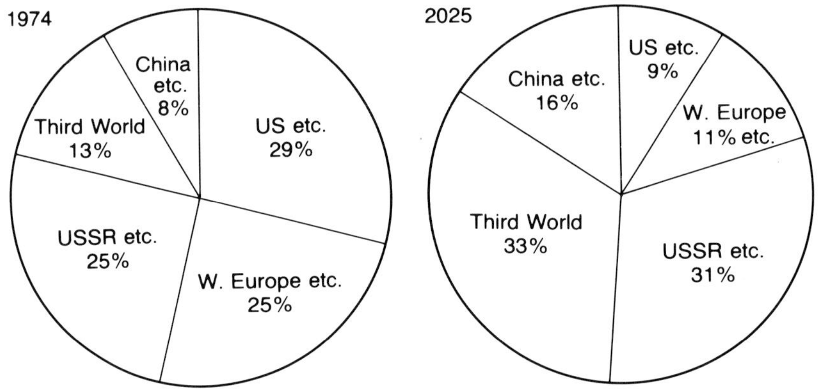

Global CO_2 Production (From J. Gribbin, *Future Weather*, Pelican, 1982.)

From J. Gribbin, *Future Weather*, Pelican, 1982.

b The following analysis highlights **some** of the changes predicted to take place in global CO_2 production.

Check your answers to *a* by reading quickly through it.

These two pie charts assume zero energy growth in the USA, 2% growth in Europe, 4% in the USSR and East Europe, 4.5% in China and 1.5% in the Third World.

It seems likely that in 2025, global production of CO_2 will be 6 times that of 1974. The proportional contribution of individual countries to this predicted figure will probably change however.

For example, whereas up to 1974 China produced only 8% of all emissions, it is likely that by 2025 this proportion will double. On the other hand, the US, which currently produces the largest proportion of CO_2 emissions, will produce proportionately less.

c Continue the passage with similar statements about the USSR, the Third World and Western Europe.

D2 *a* One line on this graph represents food production in sub-Saharan Africa and the other, food production in 6 nations of southern Asia. Which line do you think represents the African situation? Give reasons for your choice when discussing this with other students.

b Then check your answer by reading the description below.

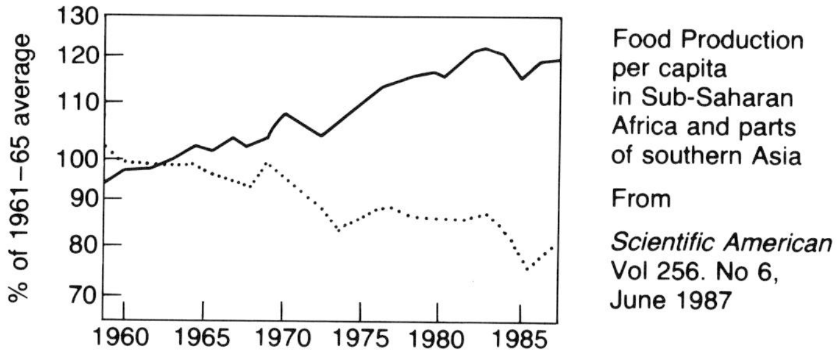

From *Scientific American Vol 256. No 6, June 1987*

This graph shows that food production in sub-Saharan Africa was at its highest point in 1960.

Between 1960 and 1985, the overall trend was a downward one. Initially this downward trend was gradual, but after 1970 the decline was marked by two troughs, in the mid-seventies and the early eighties. The only discernible peak was a small one in 1970, but even then production did not reach previous levels.

It seems likely that this trend reflects the severe drought conditions that have prevailed in the region over the past two decades.

c Now write a similar description of the trend shown by the other line.

D3 *a* Consider the table below. What trend can you discern?

b What conclusions can you draw from this information?

Percentage increases in population and energy consumption per capita between 1950 and 1970

	Population (%)	*Energy/person (%)*
World	46	57
Africa	59	73
North America	38	43
Latin America	75	122
Asia	52	197
Europe	18	96
Oceania	54	54

Source: United Nations

c Write a brief paragraph describing the table, outlining any important trends and, if possible, drawing conclusions.

SECTION 3

A Overheating

So far we have been mainly concerned with ecological problems on land. But human activity affects our atmosphere too.

1 *a* Consider these questions with a partner and note down your opinions.
- What products are we putting into the atmosphere which are likely to cause damage?
- What effects do these products have on our ecosystem?

b Listen to the interview and make brief notes on the speaker's answers to these questions.

A2 *a* Here is a list of points that are mentioned in the interview. Decide and note down what order they arise in.

(*i*) Methane and chlorofluorocarbons also influence our climate.
(*ii*) The CO_2 level in the atmosphere is rising.
(*iii*) A solution will require international co-operation.
(*iv*) Climate change will vary from country to country.
(*v*) CO_2 and other gases are making our climate warmer.

b Listen to the talk again and check your answers.

A3 We have used a mind map with a reading text. The same approach can be applied to a listening exercise.

a Working with a partner, reduce the points listed above to key words and mark them down on a mind map.

b Listen again to the interview and extend your mind map with further supporting detail. Make sure that main points are closer to the centre than supporting detail.

c Compare your finished map with those of other students. Pay special attention to visual impact.

A4 The scientist makes predictions about a number of factors:
- The level of CO_2 in the atmosphere at the end of this century.

– Future changes in climate.
– How different countries will be affected by climate change.

a What predictions did he make about these factors? With other students, try to recall what he said.

b Listen to the extracts from the talk and note down the actual phrases used.

c Are these predictions – definite?
– tentative?

B Are we draining the Gene Pool?

1 Judging from the title above, what do think the text on this page will be about?
a The pollution of lakes and ponds.
b Desertification.
c The extinction of species.
Discuss with other students the reasons for your prediction.

Look briefly at the text and see if you were right.

Exactly how many species the Earth supports is still unknown – estimates vary from 3 to 10 million. However, only 1.5 million have been scientifically recorded. The rate of discovery is still swift: in the African rain forests alone more than 200 new plant species are being recorded each year. What is clear, however, is that many species are disappearing. Current estimates are that 2,000 vertebrates are in danger of extinction as are 10 per cent of all the flowering plants known to science – about 25,000 species. Of the 145 indigenous cattle breeds found in Europe and the Mediterranean, no less than 115 are now threatened with extinction.

It is vital that as many species as possible be saved. One reason is economic. We depend for new varieties of crops and animals on the wild gene stock available from which to cultivate improved strains. As an example, in the 1860s an insect feeding on the roots of vines destroyed nearly every vineyard in Europe. Only the discovery of vines in the United States which were resistant to the insect made it possible for the vineyards of Europe to be re-stocked, by grafting European vines on to American roots – a practice which continues to this day.

In addition, almost all our agriculture and much of our medicine depend on strains which have been successfully adapted from the wild gene pool. In the United States alone, the value of medicines sold each year which are extracted from various plants is in the region of $3,000m.

Agriculture (and pharmaceutical and certain other industries) depend on infusions of fresh germ plasm imported from the genetic powerhouses which, except for a part of the Mediterranean, are all located in developing countries.

The importance of this is not simply that the wild gene stock provides something to fall back on in times of emergency. It is, in fact, being constantly used to improve species which are increasingly vulnerable to attack from different pests which are becoming more and more resistant to pesticides.

The discovery of new species also holds out the promise of new products. Rubber and quinine both came from the discovery of new trees. It is quite possible that new products of equal importance may yet emerge from the gene stock which is still waiting to be discovered, particularly in the tropical rain forests. The armadillo, for example, has recently been discovered to be the only animal other than man capable of contracting leprosy. As a result of this, a leprosy vaccine is now being developed. And in view of the growing importance of biotechnology, the preservation of microbial strains of life is also becoming urgent.

2 In what ways does the Gene Pool serve humanity?

Working on your own, read through the text again and note down as many ways as you can find in mind map form.

Compare your findings with those of other students.

C Is this the answer?

The next text provides us with a plan for protecting the environment, or at least parts of it.

1 From the title of the text, 'Biosphere reserves', can you predict what this plan might involve?

a Share your ideas with other students in the group.

b Read through the text quickly and check your predictions.

Biosphere reserves

Biosphere reserves are designed to fulfil a number of functions. They are intended to protect the flora and fauna, and the genetic diversity, of an ecological area of special interest as well as to provide a place for research, education, and training in the relevant sciences. They are linked together in a world-wide network and the computerized MAB Information System provides information on both the nature and the activities of each biosphere reserve.

Ideally, each biosphere reserve consists of a core area, surrounded by an inner buffer zone and an outer buffer zone. Typically, the core area remains undisturbed and uninhabited. Activity in this area is limited to conservation and there is a minimum of human interference. The core area serves as a baseline against which to monitor environmental changes elsewhere.

The first buffer zone contains the research station, plus other human settlements. It is used for education and training, and for 'manipulative' research on conservation and ecosystem management. There may be traditional land-use activities – logging, grazing, and fishing, for example. The second buffer zone carries this trend a stage further. In it, experiments may be conducted on alternative systems of land use; it is likely to be actively managed for the benefit of local populations, and it may even have to be 'reclaimed' for them.

By 1982 there were 214 biosphere reserves in 58 countries. However, there was a great deal of duplication of types of environment covered.

The major gaps being in tropical moist forests, warm arid zones, coastal areas, and traditional man-modified landscapes.

However, the potential role of biosphere reserves in world conservation is very large. In contrast to the idea of national parks, biosphere reserves can stimulate the active involvement of local populations in protecting and developing their own enviornments. This is an important and so far neglected area in conservation. In the past, the establishment of conservation areas has often alienated local populations, whose opinions were not solicited and whose life-styles suffered severe disruption as a result. The existence of many of these conservation areas is now threatened by an expanding and hostile local population. As Michel Batisse writes:

> The biosphere reserve constitutes a technique, among others, to reverse this very dangerous trend. Experience already shows that when the populations are fully informed of the objectives of the biosphere reserve, and understand that it is in their own and their children's interest to care for its functioning, the problem of protection is largely solved. In this manner, the biosphere reserve becomes fully integrated – not only into the surrounding land-use system, but also into its social, economic and cultural reality.

From R. Clarke 'Science and Technology in World Development'. OUP 1985

C2 The text provides a detailed description of what constitutes a biosphere reserve.

a Present this information in clear note form.

b Compare your results with those of other students. Decide which style of notes best highlights the main points.

C3 Biosphere reserves and national parks have a lot in common. However, as the writer points out, there are also considerable differences between them.

a With the help of the text, and using some of your own views as well, pick out the main points of similarity and difference.

Note these down in chart form.

b Write a short paragraph comparing and contrasting the two.

D A look to the future: Points for discussion

In this section we have considered some views of the future of our ecosystem. What are your views on the matter?

Here are some points you might like to consider.

1 Is the overall view presented in this section a pessimistic one or does it offer hope for the future?

D2 The role of the international scientific community has been referred to a number of times in this section.

Why is the role of the scientist such an important one?

What other members of the international community need to be involved?

D3 Can you suggest any direct action that could be taken to protect the ecosystem in your own environment?

E Where do YOU stand? – Preparing a short talk

1 Consider these topics and choose the one which interests you the most. You will be required to prepare a short talk (about 3 minutes) on the subject.

a We have to accept the ecological consequences of our activities in this technological world.

b Humanity has gone too far with its interference in the environment.

c 'Every day, in every way, our world is getting better and better.'

E2 With other students who have chosen the same topic, note down as many points as possible that could be dealt with. A mind map might help.

E3 *a* Working on your own, select from these points the ones that you want to talk about.

Remember that your time will be limited, so you should keep your list short.

b Arrange the points in a logical order.

c Make notes on the information you want to include to support these points.

You can refer to information in this Unit, other Units or any other sources you like.

E4 Now you are ready to draw up your final plan. You should keep the following points in mind.

a	**Introduction**	You will need to *(i)* introduce the general topic *(ii)* explain the structure of your talk Can you think of suitable phrases for these stages?
b	**Talk content**	For ease of reference, the points that you want to make should be reduced to key words only. You should not read from your notes.
c	**Visuals**	Flow charts, diagrams, mind maps, graphs and so on can be very effective ways of presenting information. But you will have to consider how you will display them – on a blackboard – in poster form – on an overhead projector The visuals should be simple and have an immediate impact.
d	**Conclusion**	In order to make sure that your main points are clear, you might summarise them at this stage and draw a general conclusion.

Now, prepare the notes you are going to talk from and any visuals you have decided to use.

E5 Before you deliver your talk, you need to design a means of assessing your performance. The notes below provide you with hints on what you should be looking for.

a Working with a partner, read the instructions in exercises 6 and 7 and draw up a suitable assessment chart.

b Compare your chart with those of other students. Agree on a common format to be used by the whole class.

Notes on delivery

Timing	Your time is limited in this case to 3 minutes.
Pace	Your speed of delivery should allow listeners enough time to take in what you are saying. On the other hand, too slow a pace can be boring.
Voice	You should be heard by everybody in the room. This involves projecting your voice to the far corners.
Stance	When speaking, face your audience. If you are referring to a visual, don't turn your back on your listeners. Don't speak to the blackboard.
Audience contact	Try to speak to all your listeners and not just a section.

E6 The talks can now be delivered in groups. There should not be more than five people in each group.

When you are listening, use your checklist to record your comments on each speaker's performance.

When you have given your own talk, note down your assessment of your performance on your checklist.

E7 Finally, when all speakers in your group have delivered their talks, compare your assessment notes. Consider the following:

a Does your assessment of your own talk coincide with other people's comments on it?

b Are there any common strengths or weaknesses in the group?

c Can you agree on any strategies for improvement?

SECTION 4 *TROPICAL RAINFORESTS*

A What do you know about rainforests?

1 Test your knowledge on rainforests by discussing the following questions with your group.

a What are rainforests?

b What regions of the earth are these forests to be found in?

c What countries can you find such forests in?

d What do you know about the flora and fauna of rainforests?

e Growth is rapid in these zones. Why?

f What do you know about the rainforest's 'canopy'?

g Rainforests are under threat at the moment. Why?

h Do you know of any attempts to preserve the world's rainforests?

i When did the destruction of rainforests begin?

j What are the reasons behind this deforestation?

k What nations are most responsible for this destruction?

l What are the consequences of deforestation?

Test the accuracy of your answers by reading quickly through the three texts on pages 82 and 85.

A2 These three texts give us different angles on the same subject. Which of the following best describe each text? More than one of these may be appropriate for each text.

a An attack on conservationists

b An attack on government policy

c An attack on Western living standards

d An outline of the various ways in which rainforests are exploited

e An outline of the effects of deforestation

f An analysis of the structure of rainforests

g An attempt to create an awareness of the problems caused by deforestation

h An appeal to people's consciences

A3 The text 'What makes rainforests so special?' on page 82 will provide you with useful information for a later activity.

a Pick out the main points and note them down. Compare your choice with those of other students.

b Complete your notes with supporting detail from the text.

You may use any note-making format you wish, as long as it is **clear, concise** and **complete**.

c Working in a group, decide which students have the most effective notes.

Text 1

What makes rainforests so special?

A vast number of species coexist in tropical forests. Why so many? The complex architecture of the canopy, and the evolutionary history of the forests, are part of the answer

Peter Moore

MOST people realise that tropical forests are by far the most diverse of the Earth's ecosystems. Less welcome but equally well publicised is the knowledge that these precious reservoirs of animals and plants are being destroyed at an appalling rate of between 50 000 and 20 000 square kilometres each year. If this rate of clearance continues, all primary – that is, undisturbed – forest will disappear in the next 30 years, and all rainforest of any sort within about 80 years.

Quite apart from moral and aesthetic objections, we must ask whether humanity can afford the immense extinction of plant and animal species that this process will entail. Perhaps as much as 80 per cent of the world's insects, for example, live in the tropical forest. Malaya alone currently boasts at

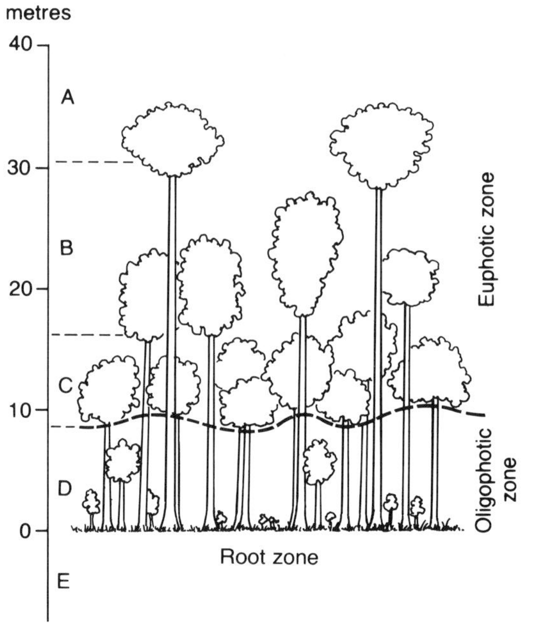

The complex architecture of the rainforest creates varied environments for a huge range of creatures. Paul Richard divides the canopy into five regions. But two divisions are most important he suggests. In the upper "euphotic" zone leaves receive direct sunlight. But plants in the "oligophotic" zone receive mostly reflected and transmitted light and the occasional sunfleck least 20 000 species of flowering plants, most of which live in rainforests. Who knows how many species have yet to be described, and what potential value they may have to pharmacology or agriculture?

But we still do not know what makes the forest of the wet equatorial regions so rich in species. Ecologists are urgently trying to discover the reason in order to determine the best way of conserving and managing what will necessarily become mere fragments of the Earth's former forests. Almost all ecological food webs start with green plants, and it is at this level that the quest for diversity must also begin.

The climate of the equatorial belt encourages the growth of plants: there is some 80 kilograms of vegetation per square metre, in these areas. Both rainfall and temperature are high and, in some regions, fairly constant throughout the year. Rainfall is usually between 2.5 and 4 metres a year, but can rise to as high as 10 metres. Temperatures often range between 20 and 28°C. There are no periods of drought or cold to limit production: equatorial forests are similar in dimensions to the vast coal forests of the Carboniferous. Just like those long-extinct communities, the forest canopy may stand at 30 metres or so, with a few trees reaching 40 or 50 metres.

One feature of the tropical forest that has attracted the attention of ecologists is the way in which the forest's canopy is arranged into layers. When Paul Richards of the University of Wales first published his classical work on tropical forests in 1952, he proposed that we could divide the canopy into five strata. Biologists have since considerably modified this generalisation to account for the wide range of structure found in nature. So we must first ask whether the forest's canopy really is stratified. Can ecologists distinguish between discrete layers, or is the forest simply a continuum of variation?

Richards now believes that some forests are stratified, particularly those in which a particular species of tree dominates, as in the swamp forests of *Shorea albida* in Sarawak, Malaysia. But we cannot determine precise boundaries to the layers of the canopy in many mixed forests. Donald Perry has closely studied the structure of the forests in Costa Rica. He describes a three-layered canopy: emergent trees occupy the upper zone, 35–50 metres high: below these, at 25–35 metres, there is a dense under-canopy; beneath that, at 10–25 metres is an understorey. Richards believes that one boundary is most important. Above this boundary the leaves receive direct sunlight (he calls this the 'euphotic' zone). Below is the 'oligophotic' zone which receives mostly reflected and transmitted light together with occasional sunflecks.

The complexity of the structure of the canopy in tropical rainforests contributes to its diversity in species. Not only does such complexity permit a great range of species of plants to coexist, it also provides varied microhabitats in which all kinds of animals, both vertebrate and invertebrate, can make a living. But the development of this complexity requires a high degree of coevolution, which takes both time and a modicum of environmental stability.

Text 2

Rainforests face attack of double standards

Catherine Caufield, San Francisco

PRESERVING tropical forests is an idea at the top of America's international agenda. The US's Agency for International Development (USAID) says it will not 'support or assist' projects that destroy rainforests. Last December, Congress passed a law that told American directors of development banks to 'vigorously promote' loans for projects that protect rather than damage rainforests.

That law has already caused the US to veto a loan of several million dollars to Brazil because the money would have paid for the destruction of Amazonian forest. Two other bills are pending which would require USAID to spend at least $10 million each year protecting biological diversity and promoting the conservation of rainforests in developing countries.

This tough approach is working: nations in the Third World are taking a close look at the social and economic benefits of looking after their rainforests.

But one country that has not stopped destroying its rainforests is the US itself.

Few Americans are aware that the US has rainforests, much less that they are rapidly approaching extinction. The main concentration is in Hawaii. Smaller forests in Puerto Rico and on Pacific islands are also under the US's control. Together, they account for less than half a per cent of the world's tropical forests. Environmentalists say that the US should be well able to protect them.

Six years ago, the US State Department recommended to the President that the US 'seek to protect and manage US tropical forests in an exemplary fashion'.

Hawaii is the most isolated chain of islands in the world. For millions of years, its remoteness and climate made the archipelago a rich source of new species. No area on Earth has as high a proportion of plants and animals that occur nowhere else. Ninety five per cent of the state's flowering plants and 99 per cent of its animals and birds are unique to Hawaii. 'For evolutionary biologists,' says Jim Jacobi of the US Fish and Wildlife Service, 'Hawaii is at least as interesting as the Galapagos Islands. It's certainly a lot more complex.'

Yet the habitats of Hawaii are

being destroyed. Deforestation began with the arrival 1500 years ago of the Polynesians and increased dramatically 200 years ago when Europeans and Americans found the islands. Since then, two-thirds of the native rainforest has been destroyed to make way for plantations, ranches and urban sprawl. Much of what remains is too fragmented to survive.

With the forests have gone hundreds of species of plants and animals. Hawaii's forests once supported 57 species and sub species of birds; now 23 are extinct and another 23 listed as endangered. Almost half the birds the US government lists as endangered are from Hawaii. Of the 3000 species of plants once found in the archipelago, 270 are extinct. Another 800 types of plant are in danger.

Jacobi warns: 'Many plants are going to be extinct before they are confirmed as endangered.' While working in the rainforest in 1973, Jacobi and a fellow student at the University of Hawaii discovered an entirely new genus of bird. The po'o-uli has such a small territory that it has been on the danger list from the moment of discovery.

Hawaii's lowland rainforests have suffered the most damage. From covering almost half the island's land surface 200 years ago, they now cover a mere 5 per cent. Upland rainforests have fared better, but the pace of deforestation has not slowed. Environmentalists are fighting what one calls 'a new boom in deforestation'.

Most destruction takes place on private lands. State and federal laws encourage it. Oswald Stender, chief executive of the Campbell Estate, a large landowner on the islands, explained the advantages of converting forest to pasture for cattle. First, the trees can be ground into wood chips and sold as fuel to the Hawaii Electric Light Company. Secondly, many rainforests fall in land that the state has zoned for agriculture. Owners in these areas pay lower taxes if they destroy forests and start a cattle ranch or plant crops.

Laws requiring the state of Hawaii to reveal how much rainforest is zoned for agriculture are stalled in the state's legislature. Last year, the Campbell Estate converted 400 hectares of land, which Dieter Mueller-Dombois, a botanist from the University of Hawaii, described as 'the best rainforest left in Hawaii' into pasture. 'We hadn't looked at it from an environmental point of view,' Stender agreed. The Campbell Estate says it no longer turns rainforests into fuel chips, but other landowners continue to do so.

Hawaii: Uncle Sam's slice of the global rainforest

The Campbell Estate is at the centre of Hawaii's most controversial development, a site covering 3500 hectares to extract geothermal heat from the slopes of Kilauea Volcano. The estate wants to lease the land to a company in Wyoming called True/Mid-Pacific. The company would drill 80 wells to tap the volcano's steam, and build as many as five power plants to generate electricity from it. Last month the state approved the scheme, but environmentalists and native Hawaiians said they will continue their battle to stop it.

For the past four years, opponents have said the project will damage a conservation zone that is home to several rare species of plants and birds. Plans for the site include roads and pipelines, ponds for silica spoil, cooling towers and drilling around the clock.

Such activities are normally banned in conservation areas. In 1984, Hawaii's state government passed a special law designating the project's area a 'geothermal subzone'.

Hawaii's main island does not need another 100 megawatts of electrical generating capacity, so the state and federal governments are spending $27 million to study the feasibility of building the world's longest deep-sea power cable to send the electricity 300 kilometres northwest to Oahu. The link would cost $400 million. 'They want to destroy our land in order to light up the skyline of Oahu,' complains Lehua Lopez, a native Hawaiian who is fighting the project.

Hawaii's dilemma is little different from those that many Third World countries face. Their governments believe that the biggest contribution rainforests can make is to create space for more profitable enterprises. The US discourages such activities overseas – but helps to pay for them in Hawaii.

Text 3

B Taking up the issue – A public enquiry

1 Hawaiian environmentalists and developers are facing a dilemma.

With other students in your group decide:
a What exactly this dilemma involves.
b Who is involved.

2 A public enquiry is about to take place to look into the whole issue.

Each interested party will have an opportunity to state their cases individually. When all cases have been heard, an open discussion will take place. The proceedings will be chaired by an independent chairperson.

a Decide who will chair the enquiry.
You may like to invite your teacher to do this.

b Decide which parties will be represented.

In all cases, it is quite likely that more than one student will represent each party. Choose at least **two** from each list:

List 1	**List 2**
US Fish & Wildlife Service.	Campbell Estate.
Members of Hawaiian public.	Hawaii Electric Light Co.
Members of Hawaiian branch of Friends of the Earth.	True/Mid-Pacific Co.
Hawaiian government officials.	US State Dept officials.

c Agree what the public enquiry should aim to achieve.
- For example, you may decide that it is sufficient for all parties to present their cases and discuss their points of view.
- On the other hand you may want to reach some kind of consensus between the parties.
- Or indeed you may want the chairperson to judge all cases and make a final decision on future policy.

d Agree on the amount of time that will be spent on:
- planning the presentations.
- delivering each presentation.
- conducting the final discussion.

B3 Divide into your groups and plan your presentations. Don't forget your presentation time will be limited.

B4 When you are ready, begin the enquiry.

C Taking sides – A report

Write a brief account of the problems and the discussion that took place at the enquiry for one of the following publications:

a an American national newspaper.

b a Hawaiian newspaper.

c a Friends of the Earth publication.

SECTION 5 *MAPPING YOUR THOUGHTS*

A Mind maps

We are going to consider the mind map below in order to assess its value.
- Do you think that it is a good summary of the skills that you have practised in this unit?
- Have any important points been left out?
- Are the four main points of the mind map clearly outlined?

Application

1 Try this note-making system out on some subject work. Working with a partner, if you can, select some notes which you have made recently in a different note form. Try to transfer them to a mind map.

Remember the following points:

a	**Key words**	The mind map should be **briefer** than the original notes and therefore easier to remember.
b	**Layout**	Make sure that it is easy to tell the difference between the central heading, sub-headings and supporting details.
c	**Linking**	Watch the direction of your arrows. Are all the links shown? Is every arrow necessary?
d	**Impact**	Don't confine yourself to bubbles. Use any shape you like. Use drawings and colours to make your map more vivid.

These same points are displayed on the mind map below for comparison.

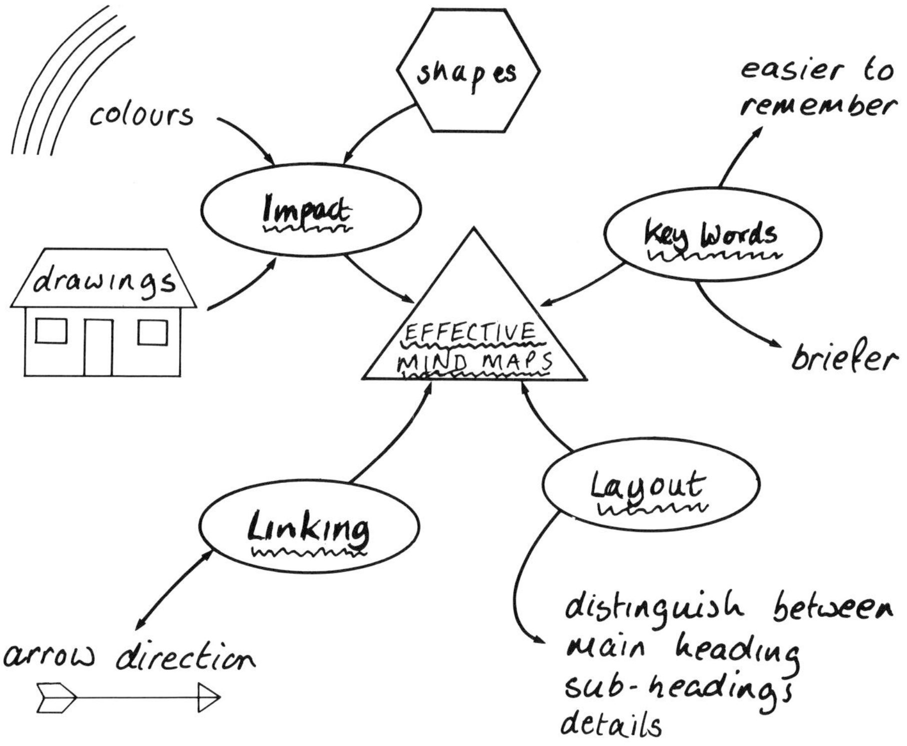

2 You may decide that you don't want to use minds maps as a note-making technique. However, you might consider using this approach as a means of revising in an active way. When preparing for a test, try following these steps:
- Draw up a mind map to break down the topic you need to study into main areas.
- Use your mind map as a check list for recording work completed.
- Transform previously made notes into mind map form. Don't try to include all the detail in the original notes. Pick out the key points only.
- See if these notes are any easier to memorise.

B Reading texts

When confronted with a large body of material that you have to read, it can be helpful to be able to predict what these texts contain, and which parts are useful to you.

We often overlook book, chapter and section titles. However, these can provide valuable clues if we give them some thought. Similarly, the first paragraph of a text can provide us with hints about what will follow. Readers often ignore these and delve straight into the text proper.

Application

So the next time you have to do some reading on your course, keep this in mind:

1 Before you begin reading in depth, scan the texts for available title clues.
2 Note down briefly what you expect each titled section to contain.
3 Read briefly through the introductory paragraphs of each one and check whether you have guessed accurately or not.
4 At this stage you may decide to discard some of the texts, if they don't seem relevant to your purpose.

UNIT 5 · *Food for thought*

SECTION 1 *IT'S NOT ALL BAD NEWS*

A1 *a* Divide into groups and choose a crop that is grown successfully in your country.

b Ensure that each group selects a different crop.

c List the factors which explain why the crop thrives naturally and is profitable economically. (Do not lose this list. You will need it later.)

A2 *a* Look at the headline below and try to predict what it is referring to.

Cameroon: Food For The People

b Quickly scan the test on the following page and see if your expection was correct.

By JOHN MADELEY

WHILE the majority of African countries battle in vain to feed ever-growing populations from home-grown food resources, Cameroon is showing how it can be done.

The West African country, with a population of nearly 10 million, represents the other face of African agriculture, the one to which the mirror is rarely held.

Since 1971, Cameroon has doubled output of major foodcrops such as maize, yams and potatoes, and now is one of the handful of African countries more than able to feed its people itself.

Only five years ago, the country was estimated to be between 75 and 80 per cent self-sufficient in food.

Isolated pockets of hunger remain today, but when the World Bank recently gave Cameroon a loan for agricultural research, it said the money was expected to 'help maintain Cameroon's self-sufficiency in food.'

In some respects, Cameroon is naturally fortunate. It has adequate rainfall for crop-growing, and since 1978 its economy has been boosted by oil revenue, giving the country a per capita income of US$800.

But there is more to its food success story than natural advantages.

The key is a pattern of government policy decisions fitting together to release the potential of the country's farmers – more than three-quarters of whom farm less than two hectares of land.

First, the government has devoted a larger slice of its national budget to agriculture than most African countries. Under the Fifth Development Plan from 1981–85, almost a quarter of the budget was ear-marked for agriculture and rural development.

Half-price fertilisers

Second, the government has given farmers the incentives they need to produce.

Rather than fixing higher prices – food is all traded on the market – it has provided farmers with new technology and half-price fertilisers, opening up the prospect of higher yields and earnings.

Ironically, shortages in some of Cameroon's six neighbouring countries have given its farmers additional incentives to produce and export food across the borders – usually unofficially.

Third, the government recognises that women grow most of the food across Africa, and every effort has been made to encourage women farmers with credit schemes, inputs, storage facilities and organisational help.

Fourth, Cameroon has cooperated with international agricultural institutes which have pioneered low-cost technology for small farmers. In particular, it has worked closely with the Nigerian-based International Institute for Tropical Agriculture (IITA).

It has tested the technology in different areas of Cameroon, adapting it to help farmers obtain the most suitable for their area.

Finally, Cameroon has attracted aid. *Donors* have been keen to lend a hand to a country whose agricultural house is in order and which stands to gain from a litle outside help.

Nowhere is this more closely seen than in the north-west province bordering Nigeria.

Until 1981 the north-west was neglected by planners, starved of development finance and marred by hunger, poor living conditions and incomes well below the national average.

In six years the province has undergone a remarkable transformation. It now is self-sufficient in food, output of which has increased by nearly 50 per cent, its small farms are thriving, and illiteracy has dropped from 80 per cent to 50 per cent.

The transformation has come through the US$44-million North-West Rural Development Project (MIDENO), which is part-funded by the Cameroon Ministry of Agriculture with help from several aid agencies.

This includes US$12 million from the United Nations' International Fund for Agricultural Development (IFAD), which specialises in helping poorer farmers grow more food.

The province includes the Nyos area, where last August 1,700 people were killed when suffocating gas erupted from a volcanic lake. Thousands of head of livestock also were killed, and farming over an area of some 10 square miles (25 sq km) was brought to a standstill.

The project aims to increase food output throughout the province, raise incomes and improve roads for faster movement of crops and goods.

A key aspect of the scheme is adaptation of agricultural techniques developed at the provincial research station for practical on-farm use.

Storage techniques

'Research has come up with 15 different varieties of maize,' said agronomist Bivina Jean-Simon. 'We adapt the research to farmers' needs.'

The new maize varieties are tested at 10 trial and demonstration centres throughout the province to find the right seeds and combination of crops for different areas.

The results then go out as recommendations, through trained village extension workers, to farmers in each area.

The link between research and extension 'is as well organised as anywhere in the world,' said extension and training adviser John Parkinson.

Farmers are not slow to accept advice from extension workers. 'We discovered farmers are very ready to accept advice when they see the prospect of definite benefits – when they can see, for example, that by growing maize in the recommended fashion they will increase output,' Parkinson said.

Results have been spectacular. Some 6,000 women farmers have increased their maize yields from 1.6 to three tons per hectare, and are earning extra money by using improved storage techniques for maize and potatoes.

For most women, the chief priority for this extra income is to educate their children – to buy uniforms and books to enable them attend school.

While Cameroon gives generous help to farmers growing food crops for home consumption, it takes a different view over export crops including coffee and cocoa. Low prices are paid to such farmers, the majority of whom are men.

Noticing how well the women are faring, many men now wonder whether they should switch from coffee to food crops. – Compass News Features

New Straits Times, Feb/Mar 1987

B As a student the format of your notes is important. A logical order using headings and sub-divisions can help recall and also leave space for making additions and comments.

B1 Below are some notes based on the first five paragraphs of the article entitled 'Cameroon: Food for the people.'

a Do you think they are effective?

b Do they bring out the main points?

c Are they concise?

d Could anything have been left out?

e Are these notes easy to remember?

Cameroon: Food for the people
Cameroon is a West African country of ten million people which has been very successful in growing food for its people, unlike many other West African countries. Since 1971 it has doubled its output of major foodstuffs such as maize, yams and potatoes. Now it is one of the few African countries able to feed itself. This was not the case five years ago when the country was only 75–80% self-sufficient in food. Although isolated pockets of hunger still remain the World Bank nowadays gives Cameroon money to sustain, not to achieve, self-sufficiency in food production.

f Can you suggest any changes to the notes that would:
– highlight the main points?
– reduce their length and save time?
– help you to remember them?

There is no one single correct way to take notes. The important thing is to select one which suits you.

B2 The secret of success

Read the text on Cameroon again, then copy and complete the outline notes given below.

A Self-sufficiency in food

1 Natural factors

a

b

2 Government policy

a

b incentives to farmers:
(i) → *(iii)*
(ii) → *(iv)*

c

d

e

B Effects of self-sufficiency in NW province

1

2

3

C Export crops

Does this style of note-making enable you to include all the major points in the article? Discuss the advantages and disadvantages of this style and suggest possible improvements or an alternative method of presenting the information.

SECTION 2 *HOW DO THEY DO IT?*

A In taking notes from talks and discussions there is less time to get information down in a clear and concise form. This means you may have to adapt your style of note-taking.

A1 *a* Listen to the informal discussion between Mr. Iddrisu, a delegate from the tiny Atlantic island of Lodos, and Mr. Bivina, a representative from the Cameroonian Ministry of Agriculture. (This discussion took place during a break in proceedings at an international conference on agricultural productivity.)

Note down the major problems outlined by Mr. Iddrisu and the solutions suggested by the Cameroonian representative.

b Compare your own notes with those of your classmates.
(i) Are the points the same?
(ii) Are the points recorded in a clear and easily recognisable form?

c If necessary, rewrite your own original notes.

A2 *a* Listen to the taped discussion again. Both speakers use certain phrases like 'due to' and 'as a result of' in order to clarify their explanations. Note down all the examples of this type of phrase.

b Note down any words and phrases not mentioned by the speakers which you commonly use in giving explanations.

c Compare and discuss the words on your own list with those mentioned by your classmates.

A3 On his return to Lodos Mr. Iddrisu decides to attempt to implement the self-sufficiency scheme but he realizes that to do so successfully he must convince the ordinary farmers of his country.

a Form into groups of four. One of you is an official from the Lodos Ministry of Agriculture. The other three are farmers.

b **The ministry official**
Try to persuade the farmers to switch from cocoa to food crops as persuasively as possible.

The farmers
You should cross-examine the ministry official as thoroughly as possible before deciding to make the switch or not. The persuasiveness of the speaker should influence your decision as much as the facts he puts forward.

c Compare the decisions reached by the farmers in all the groups in order to see which Ministry official was the most persuasive.

B Notes are often reconstituted in either an oral or written form to make explanations to a wider audience. In other words, they are useful not only to help you remember ideas but also to present those ideas to other people on a blackboard, whiteboard or overhead projector.

B1 *a* Refer to the points you jotted down in completing exercise **A1** *c* in Section 1.

b Order those points according to your preferred system of recording notes.

c Give a talk to the class which makes use of that note-taking system to demonstrate **visually** to the rest of the class why the crop you selected has been successful.

B2 In giving explanations, **how** you say something can be as important as **what** you say.

a Read the following extract and make short notes on the problems faced by Malaysian fishermen.

b Divide into groups and use the notes you have made to write a short speech to be delivered by one of the following:

(i) A politician addressing a group of fishermen in a village hall during an election campaign.

(ii) The Malaysian representative addressing a group of delegates at an international fisheries conference.

While composing your speech it is important that you consider the inter-relationship between:

- The likely attitude of the speaker towards the problem.
- What the audience already knows about the problem.
- The environment the talk is being delivered in.
- The expectations of the audience.
- The speaker's intention in delivering the speech.

Life for the fisherman has not improved

Sarah Dina

I GREW up in a fishing village. Even though my father was not a fisherman himself, I learned that the life of a fisherman is not easy. I have seen with my own eyes the fishermen going out to the high seas in the early hours of the day and hauling their catch back to sell to the *taukehs* (middlemen).

I have seen them toil under the hot sun, dragging their wet and heavy nets to dry some three miles from where they docked their boats. After a meal and a nap, they would go back to the spot, this time to mend any tears in their nets so that they can be ready to use the following day.

I must have been only about seven at that time. I still remember how excited I was when I saw the fishermen in their boats, coming back from the sea. They would haul their catch, big and small fishes, to the beach where the *taukehs* would be waiting for them.

I took delight in watching them haggle over the price. If the price was right, the *taukehs* would have the fishes packed in ice and sent elsewhere to be sold.

Life for the fisherman is full of hardships, I later learned. The fisherman earns just enough to feed the family. Usually there is little left to save. Sometimes during the rainy season when they cannot go out to the seas, there is no money to buy food.

I can still remember how my mother used to prepare dried fish when fishes were abundant and sell them cheaply to fishermen during the rainy season. Sometimes she would give the dried fish away to poorer fishermen. Even before the end of the rainy season our supply of dried fish would either be sold out or given away.

Borrow

When the weather did not improve, many fishmen had to borrow money from the *taukehs* who would deduct the amount from their catch when the fishermen are able to go out to sea again. During this time some coffee shop owners and rice stall owners closed their shops temporarily because of a lack of business.

Because the fishermen earned very little, their wives also worked to supplement their income. During low tide, it was quite common to see fishermen's wives by the beach, looking for clams and shellfish.

They would dig bucketfuls of these and then dry them in the sun. These would be sold to the *taukehs* at a very low price. One kati of dried shellfish would only fetch about 30 to 40 cents.

I did not understand why the fishermen's wives had to dig for clams and shellfish. I thought it was rather fun and my younger brother and I would have joined them had not my mother given us stern warnings not to do so. Instead we had to content ourselves with sitting by the shore watching them while they worked.

But even at that tender age, I had noticed that while the fishermen live in poverty, there were people who lived in large brick houses and drove around in big cars. I had realized that they led a totally different life from that of the fishermen who had to face hardships in their work. These people, I learned, were the rich *taukehs* and the owners of the boats.

These were the people who slept comfortably in their beds while the fishermen were already up, and in the high seas. These were also the people who made their profits from the fishermen's sweat and toil.

Many years have passed by since then. The fisherman's life has not changed for the better. The government has tried from time to time to improve the living standard of these people but the majority of them still remain poor.

I do not know what had gone wrong. But at a recent national conference on development in the country, Dr Ishak Shari, a UKM lecturer and an expert in the field of fisheries, pointed out the need to revamp the present policy taken by the government as poverty among the fishermen is still very much a reality.

In his paper 'Development and Indifference among East Coast Fishermen in Malaysia, Dr Ishak stated that despite the multiple schemes and aid to help the fishermen, problems, new and old, have cropped up from time to time. Not only has the living standard of fishermen remained low, they have to compete with 'foreign' fishing vessels for their catch.

According to Dr Ishak, the launching of the subsidy scheme would have given many fishermen access to fishing equipment and capital, and that would be able to relieve them of some of their problems.

However, he said that the scheme had been inefficiently managed and as such many fishermen do not benefit from it. 'This shows that the aim of the government to eradicate poverty among fishermen has not been successful as many fishermen still cannot enjoy the benefits of the scheme.'

c Elect a member of your group to deliver the speech in the most convincing and appropriate manner possible.

If possible try to record the speeches as this will enable you to make a more detailed analysis of the speaker's approach.

Listen critically to the speech given by the other group in order to suggest how the language used could be made more appropriate.

SECTION 3 *A GLOBAL PROBLEM*

A1 Although the world has had many successes in feeding its people certain problems still remain such as the threats posed to mankind by pests.

a Which pest poses the biggest problem in your society?

b Explain exactly why it is a threat.

A2 *a* Read the extract below and make brief notes on:
- the principal insect referred to by the writer.
- its habitat, life history and behaviour.
- the principal threat it poses to man.
- the most effective means of dealing with the insect.

Insect Fighters Gear for War

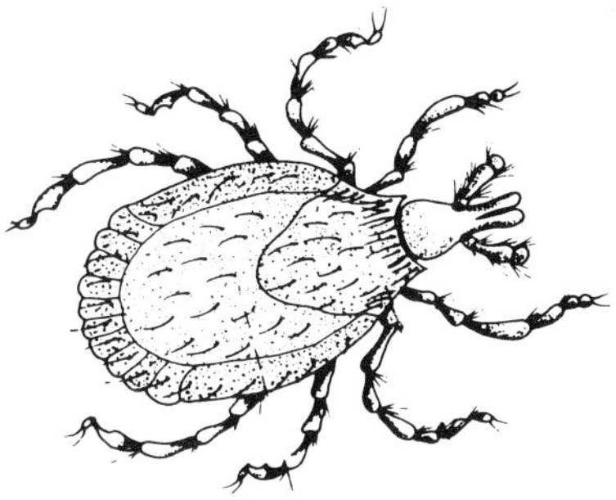

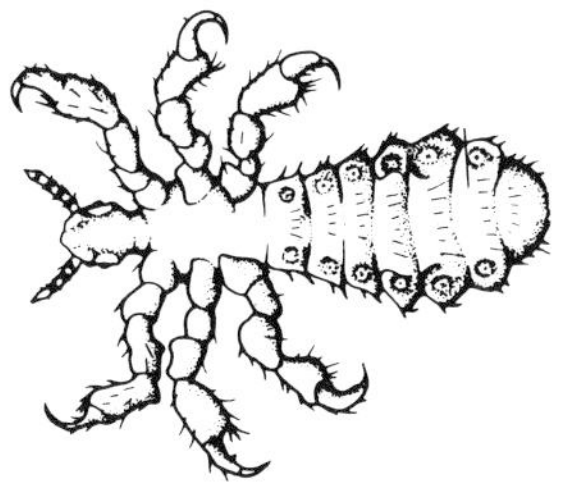

At Gainesville, FL. entomologist Gary Mount (left), computer programmer Patricia Jones, and agricultural engineer Dan Haile use a video projector hooked to a computer to view graphs of seasonal populations of lone star tick living on white-tailed deer and other wildlife.

Ticks, mosquitoes, roaches, and other insects, as well as diseases they transmit, might one day be defeated by researchers armed with personal computers.

Entomologist Gary A. Mount and engineer Danel G. Haile with USDA's Agricultural Research Service, Gainesville, FL, have already developed a growth-simulation and control computer model for the lone star tick, a blood-sucking pest that infests recreational areas and ranches, mostly in the South.

'It's still experimental, but so far, tests have verified that the population predictions and control recommendations are correct,' Mount says.

Work has begun on models for other ticks, mosquitoes, and mosquito-related diseases like malaria, yellow fever, and dengue fever, says Ralph A. Bram, the agency's national leader for research on insects affecting people and animals.

'Our scientists will also be targeting fire ants, roaches, flies, and cattle grubs in the future. We see possibilities for developing control strategies for at least those insects that are the worst pests to agriculture and humans in this country,' he says.

Each year, Americans reportedly spend more than $3 billion to rid their homes, backyards, and campsites of ticks, roaches, mosquitoes, and other insects. Many of these pests, together with diseases they can transmit, pose a health threat. And agricultural pests also cost farmers and ranchers $20 billion annually in losses and for control.

To predict a future population of one of these expensive pests, the scientists instruct the computer to compare the insect – its life history and survival needs – with information about weather and habitat in the target area.

The National Oceanographic and Atmosphere Administration supplies nationwide weather data, while research at Gainesville and worldwide yields information about insect habitat, biology, and control.

Mount and Haile put this information into their lone star tick forecasting program.

They told the computer that the pest thrives in the woods, with high humidity, warm temperatures, and plenty of white-tailed deer for hosts. This affinity for the woods makes the tick a nuisance for campers.

'Sometimes a family sets up camp and then, 2 hours later, pulls up the stakes and leaves – just because of the number of ticks that attack them for a blood meal,' Mount says. The tick is also a potential carrier of Rocky Mountain spotted fever and other diseases.

The scientists tested their tick program in three different areas of eastern Oklahoma. Its predictions agreed with actual field counts of ticks for 3 years in a row.

When asked what the population would be after a year in Peoria, IL, where the tick does not occur, the computer answered almost zero, finding from its database that Pcoria does not have high enough temperatures.

As for its ability to determine the ideal control strategy, the model is being tested in a cooperative project with the Tennessee Valley Authority a campgrounds in Land Between the Lakes in Kentucky and Tennessee.

In these tests, researchers put three possible controls for the tick into the model: pesticides, controlled burning on plants the ticks live under part-time, and fencing off or relocating white-tailed deer, the tick's first choice as a host.

They also described to the computer, in a very general way, how ticks respond to each kind of control.

The computer then decided how and when to use each method to control ticks in the cheapest, safest, and most efficient way.

The model forecast that after a year of total exclusion of deer, the tick population would decrease 95 per cent. At Land Between the Lakes, where this was tested, it decreased 98 per cent, he says.

Future programs for other pests will work in a similar manner.

Haile says, 'Officials may do in 10 minutes what it normally takes years to do in nature: observe long-term population changes of pests under various control strategies. And all they would need are the program on a floppy disk and a personal computer.' – By Jessica Morrison, ARS.

Gary A. Mount is with the USDA-ARS Insects Affecting Man and Animals Research Laboratory, P.O. Box 14565, Gainesville, FL 32604.

b Working in groups, make a similar set of notes for another common pest. *For example:* rat, locust, rabbit, *etc.*

A3 *a* Make notes on the main features of the pest control experiment set up by the researchers mentioned in the extract.

b A research institute has asked you to set up a similar experiment involving the pest you chose. In order to do this successfully you will be required to:
- suggest at least three ways of dealing with the pest.
- propose a means of assessing the effectiveness of each method.
- decide in which type of environment you wish to conduct the experiment ensuring that conditions in the environment you choose are as uniform as possible.

c Each group should present its proposal to the rest of the class.

While the other groups are making their presentations listen critically in order to suggest how the methods adopted can be improved.

B1 In reading about the experiment outlined in the previous extract you may have come across some words which were difficult to understand.

When reading an advanced text it is common to encounter unknown words or known words used in an unfamiliar way. In this situation most students refer to a dictionary. Whilst this may seem the easiest thing to do, it is a good idea to be aware of alternative strategies.

a Discuss with a partner what you do when you encounter an unknown word: *(i)* in your own language; *(ii)* in English.

b Discuss whether these techniques may be transferable from one language to another.

B2 There are a number of ways of finding the meaning of a word or phrase without reference to a dictionary.

a *(i)* Split the word into its component parts. *For example:* indiscriminately which appears *in discriminate ly* in the following text.

The prefix *in* suggests something being carried out without success or effectiveness. The word *discriminate* means being able to distinguish between two things. The suffix *ly* suggests an adverb describing the way something is done. By looking at the sentence we can see that *indiscriminately* refers to the way chemicals were applied to the land '... the chemicals were applied almost indiscriminately – often in the wrong way and at the wrong time ...'

What do you think 'indiscriminately' means?

(ii) In a similar way work out the meaning of 'pesticide' from the text.

b *(i)* Look at the sentence and paragraph in which the unknown word occurs and see if you can find any clues.

For example: 'devouring'

Find the word in the text, and read the paragraph in which it occurs. Note the part of speech of the word and the words around it.
- What part of speech is *devouring*?
- Who or what does the devouring?
- What do they devour?
- What do you think *devouring* means?

(ii) In a similar way, work out the meaning of 'despair' from clues contained in the paragraph.

B3 Not all words are of equal importance. *For example:* in understanding a sentence nouns are often more important than adjectives. You may be able to get the gist of what an author is trying to say without understanding every word he or she uses.

a In groups, underline any other words you do not understand in the following extract.

b Decide which of them are essential to your understanding of the text.

c Try to work out the meanings of the key unknown words using the strategies discussed earlier.

Harvesting poison

'FIRST they tell us to buy their poisons to help us kill the pests,' says Aguilar bitterly. 'Now they say we need new poisons to combat the problems caused by the first ones. My God, while we are doing that I think these insects will eat us alive.'

Anisar Aguilar is a Latin American peasant farmer whose fields have been swamped by a strange new plague of moths that nothing will shift. He lives in an isolated community in the high, humid subtropics. His main crop is tomatoes. Back in 1965 peasants who went to the town of Santa Cruz came back with fantastic stories. They had been told by the shopkeepers about the amazing new pesticides which would soon make the farmers rich.

'First one bought,' says Aguilar, 'then another. After that there was an avalanche of salesmen. Now look where we are.'

The energy and propaganda of the salesmen were overpowering and enormous quantities were sold. But the chemicals were applied more or less indiscriminately – often in the wrong way and at the wrong time – under the guidance of salesmen who were as badly informed as the farmers.

'It wasn't our fault,' Aguilar claims. 'We were so excited by the thought that we would soon be free of the whims of nature. What would you have done?'

But after three years they were in for a nasty surprise. Despite the mixture of powerful chemicals on the tomatoes, a few mutant moths survived. They reproduced themselves at a terrifying rate, devouring all the tomatoes they could find. The chemicals, it seemed, had disturbed the previous natural balance by killing not only the pests but their natural predators. So the new moth has the crop all to itself.

The farmers' first reaction was to increase the dose of the pesticide and then try one new chemical after another. But the story was to follow an all too familiar pattern. It just needed one or two resistant moths to survive and they could produce a new and tougher strain, immune to the most powerful pesticide.

New salesmen have now arrived with new pesticides which they say will finish off the evil moth. And indeed they have produced good results to date. But Aguilar is suspicious of what will happen in three years time. As he says 'A butterfly usually brings behind it a bigger moth.'

Some of Aguilar's friends are in despair. They have not only seen their harvests disappear but they feel they have lost the creative potential of the land itself. So serious is the situation that the suicide rate amongst the peasants has dramatically increased. 'They think they are the killers of 'Pachamama' – Mother Earth. Now they are committing suicide – by drinking the pesticide that caused all their problems,' says Aguilar sadly.

Aguilar himself is more hopeful. He has returned to more natural methods. He is letting some of his land lie fallow and changing his irrigation system around in the hope that the moths will go away.

VSO Third World Calendar, 1986

SECTION 4 *YOU CAN'T SOLVE ALL OF THE PEOPLE'S PROBLEMS ALL OF THE TIME*

A The rise of the potato

At the moment the potato is the most rapidly expanding food crop in the Third World. It is an excellent source of food energy and has a relatively high protein content for a starch crop. This, together with its potential to yield good harvests, makes it an excellent crop for farmers from developing countries where food quality and quantity can be in short supply.

A Western-based development agency is involved in a campaign to persuade your country to increase dramatically its production of potatoes. They have prepared some promotional literature (see next page) extolling the benefits and uses of the potato. Their campaign has already enjoyed some success and your Ministry of Agriculture is just about to announce the details of a new scheme aimed at quadrupling the production of potatoes within a year.

As a group of junior officials at the Ministry of Agriculture you are not happy with the proposed course of action as you feel it may adversely affect the producers, distributors and consumers of your traditional staple crop. You

The potato – uses and abuses

In the boom economies of the West, the last 20 years have seen enormous efforts by the food industry to process the cheapest vegetable and staple into ever more exotic dishes. The value-added element is out of all proportion to the original growing cost. Potato flour is used in gravy and custard powder, it is dried into instant powder mash, there are frozen French fries and potato crisps are sprayed with chemical flavours. 'Stackers' are the new breakthrough – perfectly formed chips stacked into vacuum-sealed tennis ball cans.

THE IRISH FAMINE

By the 1840s the Irish were eating an average of three pounds of potatoes a day. It was the cheapest of foods. A grossly unjust system of landholding, dominated by absentee English landlords, meant that more than half of the eight million population were in the deepest poverty. The potato blight of 1845 destroyed half the crop. Despite the famine conditions, Irish corn was still exported because no one could afford to buy it locally. In 1846 an even bigger acreage was planted with potatoes. This time the blight destroyed 90% of the crop. The winter of 1846/7 brought starvation, typhus fever and cholera which killed a million people. It was the worst disaster in European history since the Black Death.

Within five years the population had shrunk by two million. Those that didn't die, emigrated. Further rural eviction and emigration had reduced the country's population to four million by 1900. Today it is still smaller than before the famine.

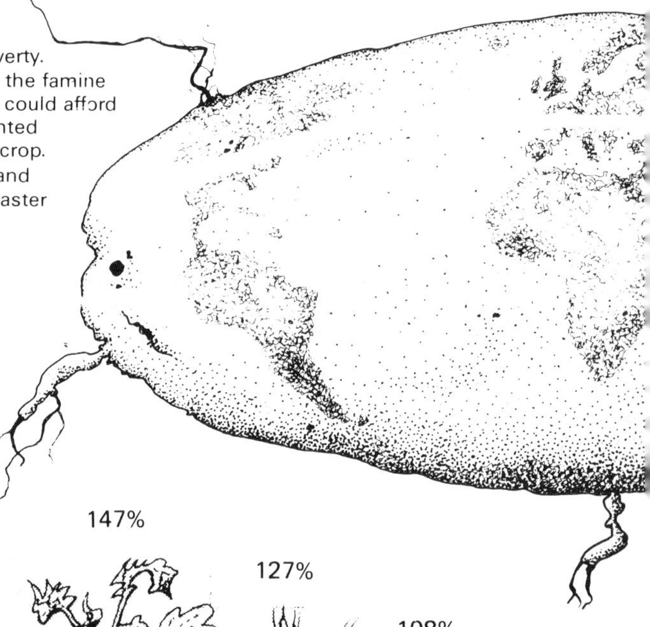

THIRD WORLD PROLIFERATION

Until 20 years ago, nearly all potatoes were grown in Europe and North America. But potato harvests in the poor world have been expanding more than twice the rate of total food production. The increase has been greatest in China, India and Indonesia. Asia now accounts for 84% of the 91 million tons grown in developing countries. Reasons for expansion include: **convenience** – it provides subsistence farmers with a high yield for little effort; **money** – high demand from the cities means good crop prices; **improvements** – new hybrids are being introduced suitable to dry conditions and more resistant to disease.

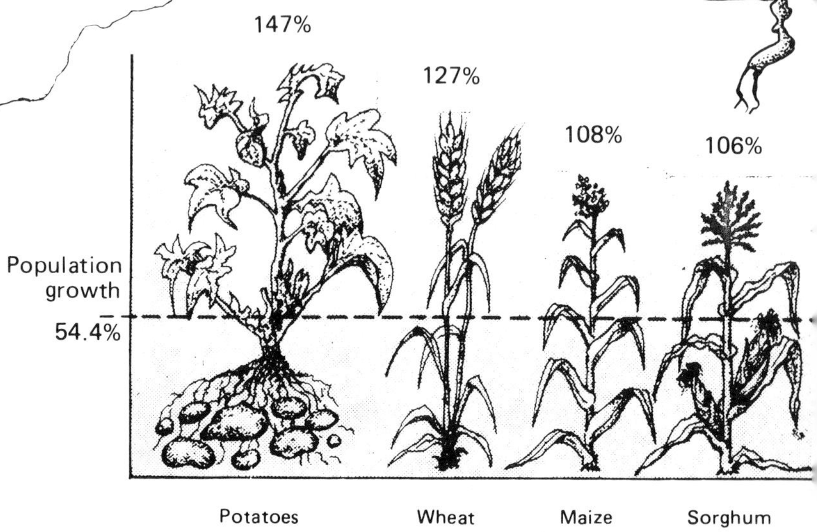

VSO Third World Calendar, 1986

decide to launch your own advertising campaign to influence public opinion.

Choose a staple crop. Working in a group, design some promotional literature explaining the importance of your traditional crop. Among the factors you may like to consider are:

a The advantages it offers to farmers.

b Its value and convenience to the consumer.

c Its nutritional and calorific value.

d Other uses of the crop in addition to food.

e Its importance to the national economy.

Crop comparison in megajoules of edible energy per hectare per day

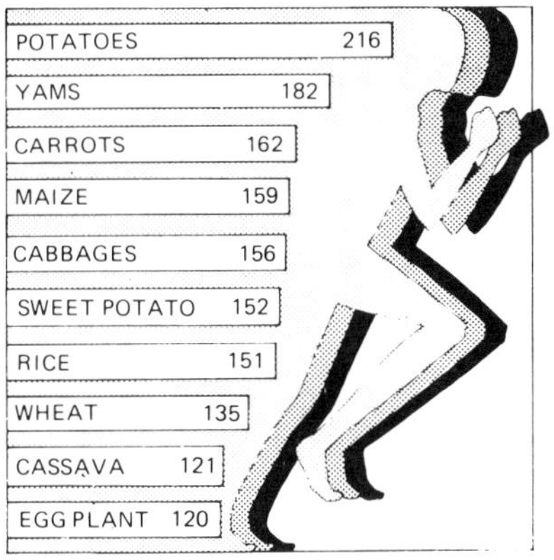

TOP FOOD CROP FOR ENERGY

Potatoes contain protein and substantial amounts of essential vitamins, minerals and trace elements. They provide more nutritious food from less land in less farming time than other major crops like wheat, maize or rice.

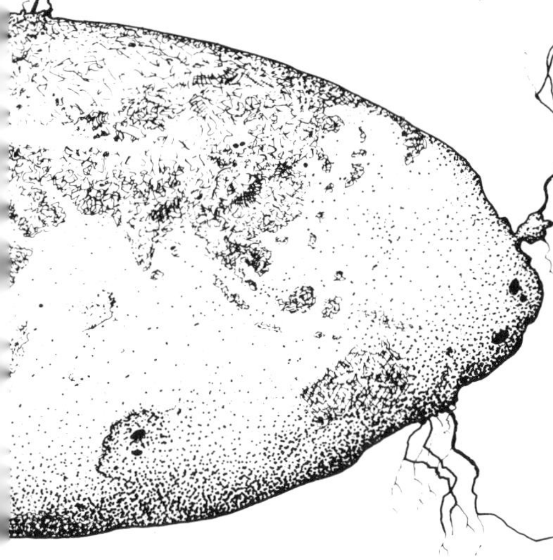

COMPARATIVE USE OF POTATOES

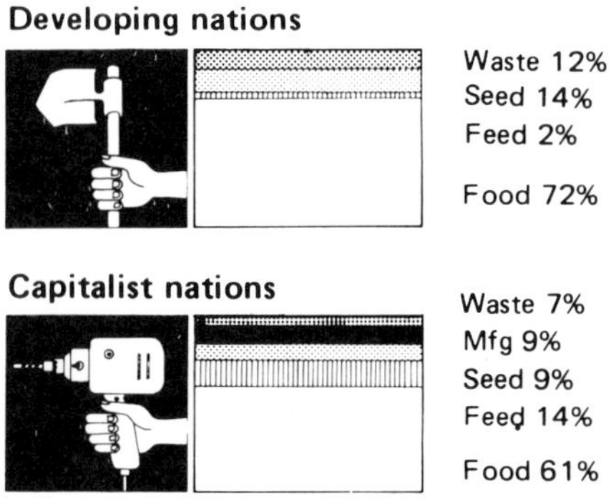

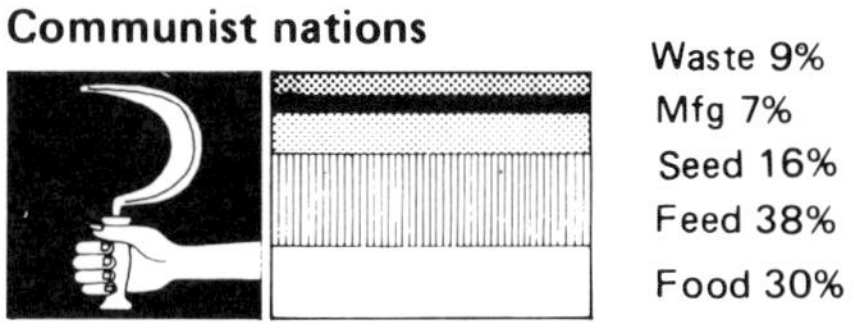

More potatoes are eaten by people in the Third World than anywhere else; and a higher proportion is wasted. Crop losses come from poor storage and transportation. As 77% of the tuber is water, it is often dried into potato flour, then used for fattening pigs and beef cattle. Manufacturing products include: **starch** used to coat paper and finish fine cottons, **dextrins** and **gums** used as glue on postage stamps and in textile printing inks, **dextrose** and **glucose** used in tanning and the drugs industries, and **alcohol**, the most famous example being Schnapps.

Per cent increase in production of selected food crops and population in developing countries, 1961/5 (average) to 1981

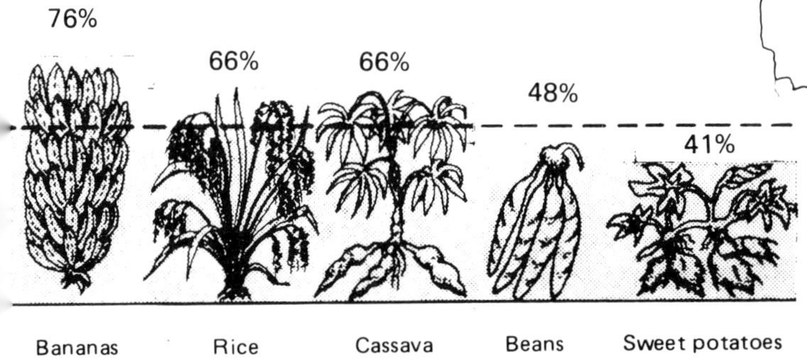

B1 The costs and benefits of change

In making decisions it is not possible to keep everybody happy. When policy makers decide upon options that favour the majority of the population certain groups are inevitably left out of the overall benefits of national development.

a Divide into groups and think of an industry or trade that has undergone dramatic change in your country.

b Describe the nature of the changes that occured.

B2 *a* Explain how and why certain groups benefited from these changes.

b Explain how and why certain groups were adversely affected by the changes that occured.

B3 Deliver a short talk to the other groups. Your talk should identify the major implications of the changes that occured.

Mechanised rice milling causes unemployment in Bangladesh

The rapid spread of small mechanised rice mills in Bangladesh has taken away from thousands of poor women their traditional source of employment in rice processing. Until recently rice milling was done by using a foot-operated pestle and mortar device known as a *dhekt* which is usually owned by the large landowners and which women from landless and low-income households operate on a contractual basis.

The alternative to the *dhekt* is a small mechanical rice mill which is considered to be more cost-effective.

Because Bangladesh is an islamic society that does not encourage free mixing between the sexes, women tend to work amongst themselves. This system of seclusion is known as *purdah*. Rice processing accounts for 50% of all income available to women from landless families since it can be accomplished within the restrictions that *purdah* imposes. With an estimated 10,000 rice mills now established in rural areas, between 1.4 and 2 million women have already lost a traditional source of part-time employment. Approximately 700 mills are being established every year displacing an additional 100,000 to 140,000 women annually.

The plight of these women who are often single, divorced or widowed is a serious economic issue. The Ministry of Agriculture has to decide whether to halt the process of mechanization or to allow it to continue.

From 'Arabia', March 1987

C1 Form into three groups. One of the groups should represent the views of the large landowners, another the interests of the *dhekt* operators. The third and final group represents the Ministry of Agriculture. Decide which interest you wish to represent and read the appropriate instructions below.

a The large landowners

You must present a case to the Ministry of Agriculture officials to persuade them to continue with the process of mechanization because of the economic benefits it is bringing. Some of the arguments you could use to back up your case are listed below. Try to be as persuasive and convincing as you can.

- The cost difference in milling between the *dhekt* and the mechanical mill is about 2:1.
- The lower cost of milling means cheaper rice for the consumers in the town areas.
- Female members of large landowning households now have more leisure time since they no longer have to supervise hired *dhekt* labourers.

b The dhekt operators

It is in your interests to resist the process of mechanization. Try to persuade the Ministry to stop the mechanization process. Some of the arguments you could use are presented below.

- Many people are losing their jobs without the prospect of alternative employment.
- Women are being denied the right to earn an honest living whilst still following the teachings of their religion.
- Displaced women are having difficulties in securing either retraining, compensation or social welfare payments.

c The Ministry of Agriculture officials

It is your job to convene and chair the meeting and to listen carefully to the point of view of both sides before making a decision. As far as possible try to base your judgement on the quality of arguments presented by both sides, not on your own opinions. If necessary, you can cross-question the two parties to gain further information. Finally, you must announce the decision you came to and give reasons why you selected this particular course of action.

Note: It may be the case that the Ministry of Agriculture officials are unable to reach a consensus, in which case a minority report may be issued.

C2 Whatever decision the Ministry makes it will be interpreted according to the vested interests of the parties concerned. Depending on the role you adopted in the simulation explain the decision in one of the following ways:

a A speech prepared by the leader of the *dhekt* workers.
b A newspaper report written from the landowner's point of view.
c One or more 'objective' accounts to be presented to the Minister of Agriculture by junior officials within his department.

SECTION 5 *FARMING IT OUT*

In this unit you have analysed and described a number of problems associated with agriculture. However, the skills you applied to do this can be applied to any problem within your own subject.

The main skills you practised in this chapter are:

- How to combine those notes with your own original ideas.
- How to identify the main points of explanation given by a writer.
- How to present your ideas to an audience in an effective and persuasive manner.

Application – revision seminars
This technique will help you to help each other in preparing for tests and examinations.

A Selection

- Form into groups and examine the contents page of one of your subject textbooks.
- Make a list of the topics **already** covered in class.
- Allocate **one** topic to each member of the group.

B Preparation

You will be required to present a short paper on the topic of your choice to the rest of the group.

- Quickly read through the relevant part(s) of your textbook(s). Make notes on the key points of explanation given by the writer.
- Reread the notes you have made and make any additions where you think your **own** ideas can further clarify the topic to your classmates.

C Delivery

- Deliver the paper you have prepared as a means of introducing a revision seminar on the topic.
- Try to ensure that anything your fellow students do not understand is clearly explained.
- Try to provide relevant answers to any questions raised by other members of the group.

D Participation

When you are **not** presenting the paper on this topic

- Reread the relevant parts of your textbook beforehand so that you can effectively participate in the discussion that follows.
- As you listen to the presentation, prepare a series of questions that will enable you to get clarification on any points you are unsure of.
- Try to participate as fully as you can in the follow-up discussion.

E Evaluation

After each presentation comment on:

- the speaker's knowledge of the subject matter.
- her ability to communicate it to the rest of the group.
- the style and appropriacy of the presentation technique adopted.
- the accuracy and effectiveness of the language used.

UNIT 6 · *A brave new world*

SECTION 1 *THE WAY DOWN*

The Fate of Previous Civilizations

In the last few thousand years many civilizations have risen to a high level of development and then collapsed. As far as we know none of them had such a sophisticated technology as we have developed, but nevertheless they produced remarkable and long lasting artefacts, such as the great pyramids and the sphinx of Egypt, the arch at Ctesiphon and the extra-ordinary stone constructions of Middle America. The civilization of Knossos in Crete even had plumbing on the third floor. Some of these civilizations were destroyed by barbarian invasions, others by earthquakes, fires or other disasters and some in Mexico apparently collapsed purely as a result of the irreversible growth of top heavy bureaucracy. In all of them, however, their collapse has had a central cause, which was the run down or degeneration of the overall motivation, spirit, or ethos of the social system.

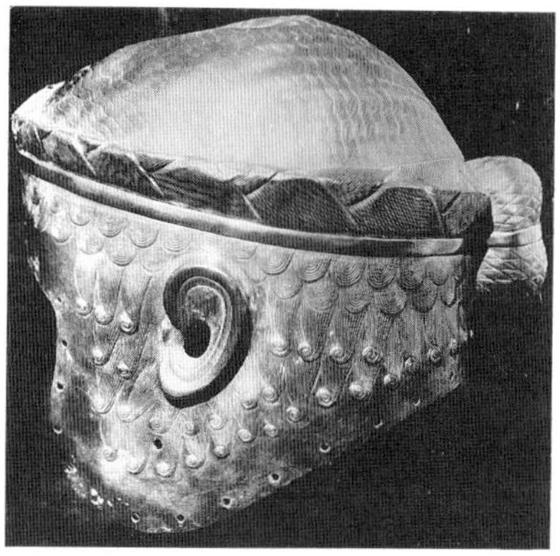

1

2

3

4

5

6

7

8

9

A1 Read through the passage above. Then discuss these questions with other students.

List any other ancient civilisations you can think of which are not mentioned in the passage.

A2 What do you know about their rise and fall?

A3 If the present technological civilisation was to collapse as they did, what artefacts would future civilisations remember it by?

A4 The title of the passage seems to suggest that this technological civilisation is now on the way down. Do you agree with this prediction? Offer some justifications for your answer.

B1 **Boom or gloom?**

Below are three further views on the state of our present civilisation.

Read through them and decide, in each case, if the author feels that we are 'on the way up' or 'on the way down'.

Excerpt 1

The case is this, the contrast between unique technological achievements and an equally unique incompetence in the conduct of its social affairs, have brought the human species to the verge of self-destruction. We who are able to land on the moon and speculate on ultimate mathematical and metaphysical problems have so mismanaged our secular affairs that starvation, race-hatred and nuclear Armageddon may soon write finish to a sordid story.

From Arthur Koestler, Janus: A Summing Up, 1978

Excerpt 2

'Thus we encounter a paradox. On the one hand, modern man is *wealthier, stronger, taller, more athletic, and longer lived than his ancestors. On the other hand he is nervous and sleepless; he cannot meditate or pray*. Even those who should have much reason for contentment cannot find it. And just as internationally the rich and the poor countries become more and more divided from each other, *so also within the same nation the gulf widens between those who have too much and those who have too little.*'

From Robert Ulich, Progress or Disaster?, 1971

Excerpt 3

> 'We are heading for a period of human misery on a scale quite unprecedented. Throughout the long history of humanity until the industrial revolution, it seems that wealth was accumulated very slowly, and the rich were those who had plundered by conquest. Then Industrial Revolution Man seemed to change all that, for wealth was created rapidly without taking it from another man; or so it seemed. But in reality we were stealing it from posterity. The accounting is about to begin.

From R. S. Scorer, The Clever Moron, 1977

B2 The main points of the three excerpts are summed up below. Read through them and decide which ones best correspond to each excerpt.

a Modern industrial man is better off than his ancestors in some ways, but worse off in others.

b Modern industrial man has grown rich at the expense of future generations.

c The gulf between rich and poor is growing.

d Man is good at managing technology, but bad at managing people.

B3 The predictions above comment on certain aspects of our present world.

a Which of the following aspects are presented as **positive** achievements of modern society?

- creation of wealth
- health and physical well-being
- man's psychological state
- technological achievements
- our conduct of social affairs

b Which of these aspects are presented in a **negative** light?

B4 The three quotations have a definite pessimistic slant.

a From the three texts pick out and note down words and phrases which have a pessimistic tone.

Can you locate any signs of optimism?

b Some of the pessimistic language used is very extreme.

(*i*) Underline what you think are the most extreme phrases on your list. Check that other students have identified similar examples.

(*ii*) Can you think of alternative phrases that would be more neutral.

B5 These writers show their depth of feeling by using emotive language.

a Try to employ some of this type of language by writing a short paragraph to describe the image of our future world in the cartoon below.

b Read some paragraphs written by other students and pick out any emotive language they have used.

C1 Rock bottom

a Seven lines are shown on the graph below.

Are any of these linked in terms of
- cause?
- effect?
- shape?

Decide on ways of grouping them and compare your answer with the suggestions in the key.

b With a partner briefly summarise the major trends shown on the graph below. Note down your conclusions.

C2 Discuss with other students to what extent this graph corresponds to the pictures painted by the three writers quoted on pages 104 and 105.

C3 Do you agree that the trends illustrated here are realistic?

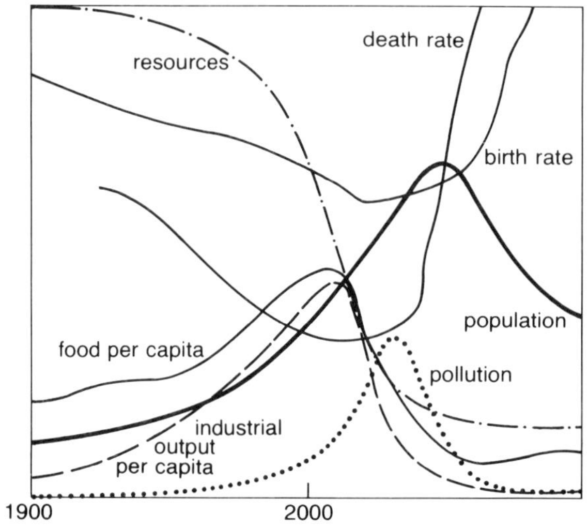

M. W. Thring, *The Engineer's Conscience.* Northgate Publishing Company Ltd., London, 1980

If you do

- Why do you think things will progress in this way?

  Discuss this with a partner and agree on the reasons?

- Compare your ideas with those of other groups who hold the same opinions.

If you don't

- Draw up a graph to show approximately how you think things will progress.
- Compare your predictions with those of other students. Be prepared to justify your forecast.

C4 Write a brief passage describing and explaining your projections for the future.

SECTION 2 *ONE WAY UP*

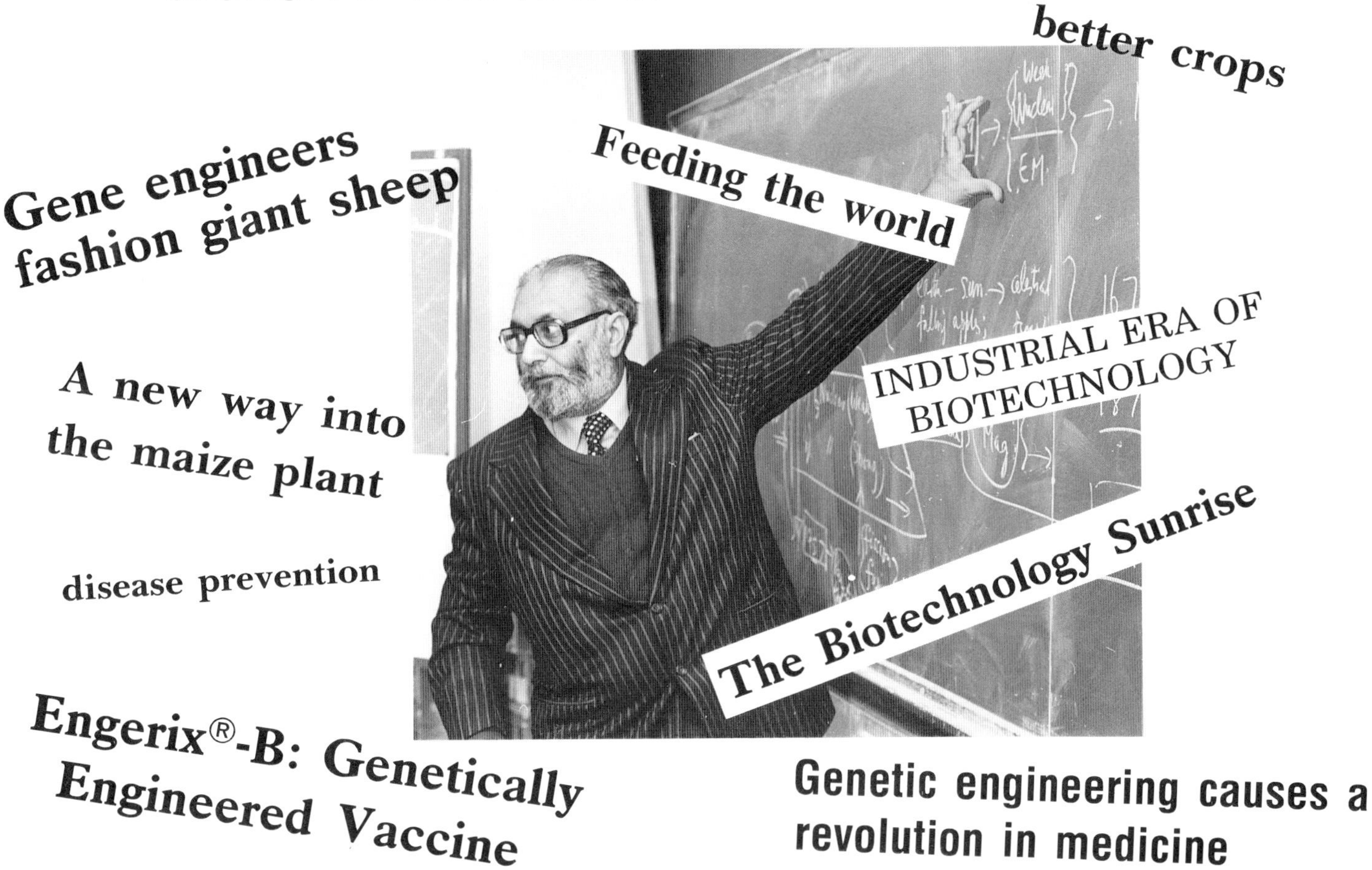

A As the headings above suggest, not all pictures of modern society are gloomy.

With a partner list any areas you can think of where advances have been made recently, which demonstrate that modern society is progressing and not regressing.

Share your ideas with other students, and extend your list if possible.

B1 Biotechnology

Everybody is talking about biotechnology. It promises to revolutionise our society.

How much do you know about it?

Test your knowledge by trying to answer the following questions.

a What areas, or fields of science, does biotechnology involve?

b What do you know about the latest attempts to find a cure for cancer, and hepatitis?

c Revolutionary new methods for increasing crop yields have been discovered. What do you know about these?

d Scientists now have new ways of dealing with waste products from industry. Do you know what they are?

e Brazilians are no longer dependent on petrol or oil to run their cars. Why is this?

B2 However successful you have been in answering these questions, you should check your knowledge by reading the following text.

The new field of biotechnology encompasses fields as diverse as genetic engineering, biological prosthetics, new fermentation processes, and the use of biological techniques to improve agricultural yields, process waste, and provide energy from biomass. The techniques involved stem from disparate areas of biological investigation. The fact that they appear to be reaching maturity at roughly the same time is not, however, accidental. To a large extent each area feeds on the next and the blossoming of applied biology which will occur over the next few decades is due to important and interconnected advances in many fields.

The most dramatic area concerns the use of recombinant DNA. The possibilities of genetic engineering have been opened up by discoveries in two areas. First, during the late 1970s techniques were developed for the rapid analysis of complicated biological molecules.

After analysis came synthesis. Although the first gene was synthesized in 1964, the technique was improved and during 1978 and 1979 it became possible partially to synthesize the genes responsible for the production of insulin and the human growth hormone; and in the latter year these genes were successfully introduced into bacterial cells. This work was made possible by the discovery of enzymes capable of cutting DNA at precise sites, of enzymes capable of sealing off the loose ends of DNA, and of other enzymes which synthesize DNA from messenger RNA.

The implications of this work were that biological molecules could be synthesized to order by implanting specific genes in various types of micro-organisms. The first chemicals to be thus synthesized were insulin, somatostatin, and the human growth hormone. Human interferon – a biological compound of potential importance in the treatment of cancer – was synthesized shortly afterwards. Production of chemicals potentially suitable as vaccines followed almost immediately – first a protein theoretically suitable as a vaccine against the hepatitis B virus, and then a protein characteristic of one of the foot-and-mouth viruses.

All these products are protentially of great medical importance. The fact that they are synthesized within a cell means that they can be obtained in essentially pure form and hence are free from other toxic products. Production of therapeutic chemicals in this way suggests that long and costly toxicity tests for new chemicals may in the future be greatly reduced. Similarly, genetic engineering opens up the possibility of new methods of medical diagnosis, in which small quantities of the DNA or RNA of an invading virus are isolated, mapped, sequenced, and replicated.

The agricultural possibilities of such techniques are almost as exciting. For example, it may become possible to transfer the nitrogen-fixing genes of certain bacteria to plants such as cereals which are unable to fix nitrogen. Should this prove possible, the savings in terms of fertilizer and improved soil fertility will be enormous. Similarly, there is the prospect of transferring to a number of different crops specific genes responsible for improved yield or pest resistance. Again, the potential savings would be immense.

Another field of application concerns the tailoring of certain yeasts and other micro-organisms to do specific jobs in industry – for example, turning the by-products of oil refineries into single-cell protein suitable for an animal feed. The carbohydrate-rich waste from sugar-refining plants may also be used in the same way. It is conceivable that similar techniques may be used to produce new ranges of compounds, such as biological polymers, solvents, and detergents, capable of substituting for petroleum-derived products.

Finally, biotechnology is already finding more and more uses in the energy field. Biomass sources, such as sugar-cane, are being increasingly used as a source of ethanol for motor fuel, and agricultural wastes are being turned into biogas, with benefits both to agriculture and the rural household which thus finds itself in possession of a new fuel and an improved agricultural fertilizer.

Exactly when most of the other expected advances are likely to materialize is harder to say. Scientists themselves are currently reluctant to commit themselves to specific predictions. However a Delphi study – in which experts repeatedly refine their own predictions as they are informed of the predictions of their own colleagues – has shown that many experts are optimistic; in the figures in Table D the first date is the one at which experts predict success with a 50 per cent probability, and the second with a 90 per cent probability. These dates, of course, represent the years in which the advance is made; the time taken to reach the market-place will be longer.

In one respect the new field of biotechnology differs substantially from that of computronics: it offers immediate and attractive prospects for developing countries. Such things as the production of bio-energy, fermentation, the treatment of wastes, particularly agricultural ones, and improved vaccine production could well find application in developing countries as quickly as in developed ones.

Table D: Delphi predictions of biological breakthroughs

Breakthrough	50 per cent probability date	90 per cent probability date
new nitrogen-fixing plants	1985	1995
single-cell edible protein	1982	1987
plants resistant to predators	1990	2000
bacteria for use in waste treatment and pollution control	1984	1990
petrochemical substitutes	1988	1995
gene therapy for diseases such as sickle-cell anaemia	1993	2010
genetic screening to isolate genes responsible for birth defects	1985	1990
mapping of human genetic code	1984	1985
better knowledge of senescence	1990	2000
understanding of immunological processes	1984	1991

R. Clarke, *Science and Technology in World Development*. OUP/UNESCO 1985.

B3 When reading texts it is helpful to be able to recognise the pattern of organisation that the author has employed. This permits the reader to pick out the main points more quickly and to predict more easily what is likely to follow.

The following questions are designed to elicit the organisation of the passage you have just read.

a Suggest a title for the passage.
Discuss this with other students and try to reach a consensus.

b Locate and write down the sentences which sum up the main points of the text.
Discuss your choice with other students and then look at the key.

c Using the main points from the core sentences as a guide, draw up a mind map.
Don't forget to reduce the main points to key words.
Make sure that you plan your mind map so that you have enough space to add further details at a later stage.

d Return to the text and extend your mind map with relevant information.

e Finally, compare your map with those of other students. Pay special attention to – visual impact.
– organisation of detail.

B4 Does the author have an optimistic or pessimistic view of the future?

In order to answer this question, you need to take a closer look at the language the author has chosen to use.

a Note down any phrases which display optimism or pessimism concerning our future.
Does there seem to be any bias towards pessimism or optimism?

b Look closely at the language you have noted.
Would you say that the writer is **enthusiastic** or **neutral** in his views?

c What words in particular help you to decide this?

C1 A brighter future

Chemicals play an important part in modern technology. Draw up a list of products which rely heavily on them.

C2 Consider the cartoon above. It seems to suggest that the days of herbicides, pesticides and other chemicals and pharmaceuticals are over.

a Can we really do without them?

b Why should we want to dispense with them?

c Would you say this cartoon comes from:
- the advertising brochure of a large chemical company?
- the advertising brochure of a genetic engineering company?
- an environmentalist pamphlet?

C3 You are now going to hear five extracts on tape, concerning biotechnology.

a As you listen, note down which areas of modern technology each one deals with.
Include these areas on your mind map.

b Do these speakers leave you with an **optimistic** or a **pessimistic** impression of development within the sciences?
Discuss this with your partner.

c The language that the speakers use will provide a good indication of their attitudes.
Listen again to the extracts and in each case note down any phrases or words which display their points of view.

Compare your list with those of other students.

C4 Consider again the cartoon above. Do the speakers on the tape:

a agree that genetic engineering will replace the use of chemicals?

b feel that genetic engineering can complement the use of chemicals?

c think that genetic engineering cannot replace or assist chemicals?

D1 **A science in action**

a The following three texts have no titles. Skim through them and then choose suitable headings.

b These texts describe further applications of biotechnology. Read through them again briefly and add relevant details to your mind map.

c The texts examine a variety of aspects of the biotechnological world.

Which of the aspects noted below are actually included in each text? You can expect to find more than one of these in each text.
(*i*) The superiority of biotechnology over traditional methods.
(*ii*) A detailed description of the latest research.
(*iii*) The commercial aspects of biotechnology.
(*iv*) The belief that biotechnology is realisable even though it seems fantastic.
(*v*) Predicted developments in biotechnology.
(*vi*) Reservations about biotechnological methods.

Text 1

So, what's really so new about biotechnology? We live in an era which saw Space become man's playground and life expectancy jump twenty years, and we almost take for granted the endless stream of products from the cornucopia of science and technology. In this context miracles of biotechnology come as no surprise. Why then do sober civil servants predict that biotechnology will 'revolutionize' our society, sceptical economists that it is the next 'industrial revolution', and cautious market analysts that it is the 'sunrise' industry?

Imagine a ranch teeming with identical cattle which started life in a laboratory test-tube. Imagine a field of crops which manufacture their own fertilizer and fight their own pests. Imagine replacing thousands of miles of green sugar-cane, rubber and tobacco by neat factories the size of football pitches, and full of gleaming steel vats. These are some of the wonders of biotechnology in agriculture. In this topsy-turvy world, corn is grown for fuel, and fuel turned into food.

We may even come to like 'fillet steak' made by biotechnology from a relative of the mushroom.

Look, too, at the smelly, sad world of human disease. Here the new gene technologies allow us, for the first time, to unravel the tangled series of events which occur within the cell as disease upsets the delicate chemical balance. Even the sinister mystery surrounding cancer is giving way to such precise scientific probing.

The real importance of biotechnology to us is that it opens up the possibility of a more natural, sensitive and yet effective way of treating disease. Genetic engineering, first of all, allows us to make large quantities of rare natural substances for treating a whole range of diseases from colds to cancers; before, these substances could only be supplied in minute amounts, if at all. These same molecular tools can help pharmaceutical companies design drugs to order, based on a new, more detailed knowledge of the disease process. With drugs costing $40 000 000 to take from laboratory bench to market, these companies hope to do away with the years of expensive 'shotgun' testing needed to develop the potions of today – potions which still often miss their target.

Along with tailoring comes targeting. Molecular biologists are already thinking of how to construct drugs which will 'dock' and 'grapple' only with specific enemies, be they invading microbes or rogue tumour cells. By attacking only certain targets, these drugs should be kinder to healthy tissues nearby, and so do away with, or at least reduce, the weakening side-effects of many of today's preparations.

However, most important is that doctors need no longer rely on very toxic chemicals to cure disease. Armed with an infinitely better idea of how the human body fights back, doctors can also try subtly enhancing with milder drugs the body's own immune system in ways tailored to the patient's needs.

In these two areas, agriculture and the treatment of human disease, we catch a glimpse of the power of biotechnology. But we must keep in mind always that biotechnology is about tampering with life. It concerns harnessing living organisms to do our will, and it uses genetic tools to control and redirect the very energy of life. In order to do this effectively we must understand more about these living processes and so learn more about ourselves. If none of the dreams were to come true, this would still be biotechnology's greatest legacy to the human race.

From S. Yanchinski, *Setting Genes to Work*. Pelican, 1985.

D2 *a* The author mixes fact with imagination in this text. Read through the following sentences taken from the text, and decide if they are facts or imagination in each case.

(i) Imagine a ranch teeming with identical cattle which started life in a laboratory test tube.

(ii) We may even come to like fillet steak made by biotechnology from a relative of the mushroom.

(iii) Genetic engineering, first of all, allows us to make large quantities of rare natural substances.

(iv) In these two areas, agriculture and the treatment of human disease, we catch a glimpse of the power of biotechnology.

b What words influenced your decision?

c Locate in the text, and note down other examples of opinions and imagination.

d Would you say that this shows a subjective or an objective view of biotechnology?

D3 *a* Throughout the text a number of words and phrases are underlined. What do they tell you about the author's attitude to biotechnology?

b Locate other phrases in the text which give the same impression.

c Who do you think the author was writing for?

(i) specialists

(ii) the general public

(iii) students of science

d What was the author trying to convey?

(i) facts and figures

(ii) a warning

(iii) an overview

Text 2

AUSTRALIAN scientists have created the world's first 'transgenic sheep' by inserting into an embryo a gene that codes for sheep growth hormone. The development is seen as a major step towards developing much larger, leaner and faster-growing animals. (i) It will cut the time required for breeding improved livestock.

The scientists say (ii) it should soon be possible to transplant a number of other genes to encourage such things as wool growth and disease resistance in sheep, and to extend the technique to cattle.

The transgenic sheep was created by inserting a gene for sheep growth hormone when the embryo comprised a single cell. The scientists then transferred the embryo into a surrogate mother. The sheep, a ewe, was born at the end of April this year.

It will be around six weeks before the scientific team know for sure if the extra genes are producing additional growth hormone, but Trevor Scott, the head of animal production at the CSIRO, Australia's largest research organisation, is hopeful of success.

Scott said laboratory examination had shown that the genes had become incorporated into the cells of the transgenic sheep. In about five weeks, the extra growth hormone will be triggered into action by a dose of zinc, which will 'switch on' the gene, by activating a regulatory sequence attached to the gene itself.

(iii) If successful, the technique could produce sheep up to 50 per cent larger than current animals. (iv) The transgenic sheep should also grow up to a third faster.

The scientists are now working to introduce new genes which code for two enzymes that allow sheep to make their own sulphur amino acids. These acids are essential for wool growth and can be obtained by the sheep only through their diet. If the gene implant is successful, the sheep (v) will no longer need additives to their diet.

Scott described the gene transplant, the result of more than three years of work, as a fundamental scientific advance which (vi) would lead to a completely new approach to animal breeding and production. It is the first time that the sheep growth hormone had been transplanted. Other teams around the world have produced transgenic mice.

From *New Scientist*, 10.7.86

D4 The author of this text describes recent advances in the agricultural branch of biotechnology. He also mentions advances that are hoped for but not yet achieved.

a From the text note down:
- what has already been achieved.
- what the desired advances are in this field.

b The phrases which are underlined in the text describe desired future advances.

How certain is it that these events will take place?

Order the phrases beginning with the most certain.

c What kind of readership do you think this article was written for?

d What message is the author trying to convey?

Text 3

Product Profile

Today, with the advent of sophisticated and highly reliable genetic engineering techniques, the production of large volumes of safe, efficaceous and cost-effective vaccines has become an achievable goal. SmithKline Biologicals* has developed Engerix®-B, a hepatitis B vaccine based on the expression (production) of the surface antigen in yeast cells.

Produced according to «state-of-the-art» technology and tested to the most stringent international quality control standards (including WHO guidelines), Engerix®-B, shows an outstanding purity profile. It is highly immunogenic, i.e. confers a high degree of immunity, as demonstrated by the most sensitive *in vivo* and *in vitro* methods.

An intensive clinical investigation program was initiated in 1984. Today, more than 3000 vaccinees have been successfully enrolled into clinical trials carried out in European, African and Asian countries. These trials,

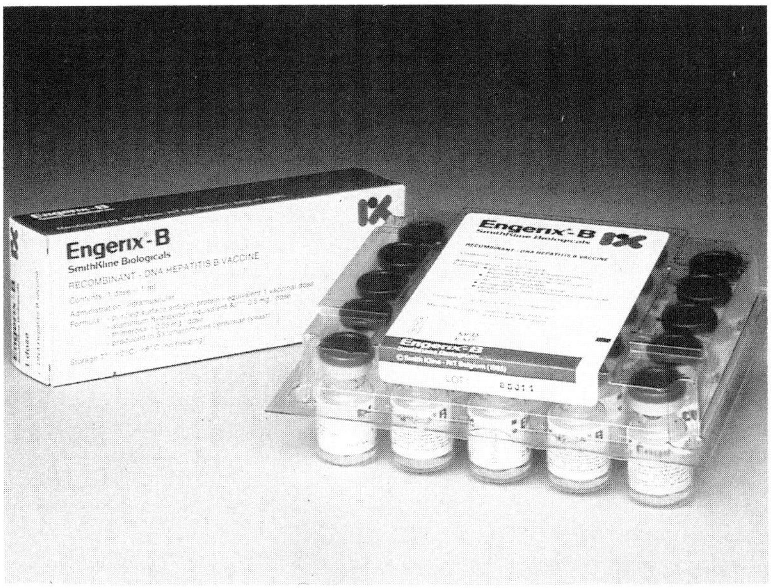

supervised by leading authorities in the field of hepatitis B prevention, have confirmed the excellent clinical profile of the product. Reactions were rare, mild and transient in nature. The incidence of reactions was similar to that observed with plasma-derived vaccines and consisted mainly of local soreness and occasionally mild and transient systemic reactions (e.g. tiredness, headache, fever).

Seroconversion rates of close to 100% have been achieved.

The very encouraging technical and clinical results achieved to date have enabled the company to invest in industrial scale production. SmithKline scientists and clinicians spare no effort to allow the world-wide medical profession to benefit from Engerix®-B, a major medical advance in hepatitis B prevention.

We expect the SmithKline Biologicals vaccine to be available in many countries as of 1986.

D5 *a* The text is overwhelmingly in favour of this genetically engineered product.

Pick out and note down phrases which display this.

Check your list with that of a partner.

Discuss the following questions with other members of your group.

b Who do you think this text was written for?

c Who do you think it was written by?

d What do you think is the purpose of the text?

D6 Discussion point

The language a speaker or writer chooses is very important in conveying a message.

The listener or reader is not always aware of this.
Can you think of any examples of this from daily life?

D7 With a partner dream up an amazing new product. Imagine that you are responsible for marketing it. Write up a product profile highlighting its advantages.

Read through other product profiles and decide which one is the most convincing.

SECTION 3 *TAMPERING WITH LIFE*

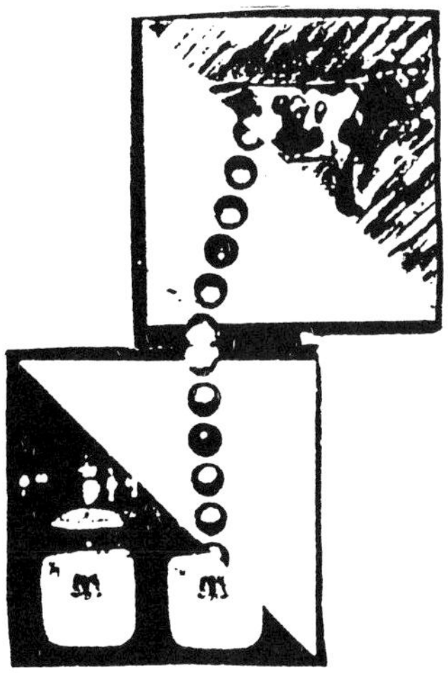

A Think of the type of world that biotechnology promises: a world of gleaming vats, test-tube cattle, giant sheep, disease-free plants, perfect health and mushroom steaks.

1 In your group, decide if such a world is achievable.
2 Is it one that you and your fellow students would want to live in?
3 Some people are disturbed by the prospect of such a future. Can you imagine why?
4 The illustration above could suggest that the sciences work in isolation.

a Do you agree with this interpretation of the drawing?

b Do you agree that scientists working in different fields are cut off from each other?

B **Plain speaking**

1 You are now going to listen to somebody talking about their view of the biotechnological future.

As you listen, decide which of the following best sums up the main speaker's attitude to genetic engineering.

a wholly in favour

b in favour, but with slight reservations

c not in favour, but can see some advantages

d firmly opposed

e uncommitted

B2 Quite a number of phrases in this interview betray the speaker's attitude. Some of these are listed below.

a Look at the phrase endings in column B, and decide which you think match those in A best.

Column A	**Column B**
(i) Its very benefit...	*(s)* ...of narrowing our genetic diversity
(ii) we run the risk...	*(t)* ...our plants
(iii) creating...	*(u)* ...supermice
(iv) we've monocultured...	*(v)* ...serious ethical questions
(v) genetic engineering...	*(w)* ...is its cost
(vi) They are huge mice...	*(x)* ...biological boundaries
(vii) bypass all...	*(y)* ...superbreeds
(viii) this creates...	*(z)* ...exacerbates that process

b Listen to the tape again and correct your choices.

c Discuss with other students the meaning of each phrase.

B3 *a* Read through the following statements about the interview. With other members of your group, decide whether or not you agree with them.

(i) The main speaker disagrees in a polite way with the interviewer's point.
(ii) The main speaker feels that a narrow genetic diversity is undesirable.
(iii) The main speaker feels that some genetic experiments are ridiculous.
(iv) The main speaker feels that genetic engineering allows man to do things which are not possible in nature.

b Listen once more and locate any phrases or sentences that confirm your impression.

B4 Would you say that the main speaker's tone was:

a tentative, but honest

b conciliatory

c forceful and direct

C A patent on life

1 *a* What is a patent?
How can patenting be applied to genetic engineering?

Genetic engineers stitched up over patent rights

GENETIC ENGINEERING:
Battle rages on patenting animals

Patent Office Decides That New Animals Can Now Be Patented

Discuss these questions with other members of your group.

b Now read through the brief explanation below to check your answer.

What is a patent?

A PATENT must first of all be new. No other inventor must have filed a patent on the same invention, and nobody must have published the discovery before filing for a patent, although in the US there is a 'grace period' of up to a year between publishing and filing a patent.

The next criterion for patenting is that an invention must involve a truly inventive step. Routine, trivial or unexpected modifications of an existing technology therefore do not count as fulfilling what patent attorneys call the 'inventive step'.

This is often the criterion that lawyers end up arguing about in the courts. The court then has to decide whether the invention is obvious 'to someone skilled in the art'. Biotechnology is such a new industry that patent lawyers often try to convince a court that something is inventive merely because the technology is so new and 'unobvious'. The recent court case in Britain between Genentech and Wellcome indicated that the court was not prepared to treat biotechnology any differently than to other technologies.

For a patent office to grant a patent, the invention must be industrially applicable.

New Scientist 20 August 1987

c Using the information you have gathered, write a brief definition of a patent.
Compare your definition with those of other students.
Decide on an acceptable one.

C2 The third part of the interview is concerned with the idea of patenting and the fact that some firms want to patent species that they have created through genetic engineering.

a You have already heard some of the views of the main speaker. Using your knowledge of her attitudes towards genetic engineering, what do you think she will have to say about patenting?

b Listen to the next section of the interview and see if you were correct.

C3 *a* What phrases do the speakers use that reveal their attitudes to the patenting of species?
Note down any that you found striking.
Were you struck by the same phrases as other students?

b Listen again and make a note of other phrases that reveal attitude.

C4 Consider these questions and discuss them with a partner.

a What kind of person do you think the main speaker is?

b Does her tone of voice or style of speaking tell you anything about her?

D1 **The complete picture**

Biotechnology has been hailed by many as a wonderful advance. Yet, certain controversial issues have developed around it. In order to gain a more complete picture, we are going to consider some of these on pages 118–127.

a What issues have you already read or heard about so far in this unit?

b Can you think of other issues involving this new technology, which could cause controversy?

c Skim the texts that follow and make a note of any further issues.

D2 Look at each text again individually, and as far as you can, answer the following questions.

You may decide that all students should examine all of the texts.

Alternatively, you may divide the task between you, allocating certain texts to certain groups. In this case, students should report to other students on what they have read.

a Who do you think wrote the text?
- *(i)* a science correspondent
- *(ii)* a scientist
- *(iii)* a non-specialist writer
- *(iv)* a publicity writer
- *(v)* an environmentalist
- *(vi)* other

b Who was the text written for?
- *(i)* the scientific community
- *(ii)* the general public
- *(iii)* the medical profession
- *(iv)* politicians and world leaders
- *(v)* genetic engineers
- *(vi)* other

c What is the view of the writer about biotechnology?
- *(i)* strongly in favour
- *(ii)* in favour, but aware of certain problems
- *(iii)* neutral
- *(iv)* against, but aware of advantages
- *(v)* whole-heartedly against

These questions are open to interpretation. It would be most profitable if you discussed your views with other students.

Text 1

BRITISH BIOTECHNOLOGY HAS COME A LONG WAY SINCE 1953

When Watson and Crick discovered the structure of DNA in 1953, few people realised its importance to medical research.

Today British Bio-technology is beginning a new era of discoveries with applications clearly in sight. As a new, innovative company we are at the forefront of medical research and development.

Through collaboration with leading pharmaceutical companies and our own independent studies we are actively involved in research into cardiovascular disease, bone and connective tissue disorders, virology and immunology.

We also market unique laboratory products including synthetic genes for the scientific community.

1953 was a good year for British science.

1987 will be a good year for British Bio-technology.

Text 2

Should Man Make Beast?

A new ethical dilemma

As a symbol of biology's moral and ethical frontier, the geep hardly cuts an impressive figure. But there it stands, with a goat's head and long neck and a sheep's bushy wool coat above knobby knees. Biologists at the University of California at Davis can make one of these odd creatures by fusing a sheep and a goat embryo in a test tube, then implanting the fused embryo in a goat's womb. A geep is a sterile hybrid and not much of a farm animal. As a scientific feat, however, it is now on center stage, along with a small number of similarly novel life forms created through modern techniques like embryo fusion and genetic engineering. The reason: the U.S. Patent and Trademark Office took notice of them and set off a complex scientific and ethical debate when it recently became the first in the world to agree to consider applications for patents on new animal varieties, just as if these beings were mere buckets of bolts.

They aren't, of course: they breathe, eat and have eyes that can stare back at you in a most unsettling way. Indeed, the notion that scientists have official sanction to create and patent new animal forms raises troubling questions for many. A coalition of 12 groups, including the Humane Society and the American Society for the Prevention of Cruelty to Animals, is lobbying Congress to narrow the patent law and exclude animals from its purview. Among other things, the critics charge that the patents will encourage cruel animal experiments, wipe out small farmers who can't afford genetically souped-up live-stock and – most sensationally – lead to a Brave New World in which people hold patents on other people. To Jeremy Rifkin, director of the Foundation on Economic Trends and an outspoken critic of bioengineering, the Patent Office was not only encouraging scientists 'to play God' but audaciously assuming it had the right to grant that power. 'Who are these people to redefine life as no different than a toaster or a tennis ball?' he asked.

Welcome action: To others, the decision was long overdue. In 1980 the Supreme Court, capping an eight-year legal fight, ruled that Ananda M. Chakrabarty, a General Electric microbiologist, could obtain a patent on a novel strain of bacteria; he had endowed the bacteria with genes from other species, enabling the bugs to digest oil and clean up marine spills. At the time neither the court nor the Patent Office extended the ruling to cover animals. But the ability of scientists to transplant foreign genes into animal embryos has grown more sophisticated, and now the Patent Office has decided that the court's ruling does apply to creatures besides bacteria. As patent commissioner Donald J. Quigg announced, 'nonnaturally occurring non-human multicellular living organisms, including animals' are patentable.

What about us, though? Ethicists are worried about what they see as a slippery slope that could lead to strange experiments on people: today it's geeps, tomorrow it's peeps. J. Robert Nelson, director of the Institute of Religion at the Texas Medical Center, said the new policy 'removes one more barrier to the protection of human life.' But to believe that the patent decision by itself will make this happen is to misunderstand patents. They are meant to protect inventions, not to evaluate whether the inventions are ethical or safe. Regarding human life, the government already prohibits laboratories that receive federal funds from experimenting on human embryos. In addition, the constitutional amendment against slavery prohibits treating persons as property, making it illegal, patent attorneys say, for one person to hold a patent on another.

What the animal-patent decision will do is speed up research on genetic manipulation of animals – for good and bad. Not surprisingly, industrial scientists applaud the new policy. Richard Godown, president of the Industrial Biotechnology Association, says the decision 'supplies a much-needed missing piece that eventually will have widespread economic impact.' But critics charge that as more researchers get involved in animal research, hoping to score a valuable patent, more animals will suffer. This is a valid concern. At the Agricultural Research station in Maryland, researchers transplanted a human growth-hormone gene into animal embryos; the animals are much larger than normal and may someday produce more meat for the dollar as researchers expect, but they are also cross-eyed, arthritic and prone to infections. John Kullberg, president of the ASPCA, says the decision is a 'profit-motive inducement to strip away some of the safeguards against cruelty that are already in place.'

A two-year-old geep: Part goat, part sheep

In coming months the patent controversy will join what one scientist calls the 'storm over biology' – the public's concern about the effects of genetic engineering. The scientific methods that are used to create patentable animals are increasingly well worked out. The still unsolved questions that need answering are mainly ethical: How will we care for these bizarre farm animals? Why are we creating them? If the Patent Office can be faulted for one thing, it is haste: its policy should have been set only after a thorough public debate.

TERRENCE MONMANEY *with* MARY HAGER *in Washington*

Newsweek/May 4, 1987

Text 3

Medical Research Council

1947 1987

Laboratory of Molecular Biology

From its outset *the aim of the MRC has been to sponsor research which will improve the health of individuals in the community*. This objective requires work on the preventive, social and environmental aspects of medicine as well as studies related to the cause, diagnosis and treatment of disease. One important ingredient for success in achieving these aims is investment in long-term basic research because the history of important practical advances in medicine shows that the routes to discovery are often unpredictable and because many of the major causes of illness, disability and premature death remain unknown. While practical problems remain unsolved the steady accumulation of basic knowledge is an essential strategy. Thus the range of research supported by the Council must encompass not only work directly related to human health and welfare but also a wide spectrum of basic disciplines. We are living at a time when great conceptual advances are being made in the basic sciences allied to medicine and the potential for practical achievement has never been greater. For example, there is a growing conviction that new knowledge in virology, molecular biology and neurobiology must lead to fundamental advances in our understanding of cancer, arterial disease and psychiatric and neurological disorders.

[Medical Research Council Corporate Plan, 1986]

Medical Research Council
20 Park Crescent
London W1N 4AL

MRC Laboratory of Molecular Biology
Hills Road
Cambridge CB2 2QH

Text 4

The gene industry

Major companies are already in hot pursuit of commercial applications of the new biology. They dream of placing enzymes in the automobile to monitor exhaust and send data on pollution to a microprocessor that will then adjust the engine. They speak of what the *New York Times* calls 'metal-hungry microbes that might be used to mine valuable trace metals from ocean water'. They have already demanded and won the right to patent new lifeforms. Eli Lilly, Hoffman-La Roche, G. D. Searle, Upjohn, and Merck, not to mention General Electric, are all in the race.

Nervous critics, including many scientists, justifiably worry that there is a race at all. They conjure up images not of oil spills, but of 'microbe spills' that could spread disease and decimate entire populations. The creation and accidental release of virulent microbes, however, is only one cause for alarm. Completely sober and respectable scientists are talking about possibilities that stagger the imagination.

Should we breed people with cow-like stomachs so they can digest grass and hay – thereby alleviating the food problem by modifying us to eat lower down on the food chain? Should we biologically alter workers to fit job requirements – for example, creating pilots with faster reaction times or assembly-line workers neurologically designed to do our monotonous work for us? Should we attempt to eliminate 'inferior' people and breed a 'super-race'? (Hitler tried this, but without the genetic weaponry that may soon issue from our laboratories.) Should we clone soldiers to do our fighting? Should we use genetic forecasting to pre-eliminate 'unfit' babies? Should we grow reserve organs for ourselves – each of us having, as it were, a 'savings bank' full of spare kidneys, livers, or lungs?

Wild as these notions may sound, every one has its advocates (and adversaries) in the scientific community as well as its striking commercial application. As two critics of genetic engineering, Jeremy Rifkin and Ted Howard, state in their book *Who Should Play God?*, 'Broad scale genetic engineering will probably be introduced to America much the same way as assembly lines, automobiles, vaccines, computers and all the other technologies. As each new genetic advance becomes commercially practical, a new consumer need...will be exploited and a market for the new technology will be created.' The potential applications are myriad.

The new biology, for example, could potentially help solve the energy problem. Scientists are now studying the idea of utilizing bacteria capable of converting sunlight into electrochemical energy. They speak of 'biological solar cells'. Could we breed lifeforms to replace nuclear power plants? And if so, might we substitute the danger of a bioactive release for the danger of radioactive release?

In the field of health, many diseases now untreatable will no doubt be cured or prevented – and new ones, perhaps worse, introduced through inadvertence or even malice. (Think what a profit-hungry company could do if it developed and secretly spread some new disease for which it alone had the cure. Even a mild, coldlike ailment could create a massive market for the appropriate, monopolistically controlled cure.)

According to the president of Cetus, a California company to which many world-famous geneticists are commercially linked, 'biology will replace chemistry in importance' in the next thirty years. And in Moscow an official policy statement urges 'the wider use of microorganisms in the national economy...'

Biology will reduce or eliminate the need for oil in the production of plastics, fertilizer, clothes, paints, pesticides, and thousand of other products. It will sharply alter the production of wood, wool and other 'natural' goods. Companies like United States Steel, Fiat, Hitachi, ASEA, or IBM will undoubtedly have their own biology divisions as we begin to shift, over time, from manufacture to 'biofacture', giving rise to a range of products unimaginable until now. Says Theodore J. Gordon, the head of The Futures Group, 'In biology, once we get started, we'll have to think about things like... can you make a "tissue compatible shirt" or a "mammary mattress" – created out of the same stuff as the human breast.'

Long before then, in agriculture, genetic engineering will be employed to increase the world food supply. The much-publicized Green Revolution of the 1960s proved, in large measures, a colossal trap for farmers in the First Wave world because it required enormous inputs of petroleum-based fertilizer that had to be bought abroad. The next bio-agricultural revolution aims at reducing that dependence on artifical fertilizer. Genetic engineering points towards high-yielding crops, crops that grow well in sandy or salty soil, crops that fight off pests. It also seeks to create entirely new foods and fibres, along with simpler, cheaper, energy-conserving methods for storing and processing foods. As though to balance off some of its awesome peril, genetic engineering once more holds out for us the possibility of ending widespread famine.

One must remain sceptical of these glowing promises. Yet if some of the advocates of genetic farming are half right, the impact on agriculture could be tremendous, ultimately altering, among other things, relations between the poor countries and the rich. The Green Revolution made the poor more, not less, dependent on the rich. The bio-agricultural revolution could do the reverse.

It is too early to say with confidence how biotechnology will develop. But it is too late to turn back to zero. We cannot undiscover what we know. We can only fight to control its application, to prevent hasty exploitation, to transnationalize it, and to minimize corporate, national, and inter-scientific rivalry in the entire field before it is too late.

From A. Toffler, *The Third Wave*. Collins 1980

Text 5

Altered organisms released in Australia

THE RELEASING of genetically engineered microorganisms into the environment to control plant production is about to spread to Australia. The first experiment there – only the third of its kind in the world – was due to take place on Tuesday of this week on a small plot at the Waite Agricultural Research Institute in Adelaide. A company pioneering work in the US is also set to begin tests in Australia.

Allen Kerr of the institute received final clearance from the university last Friday to soak the roots of almond seedlings in a solution of genetically altered bacteria to treat crown gall, a common root disease in plants and trees with stone fruits. After completing the four-month experiment, he will, as instructed by the university, sterilise and dispose of the affected soil.

Agricultural Genetic Sciences (AGS) of Oakland, California, was the first company to win approval to test a genetically altered organism in the open in the US. Environmentalists in the US vehemently opposed the tests on a product called Frostban.

Frostban consists of mutant bacteria that lack a gene for nucleating frost. The product can delay the formation of frost on plants, preventing damage to the crop.

Environmentalists argue that the mutant form, which is sprayed on to blossom, could escape and overwhelm naturally occurring bacteria, changing the environment. Members of one group, Earth First, ripped out the strawberry plants on which AGS was due to test Frostban, when the first out-door spraying was set to begin.

New Scientist

Text 6

How yesterday's discoveries have made today's developments possible

Since Wellcome's earliest days, the development and marketing of products for the promotion of human and animal health have been our prime concern.

And research has been at the heart of our work.

Today, drawing on the scientific achievements of many of the world's leading academic researchers, Wellcome Biotech is constantly developing new techniques for the treatment and prevention of disease.

Over the years we have introduced a successful range of conventional vaccines for the prevention of disease across the broadest of fronts.

Currently, Wellcome Biotech is involved not only in the production of hight-tech vaccines based on recombinant DNA, but also in the creation of therapeutic proteins for the treatment of cancer and heart disease and is a leader in mammalian cell culture.

Much of our progress owes a great deal to the original research carried out at laboratories like the Cambridge Laboratory of Molecular Biology, by men and women working at the farthest reaches of scientific discovery.

Their commitment is an inspiration to us. Our commitment is to the continuing race against disease.

Wellcome

Text 7

Court overthrows patent on gene splicing

Steve Connor

A JUDGE in the High Court in London last week ruled that a key patent on a protein made by genetic engineering is invalid. The patent would have given the company at the centre of the case, Genentech of California, rights over all versions of the protein made with recombinant-DNA technology.

The other company in the case, the Wellcome Foundation of Britain, claimed that Genentech's patent did not fulfil the criteria of inventiveness and novelty. Wellcome claimed that it had the right to manufacture and to sell its own version of the protein made by genetic engineering.

It was the fist time that a British judge has made a ruling on a patent involving the new technology of gene splicing. Patent lawyers around the world looked upon the dispute as a test case for future rows over who invented what in the technology of recombinant-DNA, in which scientists identify, isolate, modify and grow tiny pieces of genetic material.

The dispute between Genentech and Wellcome is not over, however. Immediately after the judge announced his decision last Tuesday, Genentech issued a statement from its headquarters in San Francisco saying that it intends to appeal.

Genentech's patent is for the production of a protein that occurs naturally, called tissue plasminogen activator, t-PA. Laboratory and clinical trials have shown that the protein is twice as effective as existing remedies for dissolving clots in blood vessels.

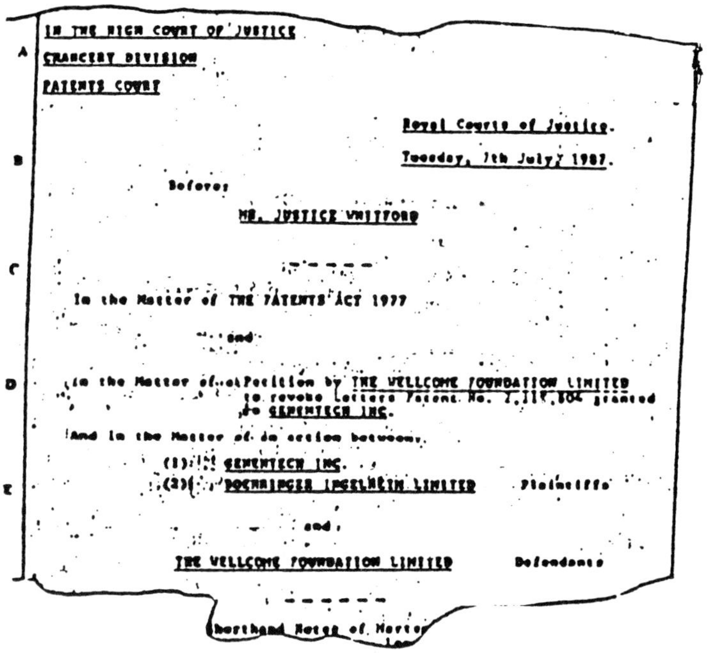
IN THE HIGH COURT OF JUSTICE
CHANCERY DIVISION
PATENTS COURT

Royal Courts of Justice.
Tuesday, 7th July 1987.

Before:
MR. JUSTICE WHITFORD

In the Matter of THE PATENTS ACT 1977

and

In the Matter of a Petition by THE WELLCOME FOUNDATION LIMITED to revoke Letters Patent No. 2,119,804 granted to GENENTECH INC.

And in the Matter of an action between:
(1) GENENTECH INC.
(2) BOEHRINGER INGELHEIM LIMITED Plaintiffs

and

THE WELLCOME FOUNDATION LIMITED Defendants

Shorthand Notes of Mert...

The ruling: patent law can cope with the techniques of biotechnology

The pharmaceutical industry expects the sale of such a drug to exceed $1 billion by the early 1990s.

The court case in London was important for Genentech because other companies may now take Wellcome's lead and start to make t-PA by genetic engineering.

Genentech fired shots across the bows of these competitors in its response last week to the judge's decision: 'This patent decision relates solely to the United Kingdom. We will continue to press our patent claims in the United States and in other jurisdictions,' the company said.

Text 8

The new age of synthetic biology

The Gene-Splicing Wars
edited by Raymond Zilinskas and Burke Zimmerman.
Macmillan, pp 288, £22.50

Eric Ashby

'WHO the hell do the scientists think they are that they can take federal tax dollars...and do research work that we then cannot come in and question?' These are the words of Alfred Vellucci, mayor of Cambridge, Massachusetts. He was referring to the scientists at Harvard and MIT who were working on recombinant DNA and similar problems.

For a time, the civic authorities, under Vellucci, succeeded in seriously obstructing DNA research. It was one of the battles in a bitter nationwide controversy in the US in the mid-1970s. Geneticists had discovered a technique with astonishing powers, and various public interest groups, inflamed by the media, were condemning the geneticists for irresponsibility and demanding that the use of this technique be banned.

At the same time, similar work was going on in England. However, the mayor of Cambridge, England, was not uneasy, and the British public was not protesting. Why was this controversy confined to the US? This is one of the questions answered in this book, the theme of which is: How did the controversy begin?

The gene-splicing war that is described is not the familiar competition between scientists for priority, fame and Nobel prizes. That story has been told already by James Watson and tarted up into a film by the BBC. This is about a much more serious struggle over a much more important issue: who should control scientific research in a democracy? The scientists who understand it or the public who pays for it? And who decides whether risks involved in the research or its consequences are acceptable? The scientists who create the risks or the public who might become victims? These are the topics covered by 14 people who were involved on both sides of the controversy: scientists, administrators, politicians, journalists, and public interest activists.

The gene-splicing war began with what was surely the most altruistic gesture made by a group of scientists. The discovery that DNA can be cut by restriction enzymes, leaving sticky ends to which other slices of DNA can be attached, opened up amazing prospects for microbiologists. Amazing and alarming: for it became possible to create new kinds of microorganisms with properties deliberately introduced by humans.

The temptation was to lock the laboratory door and get on with the research. But a committee of the US National Academy of Science under Paul Berg decided otherwise. It published a letter simultaneously in *Science* and *Nature* in July 1974, proposing a voluntary deferral of experiments which might produce dangerous strains, and asking those using the new technique to pause to consider whether the potential benefits – new pharmaceuticals, new vaccines, and much else – would outweigh the possible but unpredictable hazards.

It was a gesture that ought to have strengthened public confidence in scientists, a splendid act of integrity after decades of ambivalence over policies for nuclear power. But it misfired. The media plugged the hazards (one paper carried a picture of the DNA double helix 'topped with a snake's head dripping venom'). It was hinted that genes for cancer might inadvertently get into *E. coli*, the bacterium that flourishes in the human gut. Some of the public-interest groups got into the state of hysteria they enjoyed at the time of the nuclear accident at Three Mile Island, but no accident had occurred, and no crisis had been averted.

The condemnation of scientists for irresponsibility *after* they had made such a remarkably responsible statement generated choleric resentment among some of them, making them 'feel like a kindly person who voluteers to help an elderly lady across the street only to be mugged by the beneficiary on reaching the far sidewalk'.

In August 1976, two years after the Berg letter, a sensational article in *The New York Times Magazine* brought DNA to the notice of politicians in Washington. Several attempts were made to get bills through Congress to control gene splicing. There was a danger (and this is what made the incident in Cambridge, Massachusetts, so serious) that state and civic authorities would vie with each other in devising regulations, so that 'hazard havens' might arise where dangerous experiments would be permitted.

All this happened 11 years ago Gene splicing is being done in scores of laboratories. The output of papers on the subject doubles every year. Industry has invested enormous sums to make products from recombinant organisms. And not one individual has been harmed by the processes of research or the product. It took the media a couple of years to realise that they had been reporting a non-event. The real event, well described in this book, is the creation of a technique in biology which is very unlikely to cause physical hazards but is certain to challenge conventional concepts of ethics.

Why was there no gene-splicing war in Britain? One excellent essay in the book helps to answer this question. A few weeks after Berg's letter appeared in *Nature*, the Department of Education and Science, appointed a working party, through the Medical Research Council, to assess the potential benefits and potential hazards of the new technique. Its members were scientists who had no vested interest in gene splicing. Their job was to produce quickly a report to forestall the sort of emotional reaction which was seething in the US and to give such interim advice as they could to research workers, pending a thorough study by experts. The purpose of their report was to defuse any potential political agitation; so it had to be intelligible to the dumbest politician and the slickest journalist. (To this end, it can now be revealed, a lady aged 86, who had no scientific education, kindly undertook to criticise the draft report before it was sent to the printer.)

The Working Party reported within five months of the publication of Berg's letter to *Nature* and this was followed, two years later, by an authoritative study leading to the establishment of a Genetic Manipulation Advisory Group (GMAG) which issued guidelines even before the National Institutes of Health in the US had got around to providing guidelines for the gene-splicing work under its control.

This book summarises an important episode in the debate on 'social responsibility in the age of synthetic biology' (as one of the book's contributors calls it). Episodes like this will occur again, and the book is a useful guide for scientists and politicians on how to handle the next one.

Text 9

Third World demands justice over seeds

THIRD WORLD nations are beginning to press for 'farmer's rights' over their own genetic resources – in order to deflect a growing control by the industrialised world over the multitude of

Third World seeds and crop varieties.

The demand is a simple matter of justice, Third World representatives argue. Third World farmers, who have selected and developed crops through continual use, should have similar rights to those enjoyed by companies and industrialised nations which develop new varieties rapidly through biotechnology, they claim.

With the advent of biotechnology, fears have been growing that commercial companies in the North will use genetic material collected from developing countries for breeding programmes, with the resultant 'improved' varieties being sold back to the Southern nations at a significant profit.

The political vulnerability of the International Rice Research Institute (IRRI) in the Philippines has also worried Third World leaders. Currently, IRRI look after 50% of the world's rice cultivars – but much of its rice germplasm collection is actually held in the US. There, the Reagan administration has already barred the export of germplasm to Nicaragua and Libya, not on commercial but on political grounds.

There is also concern on the physcial collection and storage of germplasm, coordinated by the International Board on Plant Genetic Resources (IBPGR). The IBPGR has so far initiated the collection of genetic resources in 50 countries, and has organised national committees to oversee germplasm collection in 25 others.

To date, developing countries have supplied 91% of IBPGR's material. But the Third World currently holds less than one-third of all known genetic stocks. This is despite the fact that 21 of the International Board's 43 plant gene banks are actually sited in the Third World.

The Board's director, Trevor Williams, asserts that the plant germplasm from these banks is 'freely available'. But events have shown that this is not the case, with genetic material being withheld, and free access denied.

Germplasm held under the IBPGR's guidance is stored in gene banks owned by commercial companies or national governments. The FAO currently furnishes the Board's administration but a network of international centres, known as the Consultative Group on International Agricultural Research (CGIAR), actually provides the Board's funding and technical policy.

Third World nations have little representation or influence on the IBPGR, and have consequently been urging the FAO to take more direct control of the Board, in order to protect their interests.
– *Panos*

Utusan Konsumer August 1987

Text 10

Rifkin urges boycott of 'adulterated' milk

In the US, companies can lay claim to patents on higher forms of life, something that Jeremy Rifkin and others find morally repugnant

A CAMPAIGN will soon be launched in the US to encourage millions of Americans to stop drinking milk that has come from cows injected with bovine growth hormone. Jeremy Rifkin, the president of an American environmental group called the Foundation for Economic Trends, said in London this week that he plans to launch the 'massive consumer campaign' because he believes that people do not want milk from cows that have had hormones to increase their milk yields.

Rifkin's group has sued the US's Food and Drug Administration to make the administration disclose information on health and safety in connection with the approval of bovine growth engineered by inserting the gene coding for the chemical into micro-organisms. These microbes then produce the hormone in cheap enough quantities to give to cows.

Rifkin said this week that 'we are awash with milk', with vast surpluses in developed countries. If bovine growth hormone is used to increase milk production still further, he said, then a quarter of American dairy farmers will be out of business within three years.

One way of fighting this is for consumers themselves to make it clear that they do not want milk to be tampered with. 'Consumers believe that milk is the last safe product.' Rifkin said. They will turn to alternative products if they think that milk is no longer a pure natural product.

Rifkin's assault on the plan to use bovine growth hormone is the latest in a long line of campaigns designed to control what he sees as the unregulated use of biotechnology. One of Rifkin's greatest battles has been with researchers who want to release genetically engineered organisms into the atmosphere.

Last week, the US's Environmental Protection Agency (EPA) agreed to permit an American company, Bio-Technica International, to release a genetically altered bacterium. *Rhizobium million*, on a crop of alfalfa in Pepin County, Wisconsin. The bacterium contains copies of a gene that codes for an enzyme, nitrogenase, which will help to fix nitrogen, and so increase the yield of the crop.

The EPA has already given permission for two similar experiments in the US. Both concern the release of genetically engineered bacteria onto fields of either strawberries or potatoes in order to protect the crops against damage by frost.

E Agree to differ

1 As we have seen, there are a number of broad issues at stake and different people have very differing views on them. For example, in the interview that you heard in Section II, the two speakers clearly did not share the exact same view point. However, this disagreement was not immediately evident from the discussion.

a Consider these two excerpts from their discussion and decide why they are **polite** exchanges.

Excerpt 1
Interviewer: . . .And surely the new techniques are just speeding up the process of plant and animal breeding that we've had for a long long time.
Interviewee: In one sense that's true and in another sense it isn't.

Excerpt 2
Interviewee: . . .living things are to be considered manufactured processes and compositions of matter.
Interviewer: Well, I would agree with you that the idea is rather absurd. . ., but from a practical point of view. . .surely they are entitled to protect their investment. . .

b Can you think of alternative responses which would make these less polite?

E2 As these exchanges show, we often agree before we disagree. Some ways of agreeing and disagreeing are stronger than others, however.

a Working in groups, consider the phrases for agreeing and disagreeing below, and place them on a list, beginning with the strongest way of disagreeing, and ending with the strongest way of agreeing.
- We are obviously thinking along the same lines.
- couldn't agree more.
- You must be joking.
- Yes, I'm sure you're right, but. . .
- I must admit that you've got a point there.
- I'm afraid that I don't share your opinion.
- You can't be serious.

b Add to this list any extra phrases you thought of in exercise **E1*b***, in appropriate positions.

Compare your final list with that of other groups.

c Which of these phrases would you be happy to use in:
(i) a formal meeting
(ii) an informal discussion with friends

E3 You are now going to have the opportunity to take up some of the issues dealt with so far in this Unit.

a In a group, which ideally should consist of at least 5 people, choose one of the topics below for futher investigation and discussion.
– Biotechnology benefits the developed world only.
– Scientists should have free rein in their research.
– Patenting living organisms is an absurd idea.

b Decide which of the texts on the previous pages are most relevant to your investigation.

c Working alone, make brief notes on any main points you can find, relating to this issue.

E4 You are now ready to conduct the discussion.

a Decide on the time you will allow for it.

b Elect a chairperson from your group.

c Hold the discussion.

E5 Write a brief passage outlining your position on the issue you have discussed, making it clear what side you stand on, if any.

SECTION 4 *REFLEX ACTION*

Tired? Weary? Slow to react? Sleepy at work?

Are these your problems too? Poor reflexes are one of the main problems that arise as a result of stress, age and everyday wear and tear. Well, the news for all of us is good. Or is it? Read on and find out.

New Gene For Humans

SENSATIONAL NEWS FOR PEOPLE WITH POOR REFLEXES

Experiments with the super-gene HGP4[9] began 8 years ago in L.A. The gene was taken from the red ant and introduced into a variety of different species. It was firstly tried on mice and rats, and later experiments were carried out on dogs, sheep and monkeys.

The most recent experiment was conducted on an orang utan in Chicago. Professor S. Hanley, who is in charge of the experiment, said, 'The results are astounding. There's no doubt about it, this gene will change our lives.'

The main effect of the experiment is to improve the subject's speed of reaction in stressful situations.

Scientists have pointed out that such a gene, introduced into humans, would produce desirable results, especially in the areas of sport, combat and driving. Scientists also claim that the results of almost all experiments have been favourable, and without too many serious side-effects.

It has recently been decided by the Medical Research Board, that experiments may now be extended to humans on a limited scale.

A A scenario

How do you think that people would react to this kind of news?

The activities which follow are intended to replicate a variety of different reactions, and you are going to play an active role in this.

1 You are now going to break up into groups.

– Ideally the minimum size of each group should be 3, and if possible, there should be 4 groups.

At this stage it is not important that you know the identity of these groups.

If your class consists of 12 or more, choose one of the following 4 groups:
1 HRM *2* IUCS *3* ISRB *4* GELI

If your group consists of less than 12 students, choose one of the following 3 groups:
1 HRM *2* IUCS *3* GELI

If there are less than 9 students, 2 groups should be established:
1 HRM *2* GELI

A2 In your new groups, locate the relevant brief, and discover who you are. The teacher will play the role of co-ordinator in this activity.

Briefs

HRM: Human Rights Movement
You are active members of a public interest group, which is very concerned about the consequences of experiments in genetic engineering. You totally oppose them.

You are particularly alarmed about the recent developments in this field, particularly $HGP4^9$.

IUCS: International Union of Concerned Scientists
You are actively involved in the scientific world and are generally in favour of scientific and technological advancement. However, you are concerned about the implications of certain aspects of genetic engineering. Although you realise the great advantages of this branch of technology, you feel that there are limits to its application.

You fear that some scientists are irresponsible, and that you have a duty to monitor their actions.

ISRB: International Scientific Research Board
You are members of an influential body which is responsible for controlling the nature of experiments conducted in the scientific world.

Recently, a lot of your attention has been devoted to genetic engineering.

On the whole, you feel that the benefits of genetic engineering far outweigh the possible dangers. You are nonetheless aware of some dangers and endeavour to monitor them carefully.

However, you are against too much public interference in science.

GELI: Genetic Engineering Links Incorporated
You work for a multinational corporation, which is involved in the development and marketing of biotechnological products.

Your firm has just patented a new genetically engineered organism, the $HGP4^9$. You are confident that this can only benefit humans, and very little research is now needed for it to become a commercially viable product.

To date you have spent a lot of money on this research, and are eager that it should go on.

Co-ordinator

This activity involves a number of different steps and it is important for its smooth running that all groups keep up with each other. Therefore, you should impose realistic time limits on all activities. It is important that the activities move along in a lively manner.

Step 1: At the end of this step, you should make sure that the groups see each other's press releases.

Step 2: At the end of this step, you should make the articles available to all groups.

Step 3: (This step could be left out if you are short of time.) During this step, you might encourage groups to meet members of other groups for exchange of ideas. At the end of this step, those groups that have produced leaflets or posters should make them available to others, through you.

Step 4: This activity will involve some planning, regarding the availability of tape recorders.

A3 Now that you know who you are, you are ready to proceed with the activity. Work through the following steps, paying attention to time limits imposed by the co-ordinator.

Step 1 HGP4[9]

Re-read the article, 'New gene for humans', and decide on your group's reaction to it.

Write a short press release outlining your point of view, and circulate this to other groups. (Approximately 60 words)

Step 2 Stop press

It is vital that you win over public opinion as soon as possible.

Plan and write a brief article reacting to the issue and stating your position in more detail, in the strongest possible terms.

This article is to be published in a weekly current affairs magazine. You may not exceed 150 words, excluding the heading and a brief sub-heading. A visual may also be included.

Once the article has been completed, hand it to the co-ordinator for circulation.

Step 3 Plan of action

Once you have read the articles of the other groups, hold a meeting. Decisions must now be reached as to what action you should take, in order to maximise the effect of your campaign.

Among the points you might like to discuss are:

- possible meetings with other groups to establish common ground
- a poster or leaflet campaign
- written representations to the authorities
- any other ways of making the public aware of the issue and your position

Present your plan to the co-ordinator.

Put into action any of the decisions taken. Check with the co-ordinator that you have enough time.

Distribute any literature that you produce.

Step 4 Air play

The national radio station has decided to air views on the issue. Each group will have 3 minutes of air play in which to put their case to the nation.

Decide how you can best make use of this time:

- an interview

- a talk
- an advertisement
- talking to people in the street
- a combination of any of the above
- any other ideas that your group may have

Plan your programme and delegate responsibilities within the group.

If a tape recorder is available, record your programme for later broadcasting. If no recorder is available, arrange with the co-ordinator to present your programme 'live'.

SECTION 5 *VIEWPOINTS*

In this chapter you have practised a number of skills which can be applied to various areas of study.

Below are four exercises which give you the opportunity to try some of these out in your own field.

A Identifying bias

We have examined varying degrees of bias in texts concerning the scientific world. You should now be in a position to pick out such bias in texts which you encounter, both in your studies and in daily life.

- Decide on an area associated with your studies which people might have different views on.
- Locate as many sources of information as you can about that area, and compare them in terms of bias.
- Try to identify in what ways this bias is expressed.
- Decide also from what points of view the texts were written, who the texts are aimed at, and what the authors' reasons for writing were.

B Your own position

If you have managed to collect together a number of texts on one area, and you have identified their bias, you should be in a position to form your own view on the issue, and to express your personal bias.

This might be very strong in one direction, it may be moderate, or it may be entirely neutral. Your choice of language will be the main way of expressing this.

- Write a brief summary of your angle on the issue.
- Give it to a colleague who is familiar with the subject and ask him/her to identify your position.

C Speakers' attitudes

As we have seen, a speaker's attitude to a topic can often be identified; whether biased or neutral, extreme or reserved.

- The next time you are at a lecture, involved in or listening to a seminar or workshop, watching a television interview or discussion, test your ability to judge the speakers' attitudes.
- Pay particular attention to choice of language and tone of voice. Note down any phrases which give a clear indication of the speakers' points of view.

D People-watching

We have established that there is a wide variety of ways of agreeing and disagreeing, some stronger than others, and some more polite than others.

Choice of language will depend on a number of factors, for example, how

HOW can we measure health? As long ago as 1948 the WHO Constitution defined health as 'a state of complete physical, mental and social well-being.' If we were to measure all the criteria which make up such a definition of health, the list would be enormous. Apart from the more obvious ways of measuring an individual's health, we would have to look into social ills that have a bearing on our physical and mental well-being. We might look at the suicide rate, the number of murders committed or the road traffic accident rate. We might survey the rates of juvenile delinquency, drug-taking, the consumption of tranquillisers, the number of cigarettes smoked, and the average obesity of a given population.

Then there are more subtle factors that, taken together, add up to 'the quality of life.' The opportunities for leisure pursuits and cultural or sporting activities, the length of the working day or week, even such considerations as the climate – something that humans have not yet learnt how to improve – would need to be measured.

(WHO = World Health Organisation) *World Health*, October 1986

B3 In groups select two different types of society. Arrange the factors you have noted according to the extent to which they influence the health of each society.

Compare and discuss your findings with those of another group.

SECTION 2 *HEALTH MATTERS*

A1 From the following list choose the 12 'yardsticks' which you think would be most helpful in measuring a country's standard of health.

- adult literacy rate
- average life expectancy
- availability of dental care
- government commitment to health policy
- average child weight
- ratio of doctors to population
- government spending on health
- basic level of sanitation
- even distribution resources between town and country
- national diet
- country's gross national product
- average family size
- availability of basic health care to everyone
- involvement of the public in decisions on health policy
- infant mortality rate
- school leaving age
- availability of resources – from domestic and foreign sources
- distribution of small clinics throughout the country

A2 Read through the text below and decide which 12 of the 'yard-sticks' listed above match the 12 outlined by the World Health Organisation.

Twelve yardsticks for health

In order to monitor the progress of the entire planet towards the goal of Health for all, WHO has selected 12 global indicators for comparing each country's well-being

The 12 global indicators are that:

1–**Health for all has received endorsement as policy at the highest official level.** This might take the form of a declaration of commitment by the head of state; allocation of adequate resources equitably distributed; a high degree of community involvement; and the establishment of a suitable organizational framework and managerial process for national health development.

2–**Mechanisms for involving people in the implementation of**

strategies have been formed or strengthened, and are actually functioning. That is to say, effective mechanisms exist for people to express demands and needs; representations of political parties and organized groups such as trade unions, women's organizations, farmers' or other occupational groups are participating actively; and decision-making on health matters is adequately decentralised to the various administrative levels.

3–**At least five per cent of the gross national product is spent on health.**

4–**A reasonable percentage of the national health expenditure is devoted to local health care.** This includes first-level contact, including community health care, health centre care, dispensary care and the like, excluding hospitals. The percentage considered 'reasonable' will be arrived at through country studies.

5–**Resources are equitably distributed.** This means that the per capita expenditure as well as the staff and facilities devoted to primary health care are similar for various population groups or geographical areas, such as urban and rural areas.

6–**In the case of developing countries, there are well-defined strategies for Health for all, accompanied by explicit resources allocations, and the needs for external resources are receiving sustained support from more affluent countries.**

7–**Primary health care is available to the whole population, with at least the following:**

– safe water in the home or within 15 minutes walking distance, and adequate sanitary facilities in the home or immediate vicinity;

– immunization against diphtheria, tetanus, whooping-cough, measles, poliomyelitis and tuberculosis;

– local health care, including availability of at least 20 essential drugs, within one hour's walk or travel;

– trained personnel for attending pregnancy and childbirth, and caring for children up to at least one year of age.

8–**The nutritional status of children is adequate,** in that:

– at least 90 per cent of newborn infants have a birth weight of at least 2,500 grammes;

– at least 90 per cent of children have a weight for age that corresponds to the reference values recommended by WHO.

9–**the infant mortality rate for all identifiable subgroups is below 50 per 1,000 live births.**

10–**Life expectancy at birth is over 60 years.**

11–**The adult literacy rate for both men and women exceeds 70 per cent.**

12–**The gross national product per head exceeds US $500.**

The *Health for all series, No. 4* declares: 'It should be noted that the use of these global indicators implies that countries will commit themselves to use at least these and to report on them. It also implies that the WHO Regional Committees, the Executive Board and the World Health Assembly will have to commit themselves to use them and will have to take a firm stand to make sure that the information is forthcoming.'

Grizzled old age in Pakistan. Life expectancy of over 60 years is one of 12 global indicators.

New Internationalist, Feb. '87

A3 How is the WHO list different from yours?

Some indicators might surprise you, *e.g.* number 11 – the adult literacy rate. Why do you think the WHO consider this an important factor?

Discuss which factors in the WHO list surprised you.

A4 Now try to find information about these global indicators for a country of your choice. To do this effectively you must consider:

- What type(s) of book are likely to include this kind of information?
- How would you find these books in your library?

How would you use the books to find the information you want as quickly as possible?

B1 In small groups, decide on a country that you would like to investigate in terms of the global indicators suggested by the WHO.

Before proceeding, consult with other groups to ensure a wide selection of countries is being covered.

Make sure that there is adequate information available on the country you choose.

B2 In order to record the information that you gather, you now need to design a **grid** which includes the countries you have chosen and the 'yardsticks' you wish to measure with.

a In your groups, draw up such a grid.

b Check that each group is using a similar grid.

B3 Go to the library and fill out the grid for your country as far as you can.

In many cases a tick or a cross will be sufficient. If you want to include any other information, it must be brief.

B4 *a* Exchange information with other students so that you can complete your grid for the other countries on the list. This may be done in pairs or in groups.

b *(i)* Name the country which meets the largest number of criteria considered necessary for good health. Discuss the possible reasons that may account for this fact.

(ii) Name the country which meets the fewest number of criteria considered necessary for good health. Discuss the possible reasons that may account for this fact.

c Now write a brief paragraph comparing the health standards of two countries included in the grid and suggest possible reasons for the variations between them.

C How can we improve health standards?

Improving standards of health is the responsibility of both the individual and the community. No matter how much an individual tries to improve his own health he cannot improve the environment unless he co-operates with other people. Equally no matter how much a government spends on health it will have no impact unless individuals behave responsibly.

Imagine that you walk into a clinic and discover the scene below.

C1 What would your reaction be: *a* as a patient?
b as a health inspector?

C2 Working with a partner, quickly find as many faults as you can.

C3 Decide which five you consider to be the most serious and why.

C4 In groups, try to reach a consensus on the five most serious errors. Then decide on measures that could be taken to rectify them. Make notes on your conclusions and proposals.

From 'Helping Health Care Workers Learn', D. Werner & B. Bower, Hesperian Foundation, Pato Alto California 1983

D Reporting back

If you were the health inspector in this situation it is likely that you would have to turn your findings and recommendations into a formal report to your superiors.

A report can either be written in response to a specific need or as an accurate and complete account of relevant information. It should be an orderly and objective communication of facts aimed at a particular reader or readers for a specific purpose.

The main functions of a report are to:

(i) present a solution to a problem;
(ii) help the reader make a sound decision by giving him the needed facts;
(iii) allow the management of an organisation to perform its control function by providing the necessary feedback;
(iv) bring people within an organisation up to date on what is happening;
(v) communicate with people both inside and outside an institution.

To be well written and effective a report must therefore be:

Accurate. A report is of no value unless it is accurate; if it gives incorrect information this could lead to incorrect decisions.

Factual. The facts must be presented as they are and not distorted to reflect the opinions of the writer, or consciously changed in order to please the person for whom the report is being prepared.

Clear. The language used must be easily understood by the reader. If the reader knows about the subject of the report, the writer can use technical language; but if the reader is unfamiliar with the terminology of the subject, then the writer must use simpler language that is easily understood by the non-specialist.

Complete as possible in itself. The body of the report must contain all the important ideas and facts so that any extra tables or notes are only used to add details or supporting evidence.

Easy to read. A report must be well-organised with one part logically following or explaining another part, so the reader can grasp the meaning quickly.

E1 Using the criteria outlined above compile a report on the clinic shown in the cartoon following the guidelines below.

> **Report on visit to Central Territories Health Clinic week ending**
> *date*:
>
> **1** As requested I am sending you a report on the current situation at the Central Territories Health Clinic. My findings are based on personal observation and experiences in clinics of a similar nature.
>
> **2** The running of the clinic is...
>
> **3** The following factors appear to be operating to bring about this situation:
> *(i)*
> *(ii)*
> *(iii)*
> *(iv)*
> *(v)*
>
> **4** My recommendations are as follows:
> *(i)*
> *(ii)*
> *(iii)*
> *(iv)*
> *(v)*

E2 When you have completed your reports exchange them with other members of the class. Making use of the criteria above critically evaluate the reports you receive and explain whether or not they fulfil the required functions.

F Read the following 10 sentences carefully. Five of them are inappropriate in tone for a formal report.

F1 Which of the five sentences do you think are unsuitable?

a *(i)* The nurse concerned means well but merely succeeds in blundering around with the best of intentions.
(ii) The nurse concerned is hardworking but unaware of the proper procedures.

b *(i)* This class of people are of course too uncivilised to queue in an orderly manner.
(ii) The habit of queueing in an orderly manner is unfortunately not widespread.

c (i) She gave an explanation of why the laundry expenses for that period were unusually high.

(*ii*) She made a token attempt to account for the absurdly high laundry expenses.

d (*i*) Further investigations tended to indicate that her explanation was not wholly convincing.

(*ii*) We checked out the things she told me and as I expected she was wrong.

e (i) So you see it is extremely unlikely all things being equal that much can be done to improve standards in the place.

(*ii*) It is in my view extremely unlikely that the situation will improve radically in the near future.

F2 Read the following paragraphs and then check your answers to exercise **F1**.

> Simply conveying facts in a report is often not enough. The tone of what you write is as important as your message. Whilst controlling the tone doesn't change the content of your message it can influence how your reader responds or reacts to your message. The way we say something sometimes affects our readers more strongly than what we say.
>
> The tone of a report can be positive, negative, neutral, formal, informal, conversational, pleasant, sarcastic, condescending, optimistic, pessimistic, etc. Adopting an appropriate tone for a situation means thinking about how you express your message as well as what your message says. Controlling your tone involves selecting words and phrases that help you project the attitude and self-image you want your reader to see and enable you to communicate with your reader more effectively.

G While a conversational or informal tone is inappropriate to a report, there is no reason why the writer of a report shouldn't take up a constructive stance rather than a critical one or adopt a pessimistic view as opposed to an optimistic one.

G1 It is highly probable that your initial report was neutral in tone. Now that you have more awareness of what tone is, rewrite the report in a manner which is more revealing of your attitude to the problem and its resolution.

G2 Read the reports of your colleagues again and assess the likely effect they will have on the person receiving them.

SECTION 3 *LOOKING AFTER YOUR HEALTH*

A **Assessing group performance**

Few situations are as extreme as the one in the cartoon. Often, well-planned projects are designed with the best of intentions. The reasons why they fail are often difficult to predict. If future projects are not to result in failure it is important to evaluate accurately the reasons for a project's failure and to pass that knowledge on to others.

A1 Study the following report on a project that failed. Working with a partner, make short notes on the following:

a What was the objective of the programme?
b Who were selected to carry it out?
c How were they trained?
d How was the programme tested?
e Explain what the results showed.
f What reasons do the authors give for the failure of the programme?

R. N. Ratnaike, P. O'Neil, & R. Chynoweth

Village health workers and malnutrition: a project that failed

In a number of villages in the Himalayan foothills in India, after two years of using locally recruited village health workers to encourage earlier weaning, and despite the ready availability of food supplies, malnutrition among children remained at nearly 90%.

In developing countries the provision of adequate basic health care to small isolated villages presents a major challenge to health workers and is compounded by the limited financial resources available. Thus, priorities must be in areas of health that yield maximum long-term benefits. One such area is malnutrition in the under-five-year-old population, which needs to be solved as a preventive measure at village level rather than a costly curative one at a hospital or health centre (*1*).

In 1976, to assess the need and feasibility for a community health programme in surrounding villages, a community hospital in the Himalayan foothills of north India instituted a pilot study with the assistance of a voluntary health organization. Malnutrition was the major health problem of the under-five-year-olds. Poverty, diarrhoeal disease, and other chronic illnesses were not the major factors causing malnutrition but rather the failure to begin weaning until the child was at least 12 months of age. This was based on the belief that consuming solid foods at an earlier age would be detrimental to the child's health. Furthermore, despite the ready availability of food, the children's diets were insufficient in calories. Following the findings of the pilot study, the hospital established a community health programme.

Training the Village Health Workers

A major objective of the programme was to improve the nutritional status of the under-five-year-old children. It was decided that this and other health goals would be best achieved by training village health workers, who would be women selected by their own communities. They were trained in their villages for 18 months by health care personnel from the newly established community health programme, most of whom had nursing experience. The village health workers were taught in small groups using flash cards and practical demonstrations that emphasized nutrition, maternity, and child care. Other aspects of primary health care included the control of infection and diarrhoeal diseases and the treatment of simple illnesses. The preparation of food from locally available cereals for infant feeding was frequently demonstrated. The village health workers served on a part-time basis.

Testing the Programme

The programme was tested in two phases. In May 1977, the newly established community health programme, assisted by students from a high school in the district and one of the authors (P.O'N.), carried out a survey to determine the prevalence of malnutrition in the under-fives, before the training of the village health workers.

Seven villages were selected at random and the village elders contacted. The children under five years of age and their mothers were asked to gather at a central place. Some children were contacted by visits to the home or the fields. The name, age, and weight were recorded on a child health record (*1*).

In 1979, a second survey was carried out under the direction of another of the authors (R.N.R.) to determine the impact the village health workers had had on malnutrition in the under-five-year-olds.

Analysing the Results

In the 1977 survey, seven villages were visited, and the prevalence of malnutrition among 127 children was found to be 91.3%. In the 1979 survey, 156 children were weighed in 13 villages and the prevalence of malnutrition was found to be 82.1%.

The results of the 1977 survey confirmed the 1976 findings that malnutrition was a major health problem in children under the age of five. Following the introduction of the village health workers with special nutrition training, the results of the 1979 survey showed no statistically significant improvement in nutrition. Indeed the prevalence of malnutrition in the area in our study compared unfavourably with figures from other developing countries (*2–4*).

From frequent visits to the villages we gained the impression that malnutrition occurred just as frequently in the children of the prosperous families as among those of the poor, suggesting that ignorance rather than poverty was the cause of malnutrition. And we were able to confirm the existence of a widespread belief that children should not be weaned until they were about one year old. Our belief that the village health workers transmitted the teaching of better nutritional care to mothers was established by talking to the villagers; the mothers had received the advice on nutrition but apparently had not acted upon it.

Many factors may have contributed to this lack of response.

During the inception of the project, discussions with the villagers had been confined to health problems, with the result that the villagers may have withheld information about problems that were more important to them. Alternatively, they may have chosen to confine their observations to health-related matters, believing that the community health programme lacked the inclination or the resources to deal with other problems.

In fact, in 1979, two years after the programme started, the villagers often talked with us about various problems affecting their lives – wild animals ravaging their crops, flooding of the river causing crop damage, and lack of conveniently accessible sources of drinking-water. These problems were obviously associated with the nutritional status of the villagers, particularly the more vulnerable under-five-year-olds although the villagers themselves did not see them as health problems. People should perhaps have been given more encouragement in the initial stages of the programme to talk about their problems and to be assured that the programme was capable of seeking appropriate assistance for the solution of non-health problems. This might have resulted in more active participation in the community health programme.

Secondly, one wonders if there was not a divergence in the concept of health and disease between ourselves and the villagers. Ours was a broad view with many factors contributing to the total well-being of the individuals. We had identified malnutrition as a major health problem. The villagers' concept of good health, on the other hand, may have been the absence of individual sickness. Malnutrition may not have been seen as an illness.

Malnutrition was about as common among children from prosperous families as among those of the poor, suggesting that ignorance rather than poverty was the cause of malnutrition.

With this view on health and disease, their repeated request for a small hospital with a resident doctor in each village was not unreasonable, albeit unrealistic. The illiterate village health worker, lacking the real or imagined curative skills of a doctor, might thus have appeared a poor or even totally unacceptable alternative. More frequent visits to the villages by the doctor in charge of the project might have had a beneficial effect in boosting the morale and status of the village health worker in the community. However, the isolation of these villages and the often bad road conditions made visits less frequent than both the villagers and village health workers might have desired. Thus, a variety of factors might have lowered the credibility of the village health worker, making it difficult for her to induce the community to adopt a more healthy lifestyle.

There are often too many opinions on health priorities in the minds of villagers, and these may diverge from the more uniform and established views of the health professionals. However, we believe that consensus is possible through prolonged initial dialogues in which members of the community are urged to help identify health problems, set objectives, and decide on strategies.

A simpler explanation may account for our negative findings. Two years may have been insufficient time for significant changes in attitude and alterations in behaviour to have occurred in the village communities.

Perhaps some seeds have been sown, and a subsequent study may reveal that they have borne fruit.

Dr Ratnaike is Senior Lecturer in the Department of Medicine at the University of Adelaide, Australia, and Dr Chynoweth is Head of the Department of Psychiatry, located at Queen Elizabeth Hospital, Woodville, Australia, where Dr O'Neil is Senior Resident Medical Officer.

REFERENCES

1. MORLEY, D. *British medical journal*, **4**: 85 (1974).
2. BROWN, H. B. ET AL. *Journal of tropical paediatrics*, **24**: 176 (1978).
3. WYATT, J. L. & WYATT, G. B. *Papua New Guinea medical journal*. **21**: 184 (1978).
4. CHOPDAR, A. & SAMAL, N. C. *Indian journal of pediatrics*, **46**: 87 (1979).

World Health Forum, Vol. 6, 1985

A2 Study carefully the notes you have made and then discuss, in groups, ways of ensuring that the project becomes more successful in its second phase.

B As a result of your reading and discussion, write a short report for the Health Ministry of a country interested in setting up a similar project. Briefly outline the programme described here, mention what went wrong, and include your suggestions for ensuring the success of their new project.

C Assessing individual performance

1 Quickly read through the following text in order to find the phrases which refer to the qualities possessed by a good doctor.

Where docs get only 18 hours of sleep a week

WARD P1, a third-class male ward, is one of the oldest wards in the Kuala Lumpur General Hospital. On a normal admissions day, P1 can take in 60 patients. On a busy day, additional patients have to contend with camp-beds.

The ward or 'hut,' as medical officers call it, is open and breezy. Little green plants grow in empty plastic intravenous bottles hung on white washed pillars. But patients admitted into P1 are usually too ill to notice their surroundings.

P1 is usually the first male ward to receive patients if their initial diagnosis is unclear or incomplete. After additional tests are done and it is known what that patient is suffering from, he is then treated accordingly or sent to the appropriate ward.

For the medical personnel attached to P1, the ward means hard work. The four housemen are often on their feet from 7am to 12 midnight on an active or admissions day. That's a total of 17 hours a day.

For the houseman who is on call, the midnight stretch will last until 6pm the following day. That is an 18-hour stretch. Then, after about six hours of sleep at the housemen's quarters, he begins again at 7am the following morning.

Because of the volume of patients – up to 45 admissions on an active day – the four housemen have to be on call almost every other day. This means, while the average person sleeps 40 hours a working week, the houseman is lucky if he gets 18 hours sleep during the same period.

As a rule, housemen at the GH work seven days a week. On public holidays, they are expected to go on their ward rounds or be on standby for emergencies.

It is really hard work, says the Ward P1's most senior houseman, but she enjoys it.

'I am a workaholic. You learn to cope with less sleep over time and make-do with cat naps. The human body is truly marvellous.'

Tutelage

If all goes well, she will complete her housemanship in less than two months. After a couple more months in obstetrics and gynaecology, she will be a fully registered doctor.

But her beginnings in Ward P1 were difficult. Used to easier postings where she had more time to relax, she was given 'a shelling' by her supervisor who, she says, did not like her attitude.

On his teaching rounds, the supervisor checked and questioned details in her examination of patients. She learned her lesson well and accepted the guidance and advice of her supervisor. As a result, several medical officers say, she is now shaping up to be a first-class doctor.

She was not the only one subjected to such close scrutiny by the supervisor. Every houseman who underwent his tutelage under this supervisor has had similar experiences.

Some typical comments:

- 'Don't mumble. How can you mumble in front of your patient?', said the supervisor when a houseman was unable to remember the name of a thigh muscle. Surrounding the embarrassed houseman were his colleagues, a battery of nurses and this writer. And, what's worse, in front of the patient.
- 'You suffer from verbal diarrhoea,' another specialist was heard to have told one of his medical charges.
- 'Redeem yourself, doctor,' said a specialist when a houseman grinned sheepishly because he had no answer to a question about his patient.

Doctors have to be clear and accurate in their answers, most supervisors say. Vague answers like 'sometime ago' are never acceptable.

If they felt humiliated at first, they eventually got over it and learnt to accept the criticisms in the right spirit.

For 'clinical clerkship' is important. Clerking a patient means getting a history of the illness, conducting an investigation and the subsequent management of the patient.

In all three areas – general medicine, general surgery and obstetrics and gynaecology (O&G), housemen are first taught to clerk patients carefully. They also make the first arrangements for patients to see other specialists and carry out blood, urine and sometimes, bone-marrow examinations.

Trying time

In the Maternity Hospital, however, housemen are under less supervision but they are taught to recognise conditions when they need their medical officer's help.

As in P1, admissions day in the Maternity Hospital is hectic. At midnight, the houseman would still be clerking patients. At four hour intervals, she examines women in labour and helps out in the opposite ward when her colleague makes a quick dash to the blood bank.

Like she enjoys her work. She takes the long hours in her stride. She even jokes about the fact that her hectic lifestyle has not helped her lose weight.

Another earnest-looking houseman with eight month's practical experience, says one of the hardest things to do, especially when handling so many cases, was to remember that patients are human beings and not just cases.

Even though she enjoys her stint in O&G ('because I am a woman and can relate to it'), she admits that at 3am when her mind slows down and a patient is demanding, it can be trying.

Sometimes, when a mother shows no interest in her new-born baby girl (probably because she has five other daughters at home), the housemen feel depressed.

'We tell them they must take care of the child, that the baby needs their love,' says one of the doctors who, after a series of breech and vacuum deliveries, still looked fresh and cheerful at 11.30pm.

For many, the period of housemanship is long, arduous and often terrifying.

As her colleague says: 'Sometimes you have to make snap decisions. This is especially difficult when you are faced with a situation never handled before.

'You have to think fast, rely on your theoretical knowledge and act quickly'.

– ***By ROSE ISMAIL***

C2 As senior medical officer in a large hospital, you want to assess the performance of the housemen in your hospital. Using the information you have obtained, and adding any further points of your own, draw up a checklist which could be used to assess the relative competence of your housemen. Your checklist should be able to identify different levels of competence.

D Why do we damage our health standards?

Tobacco – strong words are not enough

Although we all know that smoking is bad for the individual many people assume it is enough to warn tobacco users, through the media and with labels on tobacco products, of the risks they take, and to leave them with the responsibility for their own health. It is argued that if users choose to take the risk, in return for pleasure or stimulation, that is their right.

For many governments the basis of action since the mid-1960s has been the provision of information aimed at educating smokers about their health risks and discouraging non-smokers from starting. The aim is to change society's attitude from a view of smoking as glamorous to one that sees the habit as socially unacceptable.

D1 During your studies you will often have to interpret and comment upon statistics and figures. This requires you to have a clear idea of the trends revealed by the statistics.

Suppose you were asked the following questions based on the table below.

Study the table carefully and comment on the effectiveness of Public Health educational policies in influencing the consumption of cigarettes.

In order to answer this question accurately you must establish whether Public Health educational policies actually do reduce the consumption of cigarettes.

a In interpreting statistics it is often useful to ask yourself a series of questions and then try to find the answers. Often these answers will provide you with the insights you need to analyse and interpret the statistical information.

For example, with this particular chart it is important to know the following kinds of information:

- Where has smoking increased most?
- Where has smoking decreased most?
  Compare these two.
- What restrictions do these countries have?
  Compare consumption in a country with no restrictions with consumption in a country with many restrictions.

b It is also important to select countries which are representative of a general trend. For example, if you selected Hungary/The Soviet Union/Poland to indicate the effect of government anti-smoking policies on smoking what conclusion would you reach compared to someone who had selected Bulgaria/Norway/Sweden?

Cigarette use and antismoking policies in selected countries, 1974–84

Country	Annual change in use of cigarettes(%)	Package warning label	Advertising ban		Bans in public places	
			Total	Partial	Strong	Weak
Argentina	+0.1					
Australia	+0.9	x		x		
Brazil	+1.6	x				
Bulgaria	−0.2	x	x		x[1]	
China	+6.2		x			x
Egypt	+8.7	x		x		x
Finland	+0.8	x	x		x	
France	+0.6	x		x	x	
Hungary	+0.4	x	x		x	
India	+2.9	x				
Italy	+1.6		x		x	
Japan	+0.6	x				x
Kenya	+3.9					x
Mexico	+1.0	x		x		
Netherlands	−3.3	x		x		
Norway	−1.6	x	x			
Poland	+0.3		x		x[1]	
Soviet Union	+0.8	x	x		x	
Spain	+1.6			x		
Sweden	−0.3	x		x		
United Kingdom	−3.1	x		x		
United States	0	x		x		x

[1] Includes restrictions on smoking in the workplace.
Source: Worldwatch Institute, based on R. Roemer, *Legislative action to combat the world smoking epidemic* (Geneva, World Health Organization, 1982), and on *Foreign agricultural circular*, Supplement 1–84, Washington, DC, US Department of Agriculture, Foreign Agricultural Service, 1984.

World Health Forum, Vol. 7, 1986

D2 In questions that involve the interpretation of statistics, the first part of the question often asks you to comment on what the figures themselves reveal. In many cases, however, there is often a follow-up question that asks you for your **own** opinions and ideas about what the figures **do not show**. For example, in the table you have been studying it is clear that Public Health educational policies are not the only factor that influence the consumption of cigarettes. Consequently, you may encounter a question like this.

> Can you suggest any other factors which may have influenced the consumption of cigarettes in addition to those suggested by the figures?

Discuss with a partner what other factors might be taken into consideration, and agree on a list.

D3 Taking account of the hints and guidance you have been given, answer the complete question in not more than 100 words.

> Study the table carefully and comment on the effectiveness of Public Health educational policies in influencing the consumption of cigarettes.
> Can you suggest any other factors which may have influenced the consumption of cigarettes, in addition to those suggested by the figures?

SECTION 4 *STANDING UP FOR YOUR RIGHTS*

A1 Quickly read the following Extracts and decide which ones contain the most information about the following topics:

- Diseases directly related to smoking
- The fire risks caused by smoking
- Voluntary anti-smoking campaigns in the private sector
- Policy proposals to reduce the incidence of public smoking
- The economic costs of tobacco-related diseases
- Compulsory anti-smoking laws
- The influence of smoking on workplace efficiency
- The side effects of passive smoking

Extract A

I became Surgeon General in 1981. The 1982 report clearly showed the link between cigarette smoking and cancer, particularly lung cancer, implicating cigarettes in as many as 129 000 cancer deaths per year. Our 1983 report was on the close relationship between smoking and cardiovascular disease. And the numbers were even larger: we estimated that cigarette smoking was directly related to 170 000 deaths from coronary heart disease each year. The 1984 report documented the relationship between cigarette smoking and chronic obstructive lung disease. Once again, we had a grim picture of chronic, long-term suffering among cigarette smokers.

Response of the legislators

As the evidence mounted, the United States required that anti-smoking messages should have as much time on radio and television as did cigarette advertising. Those public service messages apparently had an effect because cigarette consumption began to level off. Next, Congress banned the advertising of cigarettes altogether on electronic media, and required that every package of cigarettes and every scrap of cigarette advertising carry a warning from the Surgeon General that said 'Smoking is dangerous to your health'. During this period, certain commercial interests began to see the value, in their own terms, of the anti-smoking campaign, among them the health and life insurance companies, several airlines, and some hotels and restaurants. There were only a few to begin with, but the list continues to grow.

> **Certain commercial interests began to see the value, in their own terms, of the anti-smoking campaign.**

These and other developments combined to educate the public on the seriousness of the cigarette issue. I call this period 'Phase 1' of our fight against smoking. In 'Phase 2' the nonsmokers arrived on the scene. They were merely irritated at first, but then became annoyed and finally militant. The more militant the nonsmokers have been, the greater has been the change in social customs and in local and State law. For example, in 1973 Arizona became the first State to prohibit smoking in public places, on commercial airliners in Arizona airspace, and on buses. In 1975 the State of Maryland passed a law specifically protecting nonsmoking patients from the harmful effects of passive smoking in all health facilities.

Since then, more than 30 of our 50 States and hundreds of local communities have followed suit, enacting ordinances to prohibit or severely restrict smoking in restaurants, government offices, theatres, indoor sports arenas, bus station waiting rooms, clinics, retail stores, and so on. What do these laws say? Let me give an example. On 1 March 1984, San Francisco put into effect 'Proposition P', which the city voters had approved in an election watched by the whole country. 'Proposition P' is a tough law. It says, among other things, that every workplace and every public gathering place must separate smokers from nonsmokers. A complaint by a single nonsmoker is enough to require this separation. In addition, if the people responsible for a public place do not act after a complaint has been lodged, they are subject to heavy daily fines.

Another very interesting example of anti-smoking law is found in Virginia. This State has a law saying that if a publicly employed fire-fighter, police officer, or deputy sheriff is disabled or dies because of heart disease, respiratory illness, or high blood pressure, the State will assume that the illness was caused by the conditions of employment, and will therefore agree to be fully liable for all compensation and pension claims. However, several county governments in Virginia have gone one step further. They say that the same cardiovascular and respiratory diseases are also linked to smoking, as the reports of Surgeons General and research by others have amply demonstrated over the past 20 years, and that they will therefore reject compensation or pension claims made by any employees who prematurely bring these diseases upon themselves by smoking. And now those same counties demand that all new employees in public safety sign the following pledge: 'I agree not to smoke at any time . . . whether on or off duty, and . . . my failure to comply with the above-mentioned conditions . . . shall constitute good cause for my employer to terminate my employment'.

I would be hard-pressed to find a better example of just how completely the public accepts and believes the facts published in the 18 reports on smoking and health that have been issued by the Surgeons General of the United States Public Health Service since 1964.

Nonsmokers' rights

We are now in 'Phase 3' of the anti-smoking crusade. We are beginning to understand with more scientific precision just why the nonsmoker is so upset. We have begun to generate hard data that specifically measure the detrimental health effects of passive or sidestream smoking. The effects of passive smoking on children have been clear for some time, but the evidence regarding adults was less firm until relatively recently. Today, however, we have solid information concerning the effects of a smoker's environment upon the adult nonsmoker. One of the most significant reports on this subject was published in the *New England journal of medicine* (27 September 1984): a Japanese study measured the levels of cotinine, a metabolic product of nicotine, in the urine of passive smokers. It was concluded that if you are a nonsmoker but live with someone who smokes two packets of cigarettes a day, you will in effect be smoking three cigarettes a day yourself.

The more militant the nonsmokers have been, the greater has been the change in social customs and in local and State law.

In view of the decreasing number of smokers and the increasing interest in nonsmokers' rights, I believe that smoking will not be as acceptable in the future as it once was. In the past few years we have begun to see an active interest in the passive smoking issue, and with the increasing medical evidence that indicates a link between passive smoking and disease there is likely to be still more activity as time goes on.

There is increasing concern associated with the actual costs of illness resulting directly from smoking. The medical costs are not only a burden on individuals but also on governmental entities and private organizations. Several studies have been conducted which indicate that the cost to an organization of maintaining a smoking employee may range from US$500 to $4600 a year. These figures are quite alarming when we consider the numbers of smokers involved, and consequently I feel that we shall begin to see public and private organizations taking action to discourage smoking in workplaces. Many organizations in the United States have already begun to recognize the benefits of doing so.

Extract B

A tougher stand

The dilemma may be unique in medicine: a dangerous drug clearly should – but cannot – be banned. The economic strength of the tobacco industry is so great that it can exploit for its own purposes the safeguards built into democracies to protect minorities. In some undemocratic countries, governments may lack the credibility and motivation to tackle the problem. And under any political system, social conditioning and chemical habituation make banning tobacco a formidable task and one that would take a long time. Yet current information campaigns are failing as worldwide use increases faster than the population.

An alternative approach is inherent in a new campaign to protect nonsmokers: it stops short of an outright ban on tobacco sales, but includes either the prohibition of smoking in the workplace and public buildings or the strict limitation of smoking to specified areas. This movement may be the greatest success of the information campaign against tobacco. Its leaders insist that despite the continued sale, advertising, and use of tobacco, nonsmokers have every right not to be exposed to the carcinogens, carbon monoxide, and irritants in tobacco smoke (*2*). Such a campaign can have three important effects.

First, by banning the use of tobacco from places where nonsmokers would be exposed, thousands of lives may be saved. Second, forcing smokers to give up their habit while in the presence of nonsmokers will provide them with an added impetus to quit. If smokers must get through working days without smoking, then they are more likely to be able to quit completely. And third, by stigmatizing tobacco use as dangerous and antisocial, the campaign for nonsmokers' rights can accomplish a goal of all antismoking information campaigns: to make smoking socially unattractive.

The economic strength of the tobacco industry is so great that it can exploit for its own purposes the safeguards built into democracies to protect minorities.

This campaign focuses on the workplace, public gathering places, and public transport. Many countries now prohibit smoking on public transport and in theatres and auditoriums, though the main reason for these restrictions has usually been that of fire prevention. In a few areas, such as the state of Minnesota and the cities of San Francisco and Los Angeles, smoking is now prohibited in public buildings (except in restricted areas) and nonsmokers must be protected in restaurants and at work.

Interestingly, nonsmokers have an important ally in the workplace; their employers. Companies, at least in the United States, are rapidly realizing that most of their employees do not smoke and do not like to breathe the smoke of others, and that smokers cost employers money. Surveys indicate that inefficiency and ill-health attributable to smoking waste about 7% of a smoker's working time. Smokers also add to insurance and cleanup costs, and reduce the morale of nonsmoking employees.

A particular difficulty in banning tobacco is presented by governments that promote the use of tobacco. This happens not just in the market-oriented West, but also in centralized economies. Thus the state-owned tobacco industry in China is being carefully nurtured and rapidly expanded even as the government is telling the people that smoking is bad for them (*3*).

In the United States, the Department of Agriculture administers a price-support system to protect tobacco producers. Western European nations subsidize tobacco farmers with about US$ 60 million in price supports each year. Ironically, the systems protect small, inefficient farmers who earn higher prices than they would obtain without the subsidy. More efficient producers, who could underprice the small farmers, are not allowed to compete fully. Tobacco consequently costs more than it otherwise would, and as its use declines in response to price increases, smoking is in fact reduced by the producers' price supports (*4*). There is an even more subtle effect, however. The tobacco industry gains the powerful political support of the small farmers, and this helps to counter antismoking forces. Moreover, the official tolerance and even endorsement of the use of tobacco diminishes the effectiveness of information campaigns aimed at reducing the social acceptability of smoking.

On balance, then, the antismoking movement is holding a defensive line in industrial countries and failing to prevent an increase in the incidence of the habit in developing ones.

Effective antismoking policies are of four kinds. The first is the information campaign, which is worthwhile as a foundation for the others. The second should consist of banning tobacco altogether in those countries with low smoking rates, no indigenous tobacco industry, and a reliance on imported tobacco products. To do this would eliminate the threat of tobacco for these countries and place them in the forefront of the antismoking movement. The third requires those nations that must be politically pragmatic at least to act to protect the health of nonsmokers. Experience in the United States and in Poland shows that tobacco can be banned from public buildings and workplaces. A smoking ban in the presence of nonsmokers should be considered the minimum level of protection. All governments could pass national indoor clean air acts for public buildings, workplaces, and entertainment establishments. The fourth effective approach is to use the economic lever to reduce smoking as much as possible. Even a small tax increase would encourage light smokers to abandon the habit, would put additional pressure on the heavily addicted to do the same, and, most importantly, would discourage the young and the poor from starting.

By banning the use of tobacco from places where nonsmokers would be exposed, thousands of lives may be saved.

These measures will not be easy, nor will they solve the tobacco problem. They will not, for example, assure that children will be protected in the home against the smoke of their parents. They will not protect the newborn from harm as a result of their mothers' smoking. Parents alone can take this responsibility, though in some cases their addiction makes them risk the health and intellectual development of their children.

New measures will not guarantee that all smokers will be persuaded to quit, or that innocent young people will not become addicted. But only tougher measures than those at present being applied will have any chance of significantly improving the situation.

References

1. Buckley. W. F. The weed. In: Finger, W. R., *The tobacco industry in transition*. Lexington, Lexington Books, 1981.
2. Marwick, C. *Journal of the American Medical Association*. **253**: 2937–2939 (1985).
3. Zhao Jinming. Tobacco industry sets dual targets, *China Daily*, 22 May 1985.
4. How EEC subsidises smoking. *New Scientist*, **102** (1410): 5 (1984).

Extract C

THE BENEFITS OF SMOKING

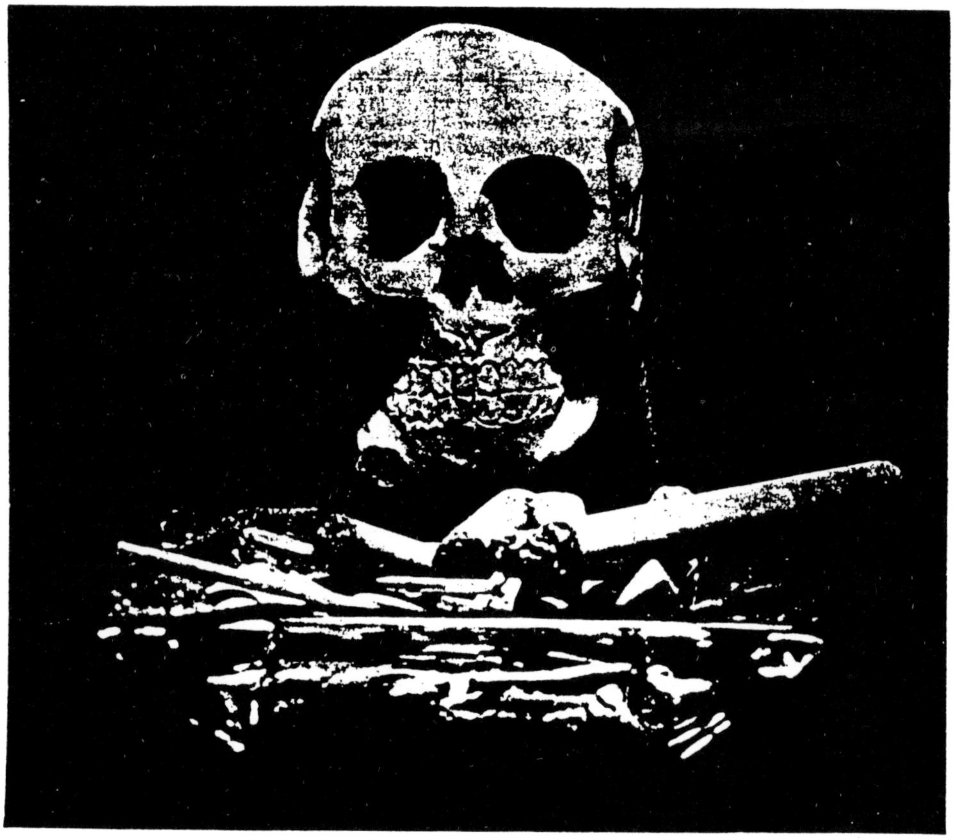

Discoloured Teeth • Cough • Premature Births • Brain Damage
Wrinkles • Reduced Birth Weights of Babies • Premature Deaths
• Bronchitis • Still Births • Yellow Nails •
Asthma • Shortened Lifespan • Bad Breath • Hardened Arteries
and **CANCER** of the Lungs Larynx

A2 You are now going to take part in a discussion about the rights and wrongs of smoking in public places.

The aim of the discussion is for the group to decide whether smoking should be banned in public places, or restricted to certain areas and times, or whether everyone should have the freedom to smoke when and where they wish.

The class should divide into two groups, each group taking one of these roles. (It doesn't matter whether you actually smoke or not.)

Role I – Non-smokers

Discuss the following questions with other members of your group. You don't necessarily have to agree on every point.

- should smoking be completely banned? Why?
- Should it be banned in certain places, or at certain times?
- Should cigarette advertisements be banned?
- Smokers sometimes claim that a ban will interfere with their individual liberty. Do you agree?

- How easy do you think it would be to enforce a ban?
- What kind of measures should be taken against people who smoke in public places?
- Is there any other way of discouraging people from smoking?

Role II – Smokers

Discuss the following questions with other members of your group. You don't necessarily have to agree on every point.

- Why do you smoke?
- Do you intend to continue?
- What effect do you think it has on your health?
- Do you think that your smoking can affect other people's health?
- What do you think about the increasing pressure from non-smokers for a complete ban on smoking in public places.

Before beginning your preparation, you will have to reach a decision on the following:

- What form the final discussion will take: a presentation of each side by one student from each group, or an open discussion.
- Who will chair the discussion.
- How much time you will allow for preparation and for the final discussion.
- How you are going to reach a final decision. *e.g.* a vote, a decision by the chair, or a decision by an observer.

Preparation

The preceding extracts are provided for your information. Refer to these texts in order to strengthen your argument. The extracts, like most contemporary literature on the subject, are heavily biased in favour of non-smokers. In preparing their case the smokers must attempt to rebut many of the points raised.

B Public Health campaigns

Smoking is one major cause of self-inflicted damage to our health. Another is excessive consumption of alcohol. There are many others.

B1 Can you think of any examples?

B2 Look at the anti-smoking poster on page 148. Do you think that it is effective in putting its message across?

B3 Devise a Public Health poster advising people about the dangers of another threat to our health.

The poster should *a* be convincing and persuasive.
b contain details of major ill-effects.

B4 Display your posters in class and decide which one is the most effective.

B5 Show your posters to another class and see if they arrive at the same decision.

SECTION 5 *TREAT YOURSELF*

By this stage in the book, you have practised most of the important skills required for further studies. But just how good are you? Now is the time to find out!

A We can work it out

You must assess accurately and honestly your ability in these skills. Make sure that the class agrees upon a uniform set of criteria to make this evaluation.

You may, for example, decide that in different areas you are now proficient, you still need practice or that you require further assistance from your teacher.

Working alone, read through the **skills matrix** at the beginning of the book and assess your proficiency in each skill according to the criteria you have developed.

Design and fill in a grid which will enable the class as a whole to identify its strengths and weaknesses.

From this grid you should be able to identify those areas in which you need practice or more help and guidance from your teacher.

B With a little help from my friends

Organise revision seminars like those in Unit 5, Section 5.

From your grid, establish areas in which several students share a similar weakness. Now form into groups with students who have the same problems as yourself. Write a short report to your teacher summarising the group's problems and making suggestions about possible ways in which the teacher can help.

UNIT 8 · *What's it all for?*

SECTION 1 *THE WORLD OF EDUCATION*

A If you are reading this then you are likely to be involved in the world of education, either as an instructor or as a learner.

The educational process is clearly not an end in itself. It has objectives. Since you are involved in this process you no doubt have objectives too.

A1 Consider the following questions on the subject.

- Why are you continuing your education?
- What benefits will your education bring you?

Try listing them in order of importance.

- How do you see yourself in 10 years time? What influence will your education have on this?

A2 Discuss your ideas on these questions with other students.

Can you pin-point any common objectives?

Well, I suppose security is what I want most. . . job security. With a good education you have a better chance of establishing yourself. . .

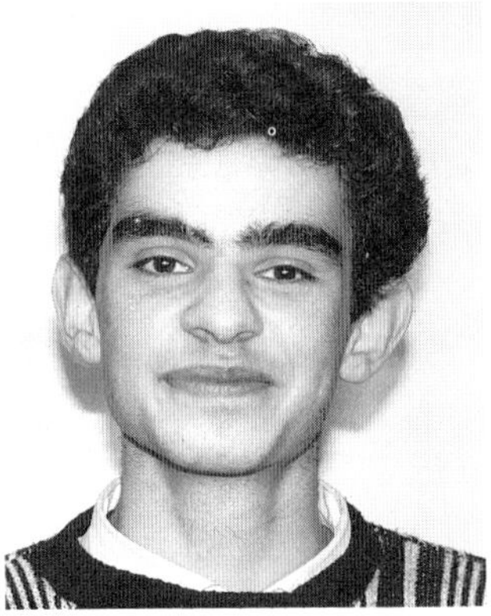

I'm interested in art. . . to continue to paint is what I really want to do. . . set up a studio maybe. Perhaps I'll be famous. . . but I don't think so.

I could have taken a job after school but I knew if I stopped studying, I'd find it hard to take it up again later. . . I suppose I want a more challenging career.

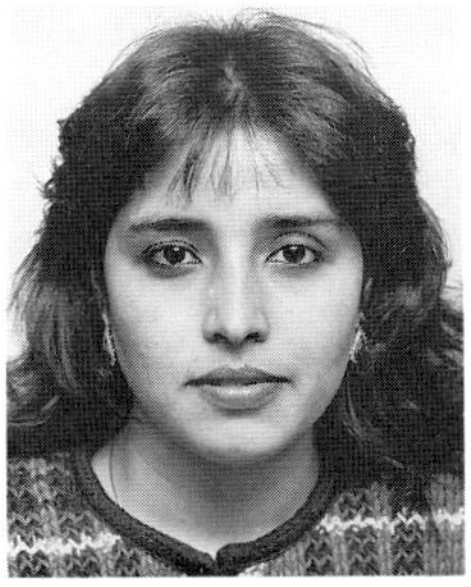

When I started uni, I left behind a more traditional family life, but this doesn't mean I'm throwing my parents' values out of the window.

Well, my parents didn't have the chance to stay at school after 14. They had to start work young so they pushed me a bit. I'm glad really. . .

B Tomorrow talking

B1 A television team conducted a survey recently to find out the attitudes of pre-university students in Britain.

a Read through the beginning of the report on this survey below, and note down how it was organised in terms of
- the target group selected
- the way it was administered

b Read on through the report and make a note of the **actual** questions that were posed by the interviewers.

Yuppie puppies

Tomorrow Talking
ITV/Granada
Wednesdays, 11.30am

The lead-in message assures us that: 'Today's sixth-formers will be running the world tomorrow.' A safe bet, barring nuclear war or Act of God.

In formal interviews set up at 10 schools in England, Scotland and Wales, sixth-form students are asked leading questions about sex, drugs, education, work, politics and religion. As these interviews take place in schools, they tend to be stilted and the students self-conscious. A more casual background might have put the students at their ease.

Even though the interviews are individual, rather than in groups, the students are not identified either by name or by school. Only by watching the credits roll can one see that the students represent a cross-section of state and public schools.

Apparently the producers, Simon Albury and David Hart, anticipated that the student identities would come across in the answers to the questions. Perhaps that is why the first question was about how the students saw themselves, specifically which social class they identified with (July 22). One girl said that the class system was no longer relevant, but all the other students had quick answers to their particular place in the social strata, including the yuppie class and the 'non-working' class.

One girl reasoned that her father was upper class, her mother middle class, so that made her upper middle class. How awful for her mother to drag her down so. But everyone, from the devout working class to the unabashedly privileged, asserted that the class system was not important, although the divisions were growing. What came across most strongly was the expansion of the middle class.

The programme title, *Tomorrow Talking*, is a misnomer. As these youngsters are still at school and being taught, their opinions are somewhat sheltered. It is really yesterday talking. This was evident on the subject of politics and authority (July 29). For the most part, these students had yet to be politicized. They admitted that they had no strong interest in political issues unless they affected them directly.

One girl was incensed about the National Curriculum, because it meant 'no individual liberty'. Another girl said that politics was the reason she lived in England rather than in her native Pakistan. Even those who had yet to be affected felt that it was important to get involved in decision-making.

The students had higher expectations for their futures than what they saw as their parent's life-styles (August 5). Several confessed to being materialistic, yesterday's taboo, and expected to have more enjoyable careers than their parents, with more mental than physical work.

Their heroes varied from world leaders and show-biz and sporting figures to Socrates and Oscar Wilde. Two black students admired Martin Luther King, one girl mentioned her appreciation of her headmaster, but the most votes went to Richard Branson. Most all agreed that the sort of people who succeed in life are those who are competitive, ruthless and hard-working. As one said; 'You gotta get your head down.'

Views were mixed on authority figures. Attitudes toward the police were fairly positive as most youngsters appreciated the safety of police presence. Yet the police were still seen as 'the agent of a repressive government'. One girl felt that the police image should be reformed as 'only a certain sort of person would want to be a policeman'.

The black students had not had any bad experiences of the police themselves, but were none the less concerned about racism. One girl asked: 'What sane black person is going to want to join the police force?'

The legal system was not seen to be fair.The students pointed out that sentences were stronger for crimes against property than for crimes against people, specifically comparing armed robbery to rape. The students also felt weak in regard to their own influence on central government. Decisions were short-sighted, focusing only as far as the next general election, and specifically orientated toward London, they said.

With the exception of one Islamic girl who wore a veil and conducted her life according to the Koran, the students were neutral about religion. They confessed to believing in God and an afterlife, but were not strong on church-going.

The double-standard still prevails in sexual behaviour (August 19), and some boys are still sexist about housework. But they will get a rude awakening from the girls of their generation, who expect equality. The attitude towards Aids is surprisingly positive. The students expect it to change behaviour by forcing people to form monogamous, long-term relationships and to treat each other with more respect.

The people who will be running the world tomorrow will pick up just where today's leaders will leave off, as one would expect. But so far, their attitudes have not been moulded by their experiences of the outside world, experiences which they will come to over the next three to five years when they have no supervision by parents or teachers. One wonders what they will think when they are on their own, and no longer yuppie puppies.

Chris Van Ormer

Times Educational Supplement 7.8.87

B2 To find out more about the attitudes of students in your learning environment towards today's society, it might now be interesting to conduct a similar survey.

In Unit 2, you will have received some guidance for this.

Within your group:

a Decide on the composition of the group you want to investigate, in terms of:
- number to be questioned
- age range
- nationality range
- specialities (faculties/subjects/jobs)

b Decide on the manner in which the survey is to be conducted.
- whether written or oral
- if in or out of class
- how long you will take to administer it

c Decide on the areas to be examined and the questions to be posed.

d Decide on the way in which you will collate and interpret the data.

B3 Conduct the survey and present the results in an appropriate way.

B4 Write a brief report on the findings.

C1 Yuppies

Compare the outcome of your survey with the report on the British survey on page 152.

a What are the areas of similarity and difference?

b To what extent are the people you interviewed yuppies, young, upwardly mobile professionals of the future?

C2 Points for Discussion

In every society the education system is to some extent designed to create desirable citizens.

- What do you think are the qualities of a 'desirable citizen' in the context of the society you come from?
- How do these compare with the 'desirable citizens' of other societies?
- Is there a 'universal desirable citizen', or do the products of education vary from society to society?

SECTION 2 *DESIRABLE CITIZENS*

A The four texts which follow present us with a variety of qualities and attributes which 'desirable citizens' might possess.

1 Divide into four groups. Each group should examine **one** of the texts.

Read through the text and pick out from the list below the main aims that the author feels the educational system has, or should have.

a To equip the individual with an armoury of facts and figures.

b To encourage responsibility towards others.

c To create an educated workforce.

d To give an understanding of values.

e To promote involvement in the community.

f To provide counselling services.

g To impart a wide scope of knowledge.

h To instil self-confidence in individuals.

i To teach technological expertise.

j To foster national pride.

k To give religious instruction.

l To promote the link between school and community.

A2 These texts portray a variety of views of education systems.

In order to compare these views, each group will now prepare a brief talk on the text they have read.

In so far as is possible, use the following headings as guide-lines for your investigation:

- The aims of the system.
- The means of achieving these aims.
- The problems of the system.

The information you require may not always be directly stated in the text, but it may be possible to infer this.

The plan you decide on should be recorded by all students in the group.

A3 Reorganise your groups so that students who have read different texts are sitting together.

Each student should present the talk in turn.

Listeners should make notes of the main points.

A4 Once all the talks have been given, you will be in a position to compare the different views.

Working with the same group, draw up a table to record the comparisons and contrasts between these views.

a Agree on a simple list of criteria to be used for the table.

b Fill out the table in note form.

c Compare your completed chart with the work of other groups.

Text 1

Scholar Decries Cultural Illiteracy in America

His new book charges that students lack, not basic skills, but a common fund of knowledge

By LIZ McMILLEN
CHARLOTTESVILLE, VA.

One of the better examples of cultural ignorance came to E. D. Hirsch not from the pages of his research notes but from his son, a high-school Latin teacher.

Mr. Hirsch's son mentioned in class one day that Latin wasn't spoken in the world anymore. One student challenged that news. 'What about Latin America?' she asked.

Mr. Hirsch, a professor of English at the University of Virginia, can cite many more examples. There's the high-school student who believes Toronto is in Italy. Others think that Socrates was an American Indian chief or that Christ was born in the 16th century.

That kind of ignorance among the young hardly makes educators bat an eye nowadays. But in a new book, Mr. Hirsch argues that gaps in this common cultural information – not a deficiency in skills, as some think – are the leading cause of illiteracy in the nation.

5,000 Facts and Figures

Americans must grasp a wide scope of knowledge to make sense of what they read in newspapers and books, to carry out their jobs, and to serve as informed citizens. Yet it is precisely this information that is absent from school curricula, Mr. Hirsch says in *Cultural Literacy: What Every American Needs to Know*, published this month by Houghton Mifflin.

E.D. Hirsch: 'You have to be superficial before you're profound. Ignorant profundity is not the answer.'

To give an idea of what Americans should know, Mr. Hirsch and two other professors have compiled a list, contained in the book's appendix, of nearly 5,000 facts and figures. Included are authors, cities, historical events, proverbs, and scientific concepts that reflect a high-school level of literacy.

According to the professors, a literate American should know something about the 'Doppler effect,' 'Pooh-Bah,' 'zero-sum,' 'Scheherazade,' and the 'nature-nurture controversy.'

The point of the list is not to create a complete catalogue of American knowledge but to establish guideposts for teachers and students. The list is not perfect, Mr. Hirsch says, and should be changed over time, just as culture and knowledge changes.

'Someone may be able to come up with a list that is more descriptively accurate,' he says. 'But let's not pretend what kids are getting now is not a list. It is, and we all agree it's a very crummy list.'

Aiming at Shibboleths

To prove his point, he offers another compilation, which he calls 'What Every American Need Not Know,' that includes authors and 'skill features' culled from school readers for 6th, 11th, and 12th grades. In the texts, Mr. Hirsch found no references to Shakespeare or Greek myths.

In his book, Mr. Hirsch takes aim at one of education's shibboleths, namely that reading and writing skills can be transferred from subject to subject, without regard to content. However, he does not blame teachers for the country's literacy problem.

'Children from poor and illiterate families remain poor and illiterate not because teachers are inept but because they teach a fragmented curriculum based on faulty educational theories,' he writes.

Americans over 50 – those who received a traditional content-based education – are more literate than those under 30, who were taught under 'well-meaning but inadequate' educational principles emphasizing generic skills, Mr. Hirsch says.

Liberating, Not Conservative

Familiarity with shared cultural information – however fuzzy – sets the literate person apart from the illiterate, Mr. Hirsch says. That is why schools should return to a traditional curriculum steeped in the information students need to know, he says.

Sensitive to charges that his ideas could fuel a conservative agenda, Mr. Hirsch argues that his conception of cultural literacy is, in fact, liberating, and that it demonstrates how American culture reflects the contributions of many different ethnic groups.

His ideas have won praise from officials as diverse as Secretary of Education William J. Bennett and Albert Shanker, president of the American Federation of Teachers (A.F.L.-C.I.O.), both of whom agree that reading cannot be separated from content.

The broad support for his work is something of a mixed blessing for Mr. Hirsch. He worries that some in higher education will reject his views simply because they have won Mr. Bennett's endorsement.

That would be a shame, he says. Although most of his ideas pertain to elementary and secondary education, Mr. Hirsch thinks colleges must do their share by creating a stronger demand for literate students. 'There is a demand now, but it's not focused,' he says.

Education Troubleshooter

Mr. Hirsh, a literary theorist turned education troubleshooter, cares a lot about the state of national literacy, and it shows. When he talks about the subject, he speaks intently – sometimes in a quiet voice, with one hand over closed eyes, and sometimes more animatedly, waving his arms to punctuate his phrases.

About a third of all Americans can neither read nor write, but many more lack a common vocabulary of the information needed to thrive in the modern world, he says.

What Mr. Hirsch does not have in mind is a list of 'great books' or a national core curriculum, although it has appeared that way to some colleagues. He takes pains to explain that cultural literacy can be conveyed in many different ways by many different texts.

He investigated the link between literacy and content in several reading experiments that tested the effect of good and bad writing on students' understanding.

Community-college students who read a well-written passage – in one example, the subject was friendship – understood it more readily than those who read a badly written essay on the same topic.

However, when the piece of writing was unfamiliar – such as a passage on Ulysses S. Grant and Robert E. Lee – the students had far greater difficulty, regardless of style. Students had trouble understanding it because they did not know who Grant and Lee were.

A Labor of Love

Developing the list of terms was a labor of love for the professors. Mr. Hirsch consulted numerous reference books in the humanities, and even sat up nights reading the entire *American Heritage Dictionary*. Joseph Kett, professor of history, and James Trefil, professor of physics, contributed items in social-science and scientific categories. More than 100 educators reviewed the list, making further changes.

The authors sent a sample of the items to 600 lawyers, on the assumption that lawyers are literate Americans. The lawyers identified 92 per cent of the items correctly, leading Mr. Hirsch to think that is an accurate gauge of American literate culture.

By putting together a 'literacy list,' Mr. Hirsch is aware that he is open to accusations of superficiality. Yet, given the state of students' knowledge, superficiality may not be such a bad thing, he observes.

'You have to be superficial before you're profound,' he says. 'Ignorant profundity is not the answer.'

One Letter's Worth of Cultural Literacy

Following is an excerpt from the list of nearly 5,000 terms and ideas prepared by E. D. Hirsch and two other professors at the University of Virginia to represent what literate Americans need to know. The excerpt includes all the items listed under the letter K.

Kabul
Kafka, Franz
kamikaze
kangaroo court
Kansas
Kansas City, Missouri
Kant, Immanuel
Kapital, Das (title)
Karachi
Keats, John
Key, Francis Scott
Keynes, John Maynard
Keynesian economics
K.G.B.
Khomeini, Ayatollah
Khrushchev, Nikita
kibbutz
Kidd, Captain
kidney
Kiev
kingdom was lost, For want of a nail the
King's English, speak the
Kinsey, Alfred
Kipling, Rudyard
Kissinger, Henry
Kitty Hawk
kleptomania
Klondike gold rush

keep the wolf from the door	Kilimanjaro	knee-jerk reflex
Keller, Helen	kill with kindness	Knesset
Kelvin, Lord	kilometer	Knights of the Round Table
Kennedy, Edward	kilowatt-hour (kWh)	Knock on wood
Kennedy, John F. (J.F.K.)	kinetic energy	Knowledge is power
Kennedy, Robert F. (R.F.K.)	King, Jr., Martin Luther	Know-Nothing
Kent State University	King Arthur stories	Koran
Kentucky	King James Version (Bible)	Korea
Kentucky Derby	King Kong	Korean War
Kepler, Johannes	King Lear (title)	kosher
kettledrum	kingdom come	Kremlin
		Ku Klux Klan (K.K.K.)
		Kuwait

April 22, 1987. The Chronicle of Higher Education

Text 2

Running a taught ship

FROM OUR SOUTH-EAST ASIA CORRESPONDENT

It is easy to see how highly education is prized in Singapore. Students pore over their books with extraordinary diligence; teachers are respected and well paid; a good examination result may get a student's photograph into the local paper; and the government has no egalitarian qualms about proclaiming that the brightest are the best. Singapore attracts foreign investors in part by advertising its educated workforce.

Just how educated is another matter. Next month a pilot scheme is being launched to give workers a basic competence in English and mathematics. It has the catchy acronym WISE, for 'worker improvement through secondary education'. It is open to any worker who did not get as far as secondary school (which begins with the ninth year of education). The surprise is that the government thinks more than 600,000 people – 53% of the workforce – will be eligible.

Now for a little creativity

Although that figure shows an improvement – in 1979 some 60% of workers had no secondary education – Singaporeans are evidently not as well-schooled as the government would like them to be. Several things may account for this. The older generation (half the workforce is over 30) had fewer schools to go to. Education is neither compulsory nor – except for the minority Malays – free (pupils have to buy books, and there are small fees for tuition and other expenses). And a fiercely elitist system, in which streaming begins at the age of nine, discourages some of the less able.

The government headed by Mr Lee Kuan Yew (who got a double first at Cambridge) fears that Singapore's hightech ambitions will fall flat unless its educational standard improves. Last year a committee chaired by the prime minister's son, Brigadier-General Lee Hsien Loong (another double first from Cambridge), pointed out that in another East Asian dragon, Taiwan, only 45% of the workforce lacked secondary education. The corresponding figure for America is a mere 6%.

Things are similar at the top of the educational pyramid. Only 5% of Singaporean workers have had any university or polytechnic level education (though the number of university graduates – 5,827 last year – has been growing by around 10% a year). That is not very good in comparison with the competition: 6% in much-poorer Taiwan and 41% in America.

Singapore's falling birth rate means that in the year 2000 its workforce will be increasing by only 1% a year. If the country is to get richer, it must do so by raising productivity and improving its technology skills. The government reckons that by 1995 a fifth of the workforce should be in professional or technical jobs, compared with less than 14% in 1980.

Identifying the problem and solving it are, of course, two different things: the WISE scheme is only the latest in a series of measures for workers' self-improvement. The real question is whether the education Singaporeans are getting is of the right kind. Brigadier-General Lee's committee emphasised that the system 'must allow for more creativity'.

THE ECONOMIST AUGUST 15 1987

Text 3

The Morals Mine Field

Teaching values in school – but whose values?

To Tennessee Williams, children were 'no-neck monsters,' while William Wordsworth apotheosized the newborn infant as a 'Mighty Prophet! Seer blest!' Most adults know the truth is somewhere in between: children are capable of moral behavior, but first they must learn the rules. Indeed, from Socratic Greece to America after World War II, schools not only taught children to read and write but to distinguish right from wrong. By the 1970s, however, the mere mention of words like 'right' and 'wrong' was enough to make teachers squirm; certainty was out, moral relativism was in. Nowhere was the loss of nerve more evident than in a popular program called 'values clarification,' which encouraged children to discuss their feelings about such issues as euthanasia and hit-and-run drivers without the imposition of adult standards. The problem: kids were called upon to identify their own beliefs long before they had enough experience to formulate them. The result, says California schools super-intendent Bill Honig: a generation of 'ethical illiterates.'

Today the pendulum is swinging back again. Political leaders from liberal New York Gov. Mario Cuomo to conservative Secretary of Education William J. Bennett are calling on teachers to confront ethics in the classroom. 'It is impossible to teach knowledge without values,' says New York City schools chancellor Nathan Quinones. The question is: whose values? Morals education remains a mine field. Some fundamentalists 'think that unless you're teaching their religious dogma, you're undermining the religious faith of their children,' says People for the American Way president Anthony Podesta. Others believe that teaching morals inevitably violates the line between church and state. The sheer sensitivity of discussing issues like abortion and teen pregnancy has made many teachers loath even to try.

In the past, instructors freely invoked Judeo-Christian precepts to buttress their own moral authority. Now, says Ruby Sitea, a teacher of values at Pacific High School in Brooklyn, 'we're talking about the conversion of what was moral under religion into what is moral for society.' The process is not always easy. When the Baltimore County, Md., school district first set about adopting a 'common core of values' four years ago, it convened a round table on how best to instill compassion, courtesy, honesty and tolerance in young students. Recalls associate super-intendent Mary Ellen Saterlie, 'A fundamentalist minister asked one of the best questions: 'Who or what is your moral example?' He said he could use the Bible and Jesus Christ. We obviously could not. We finally concluded that the Constitution and the Bill of Rights would be our moral example.'

Indeed, values education is often just another name for that traditional school staple, civics. New York City's 'Citizenship' program got under way, says Board of Education official Charlotte Frank, 'when the police, fire and sanitation departments came to us, saying, "You have to do something about helping kids understand how to keep the city clean, how to keep it from burning down".' At Seth Low Intermediate School in Brooklyn, students now face issues such as fairness, discipline and responsibility in a mockcourt program. Acting as judges, jurors and lawyers, kids try their peers for actual infractions, from forgetting a pencil to carrying a weapon; they also mete out the punishment – often more severe than the teachers' would have been. And since 1984, Atlanta high schoolers must demonstrate a sense of community by completing 75 hours of volunteer work before graduation.

Parental abdication: This energetic commitment to teaching values has come about partly by default. 'A great many adults in general have abandoned their own responsibilities and said it's the school's job,' says Bruce McClellan, headmaster of the Lawrenceville School in New Jersey. 'It is the school's job, but not the school's alone.' Some experts cite the breakdown in family stability and increased financial hardships as explanations for parental abdication of their traditional roles. But the problem is hardly limited to one social or economic class. Most parents want to take a stand, but some are confused about the limits of their own authority and the wisdom of their own beliefs. This may be particularly true, suggests Baltimore's Saterlie, because today's parents came of age in the skeptical '60s.

But the children of the '60s children are proving, once again, that character traits skip a generation. Kids today 'want the rules set down for them,' says Seth Low principal John Mancini. Living up to basic ethical standards in the classroom – discipline, tolerance, honesty – is one of the most important ways children learn how to function in society at large. For good or ill, schools will continue to be what Cornell child-development specialist Urie Bronfenbrenner calls 'brokers between the world of children and the world of adults.'

ELOISE SALHOLZ with
RENEE MICHAEL in *New York and*
PAT WINGERT in *Washington*

NEWS WEEK/OCTOBER 20, 1986

Text 4

An African Perspective

We know that something called 'education' is a good thing. And all African states therefore spend a large proportion of government revenue on it. But, I suspect that for us in Africa the underlying purpose of education is to turn us into black Europeans, or black Americans, because our education policies make it quite clear that we are really expecting education in Africa to enable us to emulate the material achievements of Europe and America. We have not begun to think seriously about whether such material achievements are possible or desirable.

The primary purpose of education is the liberation of man. To 'liberate' is to 'set free'. It implies impediments to freedom having been thrown off. But a man can be physically free from restraint and still be unfree if his mind is restricted by habits and attitudes which limit his humanity.

Education is incomplete if it enables man to work out elaborate schemes for universal peace but does not teach him how to provide good food for himself and his family. It is equally incomplete if it teaches man to be an efficient tool user and tool maker, but neglects his personality and his relationship with his fellow human being.

There are professional men who say, 'My market value is higher than the salary I am receiving in Tanzania.' But no human being has a market value – except a slave. When people say such things, in effect they are saying: 'This education I have been given has turned me into a marketable commodity, like cotton or sisal, and they are showing that instead of liberating their humanity by giving it a greater chance to express itself, the education they have received has degraded their humanity. Their education has converted them into objects – repositories of knowledge like rather special computers.

We condemn such people. Yet it is our educational system which is instilling in boys and girls the idea that their education confers a price tag on them – which ignores the infinite and priceless value of a liberated human being, who is co-operating with others in building a civilization worthy of creatures made in the image of God.'

A formal school system, devised and operated without reference to the society in which its graduates will live, is of little use as an instrument of liberation for the people of Africa. At the same time, learning just by living and doing in the existing society would leave us so backward socially and technologically that human liberation in the foreseeable future is out of the question. Somehow we have to combine the two systems. We have to integrate formal education with the society and use education as a catalyst for change in that society.

Inevitably it takes time to change. We have not solved the problem of building sufficient self-confidence to refuse what we regard as the world's best (whatever that may mean), and to choose instead the most appropriate for our conditions. We have not solved the problem of our apparent inability to integrate education and life, and education and production. We have not solved the problem of overcoming the belief that academic ability marks out a child or an adult as especially praiseworthy, or as deserving a privileged place in society.

This is not a failure within the formal education system. It is a failure of the society as a whole. Indeed, the educationalists have advanced in these matters more than other sections of the community. We have downgraded examination results in selecting pupils for secondary school, we have included course work assessment in degree awards. But our society has not yet accepted that character, co-operativeness and a desire to serve are relevant to a person's ability to benefit from further training.

An abbreviated version of an address given by President Julius Nyerere of Tanzania at a major international conference held in his country in 1974.

Taken from K. Ottosson, *Thinking About Education*. Lutterworth Educational Guildford and London, 1978.

B Deschooling

You are about to hear some more views on education.

B1 There are three speakers in this discussion. They are Alan Fox, Shirley James and Ronald Baker.

As you listen, decide which of the following descriptions best matches the position they take.

a Critic of present educational policy.

b Neutral, not expressing any strong opinion.

c Defender of present educational policy.

B2 Listen again to the discussion and note down the phrases which the speakers use to:

a interrupt another speaker.

b change the direction of the discussion.

c agree.

d disagree.

To make your task easier, you could divide it up, so that different students are listening for only one of the different types of phrases. Once you have listened to the tape, pool your findings.

B3 Considering the language that the speakers use and the tone of their discussion:

a How well do you think the speakers know each other?

b Would you say the discussion is formal or informal?

B4 Do you know any other phrases, similar in meaning to those you noted in **B2**?

Try to arrange any phrases you can think of in lists, beginning with the most formal and ending with the most informal.

C Education for the individual or the citizen?

'Children,' wrote Bertrand Russell, 'should be free citizens of the universe.'

In the excerpts which follow, the British writer discusses whether education systems should be geared towards preparing citizens or encouraging individuality.

C1 Read quickly through the excerpts and decide whether he was in favour of education for the citizen or for the individual.

The Individual versus the Citizen

That education is desirable is the opinion of all modern civilised States, but is, nevertheless, a proposition which has at all times been disputed by some men whose judgement commands respect. Those who oppose education do so on the ground that it cannot achieve its professed objects. Before we can adequately examine their opinion, we must, therefore, decide what it is that we should wish education to accomplish if possible: on this question there are as many divergent views as there are conceptions of human welfare. But there is one great temperamental cleavage which goes deeper than any of the other controversies, and that is the cleavage between those who consider education primarily in relation to the individual psyche, and those who consider it in relation to the community...

...In practical daily life the education which results from regarding a child as an individual is very different from that which results from regarding him as a future citizen. The cultivation of the individual mind is not, on the face of it, the same thing as the production of a useful citizen. Goethe, for example, was a less useful citizen than James Watt, but as an individual must be reckoned superior...

...With the exception of Robinson Crusoe we are of course all in fact citizens, and education must take account of this fact. But it may be held that we shall ultimately be better citizens if we are first aware of all our potentialities as individuals before we descend to the compromises and practical acquiescences of the political life. The fundamental characteristic of the citizen is that he co-operates, in intention if not in fact...

...For the reasons which we have been considering, education in citizenship has grave dangers. Nevertheless, the argument in favour of some education designed to produce social cohesion is overwhelming...

...Apart from national cohesion within the State, which is all that State education attempts to achieve at present, international cohesion, and a sense of the whole human race as one co-operative unit, is becoming increasingly necessary if our scientific civilisation is to survive. I think this survival will demand, as a minimum condition, the establishment of a world State and the subsequent institution of a world-wide system of education designed to produce loyalty to the world State. No doubt such a system of education will entail, at any rate for a century or two, certain crudities which will militate against the development of the individual. But if the alternative is chaos and the death of civilisation, the price will be worth paying. Modern Communities are more closely knit than those of past times in their economic and political structure; and if they are to be successful there must be a corresponding increase in the sense of citizenship on the part of individual men and women. Loyalty to a world State would not, of course, entail the worst feature of loyalty to one of the existing States, namely, the encouragement of war. But it might entail considerable curtailment of the intellectual and of the aesthetic impulses. I think, nevertheless, that the most vital need of the near future will be the cultivation of a vivid sense of citizenship of the world...

...Considered *sub specie aeternitatis*, the education of the individual is to my mind a finer thing than the education of the citizen; but considered politically, in relation to the needs of the time, the education of the citizen must, I fear, take the first place...

Bertrand Russell, *Education and Social Order*. George Allen & Unwin 1932.

C2 You are going to take part in a discussion on the topic, 'Should education be for the individual or the citizen?'

a Working with a partner, consider your views on the topic. Think about the question in terms of your own society. Make notes of any points you think relevant.

b Form groups of approximately five students and elect a chairperson. Then hold the discussion.

c The chairpersons should give spoken summaries of the views of their respective groups after the discussions.

C3 *a* In your discussion group, draw up a plan for an essay based on your discussion.

This could take the form of an argumentative essay, giving two or more sides to the question. Alternatively, you may decide to concentrate on one view.

b When your plan is complete, compare it with the plans of other groups.

c Working on your own, write the essay.

SECTION 3 *THE CHANGING WORLD OF INFORMATION*

A Consider the following points and discuss them with other students.

1 Have you had any experience of 'information technology' during the course of your education?

2 Is it necessary for all students to become acquainted with information technology?

3 Is information technology bound to certain subject areas or professions?

4 What, in your opinion, are the uses of information technology?

B The shape of things to come

> 'From primary school to the largest companies, from one end of the world to the other, information technology is about to take over.'

Your eventual task in this section is to write a report, commenting on the quote above.

Step 1 Initial reactions

Form into groups of at least three students, and discuss your initial reactions to the quote.

Jot down your ideas on a mind map.

Step 2 Skimming the surface

The following texts are all in some way related to the topic.

In your groups, skim through them and decide which ones would be most useful to your investigations.

Step 3 Delving deeper

In your groups, divide up the texts between you for closer study.

Working alone, read through the text(s) you have been allocated and note down the relevant main points.

Report back to the rest of the group and together decide which ideas you want to include.

Look again at your original mind map and try to work these ideas in.

Step 4 Breaking it down

From your extended mind map, you should now agree on a detailed plan for a report.

Divide the agreed plan into sections, according to the number of students in the group.

Each member should now write up his/her section.

Step 5 Putting it all together

The group should now come together again in order to examine the sections written by the individual students.

Make sure that
- each section is complete.
- the sections follow in sequence.
- the sections form a coherent whole.

Some adjustments will doubtless be necessary.

You may wish to write the concluding paragraph of your report together, at this stage.

Step 6 Technophiles or technophobes?

Exchange reports with other groups and decide how similar or different they are from your work.

Evaluate these reports in terms of whether the arguments they present are logical and coherent.

Can you establish whether the students in your class tend to be technophiles or technophobes?

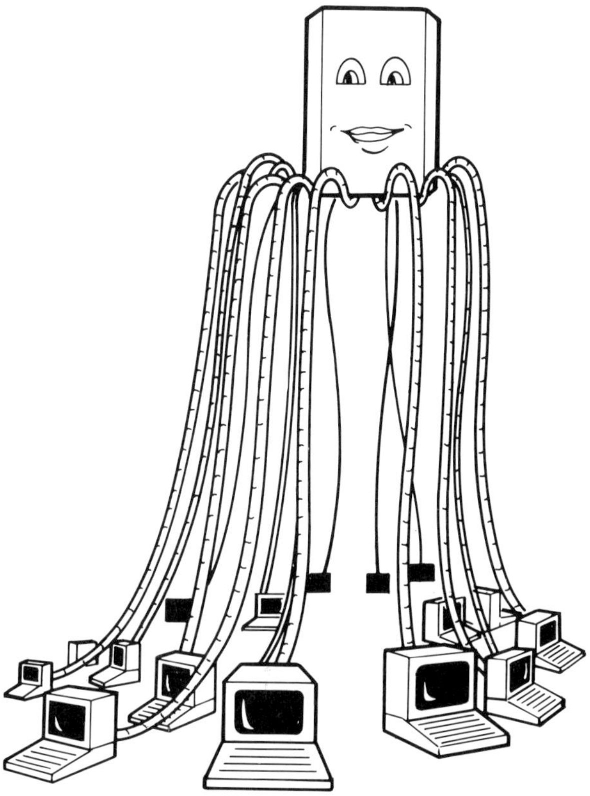

Growing up with computers

Adrian Furnham assesses young people's attitudes to 'new' technology

THERE ARE, it seems, two types of people in this world: those who believe there are two types of people and those who do not. But when it comes to attitudes to computers and new technology, adults appear to fall into two dramatically opposite groups.

There are the technophobes, who remain scared, but pretend to be sceptical, about all forms of new technology, from microwave ovens to word processors. Many fixate on the very first level of technological sophistication: they write with a fountain pen; they have never got into ballpoints let alone manual or electric typewriters, or, of course, the now ubiquitous word processor. Despite increasing evidence to the contrary, technophobes advocate the use of old technology (or preferably none at all) on the basis of a range of weak arguments about hidden dangers and alienation, though they tend to restrict their latter-day Luddism to dinnerparty snipes at 'conformist modernists'.

Technophiles, on the other hand, behave like children who, deprived of an electric train-set at some crucial age, spend the rest of their lives making up for this early loss by surrounding themselves with adult toys of every shape or kind. They are a manufacturer's dream, because they are eager to discard perfectly usable apparatus in favour of the new improved model which can do so many more tricks. Technophiles are the computer bores at dinner parties who lapse easily into competitive software-speak, which may appear to some as the language of the hard of thinking.

Some adults are thrust, dragged or bullied into using new technology at work. They have no option but to become competent in a new range of skills, even if they never become enthusiastic about the microchip revolution. But what about the young? Today's schoolchildren have the advantage that they are growing up with computers which are as natural a part of home furnishings, office decor and school apparatus as radio, typewriters and bunsen burners were, respectively, to earlier generations. What do *they* think of the new technology?

A colleague and I recently conducted a nationwide survey of the attitudes of more than 500 young people in Britain, aged between 12 and 19, which included questions about computers. Ninety per cent of the young people we sampled claimed to have used a computer, and 43 per cent said that they had a computer at home. As it happens, exactly the same proportion (43 per cent) had a videogame set at home as well, which might suggest that some households are technologically deprived, whereas others are over-stocked. Interestingly, a quarter of the sample claimed to use the home computer every day, and another quarter a few times each week, which puts them well on to the road to becoming 'hacks'. Nearly 60 per cent had also used video recorders and, unlike many adults, appeared to be quite familiar with, and competent at, recording programmes.

As many as 93 per cent of the young people, who came from all backgrounds, said that their school had computers that pupils could use. Roughly a quarter used their school computer daily or a few times a week, a third once or twice a month and the rest hardly ever or never. Yet nearly 60 per cent had had formal classes in how to use the computer.

The young people in our survey had firm beliefs about the place

of new technology in the world, though, perhaps as one would expect, their attitudes were rather ambivalent. For instance, 72 per cent agreed that computers were improving our quality of life. Two-thirds of the sample believed that everyone should be taught how to use computers, and roughly that number believed that knowing how to use a computer would help them find a job.

On the other hand, these results suggested that a third of the sample were against new technology. When we asked specifically whether they thought it a good or bad thing (or both) that today more and more things that people used to do are done by machines, only 15 per cent thought it a good thing and 28 per cent a bad thing. Similarly, nearly two-thirds thought that computers would increase unemployment. In this sense, the young people appeared to admit or accept the inevitability of new technology, even if they did not fully welcome it.

There are a number of possible explanations for this hesitation about the benefits of new technology. First, one could simply argue that young people are being realistic: new technology will reduce the number of jobs available, particularly in some traditional occupations, though it could also, perhaps, increase the number of jobs in other, much more desirable, occupations.

Secondly, one could argue that these beliefs are evidence of a growing post-materialism among young people, a yearning back to the simple good life (if it ever existed). Technology is associated with industrialism, alienation and materialism, all of which are antithetical to 'green environmentalism'. It would be fascinating to compare young people's attitudes to new technology in different countries with the gross national products of those countries: I suspect that those in the richer countries would be against it.

Thirdly, the negative or at least cautious attitude of young people towards new technology may simply reflect a natural conservatism in a section of the population, which finds everything new bad and all change undesirable.

We were also interested in differences in attitudes between the sexes. Overall, 82 per cent of the young people did not believe that it was easier for boys, rather than girls, to learn to use a computer, but there was a predictable difference between the sexes, with many more girls disagreeing than boys. However, only 55 per cent disagreed with the statement that men are better at programming than women (42 per cent of boys disagreed compared to 70 per cent of girls). Both sexes agreed that, as computers at work become more common, there will be less and less difference between the jobs done by men and women. Overall, the young women appeared to be less convinced of the benefits of new technology, but certain of their ability to use it.

In many ways, it seems that young people are not unlike their parents in their attitudes to new technology, despite the fact that they have probably had more experience of using it. Few are totally for it and few totally against it, the majority seeing both advantages and drawbacks. But there is some evidence of the beginnings of technophobia and technophilia in school-children. Better educated, more able and more ambitious adolescents, often from middle class homes, tend to be technophiles, while those with less education, who are not so talented or ambitious, tend to technophobia. But precisely because they are young their attitudes and behaviours are more easily changed than those of adults. With enough resources and inducements, all young people could become at least computer literate or learn not to fear the new technology.

Adrian Furnham is a lecturer in psychology at University College, London.

New Scientist 26 March 1987

Text 2

Computing for young superbrains

My First Computer Library
by David Marshall, *Macdonald, pp 30, £3.95 each*

Lynne Murray

On the face of it, this series is a brilliant idea – a set of books for the library and a way to help children to help themselves with the school computer. Wonderful for the hard-pressed primary teacher, with little or no computer training, expected to promote the white hot message of the new technology.

At first, everything looks great. Each book (*Living with animals, Colour and Shape, Living Things*) is attractively produced, full of beautiful, photographs and drawing with each two-page spread self-contained. Each deals with the subject matter in a broadly 'scientific' way, encouraging its young reader to look at the world and learn a little about how it works – how a fish breathes, why grass is green, how trees grow.

The format is a tried and proven one; the clever bit is that each spread has a computer activity built into it. The user reads through the spread and then turns to the back of the book where there is a collection of words, each rather like the sort of recipe card that is sometimes handed out free in supermarkets. This time, the 'recipe' is a program to be typed.

It would be brilliant, if it worked. The snag is that mortal child is apt to make mistakes. During the past month I've tried every program in every book with bright 8-, 9-, and 10-year-olds. When the programs are typed with scrupulous accuracy the results are good; but (surprising though the news may be to author David Marshall) not one of the children who used the cards could type a program in first time without making an error.

An 8-year-old who makes one abortive attempt at typing a program can get rather cross. After four abortive attempts they verge on the murderous, which is a pity because once the programs are running the effects are very entertaining. Some, however, are 15–20 lines long and have up to 50 characters in a line – alright for the nimble-fingered superbrain but a bit tough for everyone else.

It was interesting, however, that even though the children made endless frustrating mistakes, they were a good deal more accurate than the teachers, not one of whom was prepared to fight on past the mistakes to make even one program work.

The most perplexing thing about all this is that while the DIY computer programs require considerable computer familiarity and strongly hint that the author is used to working with children of powerful intellect and innate touch-typing ability, the actual text of each book is simple to the point of being patronising and twee. Could it be that the children Marshall is writing for spend so much time during their formative years working on their computers that they fall behind a bit on the reading and writing?

Carping aside, these books are good-looking, potentially useful and entertaining. But they do require the best of all possible worlds – plenty of computers and teachers already trained to use them. From my experience, roughly one teacher to two children would be okay. Some hope.

New Scientist 26 March 1987

B. Sc. courses in computer science at the University of Sussex

The first computers were built less than forty years ago. Within this short space of time, their impact has grown to such an extent that they find application throughout an enormous range of activities in modern society. From space exploration to the organisation of libraries, from banking to stylistic analysis, from architecture to telecommunications, computer systems play an active role in every sphere of life. This trend is set to continue so that computers will eventually permeate the philosophical and technological basis of our society.

Computer science embraces the study of computationally related phenomena. This includes the study of hardware systems or the physical machines which perform the actual computations, the software systems or languages for instructing the machines and the mathematical foundations which inform our understanding of the organisational principles underlying these systems. Continuing advances in electronics and in our understanding of the nature of computational processes mean that computer science is a fast-evolving discipline; its domain of interest is difficult to encompass and its future development impossible to predict.

Computer science at Sussex

Computer Science has much in common with subjects such as Electronic Engineering, Mathematics and Artificial Intelligence. Each of these is well established in the University of Sussex, with strong undergraduate curricula and dynamic research programmes. The new Major (degree course) in Computer Science takes considerable advantage of this existing infrastructure which already contains many aspects of computing. The overall aim of the new degree is to give students a thorough understanding of the fundamental principles of computer science, together with considerable experience in their practical application. Students may belong either to the School of Engineering and Applied Sciences (EAPS) or to the School of Mathematical and Physical Sciences (MAPS). In the EAPS version of the Major more emphasis is placed on hardware, while students in MAPS concentrate more on software. However, most courses are common to both streams. The first two years of the Major cover the fundamental concepts of computer science and the necessary prerequisites in allied subjects such as mathematics and engineering. In the third year, students choose from a range of optional courses which allow them to pursue their individual interests. A final year project is also required, where students show their in-depth knowledge of particular topics. Students from the School of Mathematical and Physical Sciences tend to choose software-based projects and those in Engineering and Applied Sciences are more attracted to hardware.

Entrance requirements

A formal statement of the general entrance requirements for the University appears in the Sussex Prospectus. The minimum requirement for the Major in Computer Science is an 'A' level pass (or an equivalent) in an approved mathematical subject together with an 'A' level pass in another subject; in the case of applicants for the EAPS version of the Major we prefer this second subject to be 'A' level physics.

You will find the UCCA number code for these courses in the Prospectus (or in the UCCA handbook):
Computer Science in the School of Engineering and Applied Sciences Computer Science in the School of Mathematical and Physical Sciences

Facilities

Students have access to modern computer workstations to support the teaching in several of the courses which form part of the Computer Science Major. A wide variety of microprocessor systems are also available and are used primarily for practical teaching in the hardware courses. They are also used in some student project work. Additionally students have access to the computer facilities offered by the University Computing Centre. Most of the Centre's computing power is supplied by a group of linked VAX 11/780 machines but various other computers are also available. Support is provided for a very wide range of language and software systems including Pascal FORTRAN, *C*, *ML*, LISP, POP-11 and Prolog (in the POPLOG system).

Careers in computer science

Graduates in computer science have excellent career opportunities in the rapidly expanding field of information technology. There is a great demand for skilled staff in this challenging and fast-moving area. Software skills are in particularly short supply. The Sussex Computer Science course is designed to offer an excellent preparation for a wide range of employment areas such as the computer industry, software houses, research and development in industry or in higher education, commercial computing – in fact, the material in the course would be of relevance for a career with most organisations making use of computers.

Computing has a very attractive future and a degree in computer science prepares the graduate for an interesting and exciting career.

Text 4

All for IT

Adrian Low on information technology

Sooner or later the powers that be will realize that it is not 'computing' that should be taught to every school child, but 'information technology'. But merely presenting the term 'information technology' to a staff meeting to formulate a school plan is likely to result in a lot of blank looks.

Information technology (IT) is not a specialized subject in its own right nor is it an umbrella term for a variety of subjects like business studies. Like the 3 Rs, IT is as much to be taught as it is to be used in teaching learning or school administration.

A real appreciation of IT is a must for any national core curriculum, from primary onwards. Currently it is found in most vocationally oriented courses, often labelled as 'computing', and there's the rub. For a lot of educational centres, computing means what it says: just computing.

It's not good enough to satisty a real commercial and industrial demand. Our forthcoming workforce should not be frightened of wires, printers, booting, word processing, networks, sending electronic mail or using robots. Indeed, apart from a specialized few (programmers or software engineers), they should be wary of programming. More often than not, it is just massively time-wasting and makes company data more vulnerable. Yet, while most large companies have invested in high-tech – such as data handling telephone systems – few school leavers have any more idea how to use this new technology than Bell did a century ago.

Teaching IT is one thing. Using IT in education is another. Its application is so broad as to concern all but the most detached and insular subject and teaching method. IT can be a teaching tool or a learning aid, so it must become part of the natural curriculum planning process. In administration, IT turns a day's report writing, register keeping and dinner money records into that much less of chore.

Times Educational Supplement 5.6.87

Text 5

You should be pleased to learn you can now have a modern communications system without lots of cables, extra telephones or equipment. Simple is beautiful again. But, more importantly, simple is efficient.

So with our MD110 digital exchange (PABX if you'd rather be technical) you can do things with your telephone system you'd never have believed possible. And that includes data transmission and net-working. Without cluttering your desk. Or anyone else's for that matter. Of course, the MD110 makes light work of conventional exchange functions as well.

We've taken our time developing this exchange (110 years in fact) but then the MD110 is going to define the state of the art for a pretty long while. So why not find out more about what you should be expecting from *your* exchange, and about how the Ericsson

MD110 can help you, by clipping the coupon today or by phoning us.

Unless, of course, like Roger you get off on lots of cables.

ERICSSON

Text 6

Information

Since about 1950 the world of computing and information handling has undergone a revolution so profound that it is difficult to bring it into sharp focus. During the past three decades the number of bits of information that can be stored in a unit surface area has increased by 10^{5-6} times and the speed at which information can be processed has increased by almost the same amount. Yet, at the same time, the quantities of raw materials and energy needed to achieve this increase in speed and capacity have actually decreased by 10^{4-5} times; and the unit cost of an electronic device has decreased by 10^{3-4} times.

These facts can be illustrated more dramatically. The number of logical/mathematical operations which it would once have taken a man his whole life to perform can now be done by a single microprocessor in just one minute. Whereas in the 1950s a computer with the information processing capacity of the human brain would have occupied the physical size of a large city, such a computer would now be no bigger than a brain. Cost comparisons are even more dramatic. If costs in the car industry had declined over the past thirty years as rapidly as they have in the electronics industry, the most expensive car would now cost about $1.

The speed at which information technology advanced during the 1970s was due to the silicon chip. Between 1971 and 1978 the number of bits of information which could be housed on a single chip rose from 1,000 to 64,000; during the same period the cost of the chip stayed constant. Within another ten years, the million-bit chip is likely to be in widespread use. Costs seem likely to continue to fall, and the pace of advance to continue unabated.

This massive cost reduction in information storage and processing has brought the chip into use in many places where it had not previously been available: in the home computer, the small office, the car engine, at the paying exits to parking facilities, at cash withdrawal points at banks, at airline booking-offices, and in the provision of raw data via the television to homes which subscribe to a service. All this seems likely to be greatly extended in the very near future. As the National Science Foundation comments in its report on the next five years: 'The coming period will see the spread of computing power to more people than ever before.'

Three decades ago futurologists talked confidently of the coming nuclear age. Their optimism has proved misplaced and nuclear technology now occupies a hotly debated and somewhat ambivalent position in the list of future priorities. But, as often happens in technical advance, the nuclear age has been replaced in short order by the information age. In the next decade, the word processor will enter nearly every major office in both the developed and the developing world. In the place of the piece of rectangular paper, on which information has been stored for more than two millenniums, will come the plastic disc, a few centimetres in diameter, storing the information content of a small book.

Unlike mamy other technologies, microcomputing depends for its effectiveness essentially on decentralization. The microprocessor has brought computing power to the individual desk and into the individual living-room. Several manufacturers now even offer genuinely portable microcomputers – some of them of considerable power. As the technology continues to develop – with computers becoming yet faster and smaller, and being able to accept input in the form of either the human voice or visual patterns – this trend will continue. Every human activity in which data handling is involved will be affected. The implications of this are so huge that few have yet attempted concrete social forecasts of the impact of microprocessors.

The one area where advance is sure to be extraordinarily rapid is the interface between communications and computing – a field which Anthony G. Oettinger of Harvard University has called 'compunications technology'. France is already looking to the time – only a few years ahead – when every telephone subscriber will have a computer terminal in his home. As fibre optics and satellite communiation become more and more common, two-way access to data banks, the ability to shop and pay for goods without leaving the home, and the possibility of communicating with other individuals via systems of electronic mail will be quickly translated from fantasy to reality.

Already, however, it is clear that some new information technologies have not developed in the ways originally predicted. Twenty years ago scientists were preoccupied with concepts of 'artificial intelligence'; computers that wrote poetry, composed music, and manufactured art were talked of in glowing terms. The comparison between the computer and the brain has not stood the test of time. The creativity of the human being has not been threatened by electronics, as most humanists knew it never would be, and the computer is now seen more simply as an efficient and fast means of handling data – a task which was hardly ever creative in human terms. Its disappearance from the vocabulary of human employment will be regretted only to the extent that it creates unemployment.

There are, however, still bottlenecks to the advance of the microprocessor. One of these is the development of the software, which has not progressed with the same rapidity as the hardware. Programming has turned out to be one of the most complex human tasks ever undertaken, and those with the knowledge and patience to do it have been richly rewarded by society. One of the strangest phenomena of the computer explosion is the ability of the young to come rapidly and easily to terms with the chip. As many experts have pointed out, the computer revolution will really occur only when the current generation of computer-literate youngsters reaches positions of social responsibility.

It is not difficult to forecast some obvious social implications of the computer age. Intelligent and appropriately trained people will find themselves once more in great demand while those without the necessary training and ability will face increasing unemployment. One estimate is that by 1990 more than 50 per cent of the work-force in industrialized countries will be employed directly or indirectly in the information business. This is already the case in the United States.

At the same time ease of communication will lessen the need for travel and personal encounter. The home will become more attractive as new types of information and entertainment become directly accessible from it. Interestingly, nearly all these advances can be made without environmental costs – indeed, many will involve environmental gains because the new information technologies consume almost negligible quantities of energy and natural resources, in contrast to newspaper technology (the Sunday edition of the *New York Times* consumes 25 hectares of forest per issue).

A French technologist, André Danzin, believes that the nature of the coming information society will be as different from the industrial society as that was from its predecessor, agricultural society. He writes:

> Imagine two average Frenchmen, one born in 1900, the other in 1980. If they are 12–16 years old, the first is working, the second is at school. If they are both working, there is more than a 50: 50 chance that the first will be on the farm and the second in an office. The amount of free time they will have during their lives is respectively 5 and 19 years. If we ask how they will spend their free time, the first will spend, outside his work, at most two years informing himself, through reading or communication, while the second will spend more than 12 years in front of his television, on the telephone, listening to the radio or at his computer terminal. These are not the same men: work has changed; the way time is used has changed; education has changed; use of leisure time has changed, radically. The most important commodity has become information and not, as official statistics might have us now believe, energy, primary materials or machines. the centre of gravity of human activity has been shifted towards the immaterial.

Danzin has summarized these profound changes, which are already affecting industrial society, in Table C.

It is only when information is considered as a resource along with other resources, such as materials and energy, that the scope of what is about to happen to society can be fully appreciated. Many writers have pointed out that the information revolution now taking off is comparable in magnitude to the Industrial Revolution which occurred two centuries earlier. As Oettinger argues, action of any kind depends on materials and energy. Without materials there is nothing and without energy nothing happens. But without information nothing has meaning: materials are formless, motion is aimless.

Robin Clarke, *Science and Technology in World Development.* UNESCO/OUP, 1985

Table C: Major characteristics of three types of society

	Agricultural society	Industrial society	Information society
importance of research	minor 0.3% GNP or less	strong 1–2% GNP	very strong 2–3% GNP
importance of education	minor 1% GNP or less	strong 2–4% GNP	very strong 6–8% GNP
importance of communications	unknown	3–5% GNP	about 10% GNP
proportion of work-force			
in agriculture	up to 40%	10–20%	10% or less
in industry	15–25%	40% or more	20% or less
in information	12%	15–20%	50% or more
use of time			
life expectancy	36 years	60–70 years	70 years plus
free time	3 years	12 years	19 years
on transport	1.8 years	4–6 years	diminishing
level of urbanization	up to 25%	70%	diminishing
role of mass media	minor	strong	enormous
level of organization	simple	complex	extremely complex
degree of interdependence	weak	strong	very strong
population growth	high	low	very low

Source: Danzin, André, 'Entreprise et évolution'. In *Connaissance Politique*, No. 1, Feb. 1983, 116.

Text 7

Bold numbers refer to LocoScript: Light numbers refer to CP/M

618 **PCW9512 User Guide: Index**

PCW User Guide, Amstrad, 1987

Text 8

Sources of Additional Information

How to Live in Britain (Bell and Hyman for The British Council, biennial). £1.35.

Information Sheets for School Leavers (Department of Education and Science). Free.

Polytechnic Courses Handbook: Full-time and Sandwich Advanced Courses, England and Wales (Pitman Press for the Committee of Directors of Polytechnics, annual). 1983 edition, £6.95.

Postgraduate Courses in United Kingdom Universities (Association of Commonwealth Universities for Committee of Vice-Chancellors and Principals of the Universities of the United Kingdom, annual). 1983–84 edition, £4.75.

Research in British Universities, Polytechnics and Colleges: Vol 1–*Physical Sciences*; Vol 2–*Biological Sciences*; Vol 3–*Social Sciences* (The British Library, annual; prices shown are for 1982 edition).

Residential Short Courses (National Institute of Adult Continuing Education, twice yearly).

Scottish Universities Entrance Guide (Scottish Universities Council on Entrance, annual). £1 (UK), £1.50 (overseas).

Which Degree 1983–84 (VNU Business Publications, 5 volumes, annual). £34.75.

Some subject guides

Agriculture, Horticulture and Forestry: Choose Your Course (Department of Education and Science/Welsh Office, annual). Free. Also *Opportunities in Agriculture* (Scottish Agricultural Colleges). Free.

A Career in Metallurgy or Materials Technology (Institution of Metallurgists, London, 1983). Free.

Compendium of UK Postgraduate Studies in Psychology (Department of Psychology, University of Surrey). 7th edition, 1983. £4.50.

Courses in Agriculture, Horticulture & Forestry. List of Full-Time and Sandwich Courses in England and Wales 1983–84 (National Consultative Committee for Agricultural Education, annual). Free.

Degree Course Guides, covering the main subjects studied at universities (Hobsons Press for Careers Research and Advisory Centre). Individual booklets, £.2.70.

Degree Courses in Building (Building (Publishers) for the Builder). 1982 edition. Free.

Degree Studies and the Accountancy Profession (Accounting Education Consultative Board, annual). Free.

Design Courses in Britain (Design Council). 1983 edition, £3.20 (plus postage).

Development Studies in the UK: a Guide to Postgraduate, Undergraduate and Shorter Courses (Institute of Development Studies, University of Sussex). 1983 edition.

Development Studies: Register of Research in the United Kingdom (Institute of Development Studies, University of Sussex). 1983 edition.

The Directory of Schools of Medicine and Nursing: British Qualifications and Training in Medicine, Dentistry, Nursing and Related Professions (Kogan Page on behalf of International Hospitals Group). 1983. £14.95

A Guide to Degree Courses in English 1983–84 (The English Association). 1982 edition, £6.00.

Guide to Language Courses in Polytechnics and Similar Institutions (Centre for Information on Language Teaching and Research). 1982–83 edition, £3.95.

Guide to Postgraduate Degrees, Diplomas and Courses in Dentistry (Council for Postgraduate Medical Education in England and Wales on behalf of the three Councils of the UK). 1983 edition, £4.85.

Guide to Postgraduate Degrees, Diplomas and Courses in Medicine (Council for Medical Education in England and Wales on behalf of the three Councils of the UK, annual). 1983 edition, £4.50.

Local Authority Full-time Courses in English for Overseas Students (The British Council, annual). Free.

Long Courses for Teachers (Department of Education and Science and Welsh Office Education Department, annual). Free.

A Matter of Degree. A Directory of Geography Courses (Geo Books, annual). 1983 edition. £1.50.

Physics Courses in Higher and Further Education (special issue each year containing survey of courses of school-leavers) (Institute of Physics).

Postgraduate Courses in Business Studies, Management and Related Subjects at Universities and Business Schools in the United Kingdom (Conference of University Management Schools, Durham University Business School). 1981 edition, £1.00.

Postgraduate Opportunities in Meteorology and Oceanography 1984–85 (Royal Meteorological Society). 1983 edition, £0.50.

Postgraduate Qualifications by Courses in Psychology (British Psychological Society). 1981 edition, £0.50.

Research Fields in Physics at UK Universities and Polytechnics (Institute of Physics, 7th edition, 1984).

Schedule of Courses in Translating, Interpreting, Practical Linguistics, and Degree Level Courses in Languages Combined with Scientific and Technical Subjects (for students whose native language is English) (Institute of Linguists Educational Trust). 1982 edition, £1.00.

SSRC/Handbook Studentships (Social Science Research Council, annual). Free. Awards quoted are solely for residents of the UK.

Summer and Short Courses in TEFL, EFL and ESP (The British Council, annual). Free.

TEFL/TESL Academic Courses in the U.K. 1984–85 and Other Courses Relevant to the Teaching of English to Speakers of Other Languages (British Council, Design, Production and Publishing Department, annual). £5.50. A shorter form, known as the *Brief List*, is also produced annually; it is free.

University Courses in Education Open to Students from Overseas 1984–85 (Universities Council for the Education of Teachers and the British Council). Free.

Scholarships and grants

Awards for Commonwealth University Academic Staff (Association of Commonwealth Universities, biennial). 1984–86 edition, £8.40.

Financial Aid for First Degree Study at Commonwealth Universities (Association of Commonwealth Universities). 1984–86 edition, £2.25.

Grants for Study Visits by University Administrators and Librarians (Association of Commonwealth Universities). 1983–85 edition, £2.00.

Grants Register (Macmillan Press, biennial). 1983–85 edition, $25.00.
Scholarships Abroad (British Council, Design, Production and Publishing Department, annual). £2.00 including postage.
Scholarships Guide for Commonwealth Postgraduate Students (Association of Commonwealth Universities, biennial). 1983–85 edition, £7.90.
Study Abroad (UNESCO, Paris). 1983–84, 1984–85, 1985–86 edition, £8.25. An international handbook of fellowships, scholarships, grants etc.

Higher Education in the UK 1984–86, Longman, Revised Edition, 1984

Text 9

The death of the secretary?

As fewer workers in the rich nations have engaged in physical production, more have been needed to produce ideas, patents, scientific formulae, bills, invoices, reorganization plans, files, dossiers, market research, sales presentations, letters, graphics, legal briefs, engineering specifications, computer programs, and a thousand other forms of data or symbolic output. This rise in white-collar, technical, and administrative activity has been so widely documented in so many countries that we need no statistics here to make the point. Indeed some sociologists have seized on the increasing abstraction of production as evidence that society has moved into a 'post-industrial' stage.

The facts are more complicated. For the growth of the white-collar work force can be better understood as an extension of industrialism – a further last surge of the Second Wave – than as a leap to a new system. While it is true that work has grown more abstract and less concrete, the actual offices in which this work is being done are modelled directly after Second Wave factories, with the work itself fragmented, repetitive, dull, and dehumanizing. Even today, much office reorganization is little more than an attempt to make the office more closely resemble a factory.

In this 'symbol-factory', Second Wave civilization also created a factory-like caste system. The factory work force is divided into manual and nonmanual workers. The office is similarly divided into 'high abstraction' and 'low abstraction' workers. At one level we find the high abstracters, the technocratic élites: scientists, engineers, and managers, much of whose time is taken up with meetings, conferences, business lunches, or in dictating, drafting memos, placing phone calls, and otherwise exchanging information. One recent survey estimated that 80 per cent of the manager's time is spent in 150 to 300 'information transactions' daily.

At the other level we find the low abstracters – white-collar proletarians, as it were – who, like factory workers throughout the Second Wave period, perform endlessly routine and deadening work. Mostly female and nonunionized, this group can justifiably smile with irony at the sociologists' talk of 'post-industrialism'. They are the *industrial* work force of the office.

Today the office, too, is beginning to move beyond the Second Wave and into the Third, and this industrial caste system is about to be challenged. All the old hierarchies and structures of the office are soon to be reshuffled.

The Third Wave revolution in the office is the result of several colliding forces. The need for information has mushroomed so wildly that no army of Second Wave clerks, typists, and secretaries, no matter how large or hard-working, can possibly cope with it. In addition, the cost of paper work has climbed so calamitously that a frantic search is under way to control it. (Office costs have swelled to 40 or 50 per cent of all costs in many companies, and some experts estimate that the expense of preparing a single business letter can run as high as $14 to $18 when all the hidden factors are taken into account.) Moreover, while the average factory worker in the United States today is supported by an estimated $25,000 worth of technology, the office worker, as one Xerox salesman puts it, 'works with $500 or $1000 worth of old typewriters and adding machines, and is probably among the least productive workers in the world'. Office productivity has climbed a bare 4 per cent over the past decade, and conditions in other countries are probably even more pronounced.

Contrast this with the extraordinary decline in the cost of computers, as measured by the number of functions performed. It has been estimated that computer output has increased 10,000 times in the past fifteen years, and that the per-function cost today is down 100,000-fold. The combination of rising costs and stagnating productivity on the one hand and computer advances on the other make an irresistible combination. The result is likely to be nothing less than a 'wordquake'.

The main symbol of this upheaval is an electronic device called the word processor – some 250,000 of which are already at work in US offices. Manufacturers of these machines, including such titans as IBM and Exxon, are bracing themselves to compete in what they believe will soon be a $10-thousand-million-a-year market. Sometimes called a 'smart typewriter' or a 'text editor', this device fundamentally alters the flow of information in the office, and with it the job structure. It is, however, only one of a great family of new technologies about to deluge the white-collar world.

In Chicago in June 1979, at the

convention of the International Word Processing Association, some 20,000 perspiring visitors trooped through an exhibition hall to examine or try out a bewildering array of other machines as well – optical scanners, high-speed printers, micrographic equipment, facsimile machines, computer terminals, and the like. They were looking at the beginning of what some term the 'paperless office' of tomorrow.

The key to such an office of the future is ordinary correspondence. In a conventional Second Wave office, when an executive wants to fire off a letter or memo, an intermediary is called in – the secretary. This person's first task is to capture the executive's words on paper – in a notebook or a typed draft. Next the message is corrected to eliminate errors, and perhaps retyped a few times. After that it is clean typed. A carbon or Xerox copy is made. The original is dispatched to its destination through the mailroom or the post office. The duplicate is filed. Not counting the initial step of composing the message, five distinct sequential steps are required.

Today's machines compress these five steps into one, making the sequential all but simultaneous.

Messages and memos move silently and instantaneously. Terminals at every desk – thousands of them in any large organization – flicker quietly as information flows through the system, bouncing up to a satellite and down to an office halfway around the world or to a terminal in an executive's home. Computers link the company's files with those of other companies where necessary, and managers can call up information stored in hundreds of outside data banks like the *New York Times* Information Bank.

Just how far events move in this direction remains to be seen. The image of the office of the future is too neat, too smooth, too disembodied to be real. Reality is always messy. But it is clear that we are rapidly on our way, and even a partial shift towards the electronic office will be enough to trigger an eruption of social, psychological, and economic consequences. The coming wordquake means more than just new machines. It promises to restructure all the human relationships and roles in the office as well.

Pressures on the job market may well increase dramatically in the years ahead. But it is naive to single out the computer as their source.

What is certain is that both the office and the factory are destined to be revolutionized in the decades ahead. The twin revolutions in the white-collar sector and in manufacture add up to nothing less than a wholly new mode of production for society – a giant step for the human race. This step carries with it indescribably complex implications. It will affect not only such things as the level of employment and the structure of industry but also the distribution of political and economic power, the size of our work units, the international division of labour, the role of women in the economy, the nature of work, and the divorce of producer from consumer; it will even alter so seemingly simple a fact as the 'where' of work.

Alvin Toffler, *The Third Wave*. Collins 1980.

Text 10

The electronic cottage

Hidden inside our advance to a new production system is a potential for social change so breathtaking in scope that few among us have been willing to face its meaning. For we are about to revolutionize our homes as well.

Apart from encouraging smaller work units, apart from permitting a decentralization and de-urbanization of production, apart from altering the actual character of work, the new production system could shift literally millions of jobs out of the factories and offices into which the Second Wave swept them and right back where they came from originally: the home. If this were to happen, every institution we know, from the family to the school and the corporation, would be transformed.

Watching masses of peasants scything a field three hundred years ago, only a madman would have dreamed that the time would soon come when the fields would be depopulated, when people would crowd into urban factories to earn their daily bread. And only a madman would have been right. Today it takes an act of courage to suggest that our biggest factories and office towers may, within our lifetimes, stand half-empty, reduced to use as ghostly warehouses or converted into living space. Yet this is precisely what the new mode of production makes possible: a retum to cottage industry on a new, higher, electronic basis, and with it a new emphasis on the home as the centre of society.

To suggest that millions of us may soon spend our time at home, instead of going out to an affice or factory, is to unleash an immediate shower of objections. And there are many sensible reasons for scepticism. 'People don't want to work at home, even if they could. Look at all the women struggling to get *out* of the home and into a job!' 'How can you get any work done with kids running around?' 'People won't be motivated unless there's a boss watching them.' 'People need face-to-face contact with each other to develop the trust and confidence necessary to work together.' 'The architecture of the average home isn't set up for it.' 'What do you mean work at home – a small blast furnace in every basement?' 'What about zoning restrictions and landlords who object?' 'The unions will kill the idea.' How about the tax collector? The tax people are getting tougher on deductions claimed for working at home.' And the ultimate stopper: 'What, and stay home all day with my wife (or husband)?'

Even old Karl Marx would have frowned. Working at home, he believed, was a reactionary form of production because 'the agglomeration in one workshop' was 'a necessary condition for the division of labour in society'. In short, there were, and are, many reasons (and pseudoreasons) for regarding the whole idea as silly.

Doing homework

Yet there were equally, if not more, compelling reasons three hundred years ago to believe people would never move *out* of the home and field to work in factories. After all, they had laboured in their own cottages and the nearby land for 10,000 years, not a mere 300. The entire structure of family life, the process of childbearing and personality formation, the whole system of property and power, the culture, the daily struggle for existence were all bound to the hearth and the soil by a thousand invisible chains. Yet these chains were slashed in short order as soon as a new system of production appeared.

Today that is happening again, and a whole group of social and economic forces are converging to transfer the locus of work.

To begin with, the shift from Second Wave manufacturing to the new, more advanced Third Wave manufacturing reduces, as we just saw, the number of workers who actually have to manipulate physical goods. This means that even in the manufacturing sector an increasing amount of work is being done that – given the right configuration of telecommunications and other equipment – could be accomplished anywhere, including one's own living-room. Nor is this just a science fiction fantasy.

When Western Electric shifted from producing electromechanical switching equipment for the phone company to making electronic switching gear, the work force at its advanced manufacturing facility in Northern Illinois was transformed. Before the changeover, production workers outnumbered whitecollar and technical workers three to one. Today the ratio is one to one. This means that fully half of the 2,000 workers now handle information instead of things, and much of their work can be done at home. Don Cuomo, director of engineering at the Northern Illinois facility put it flatly: 'If you include engineers, ten to twenty-five per cent of what is done here could be done at home with *existing* technology.'

Cuomo's manager of engineering, Gerald Mitchell, went even further. 'All told,' he stated, '600 to 700 of the 2,000 could *now* – with existing technology – work at home. And in five years, we could go far beyond that.'

These informed 'guesstimates' are remarkably similar to those made by Dar Howard, manufacturing manager of the Hewlett-Packard factory in Colorado Springs: 'We have 1,000 in actual manufacturing. Technologically, maybe 250 of them could work at home. The logistics would be complicated but the tooling and capital equipment would not prevent it. In white collar research and development, if you're willing to invest in [computer] terminals, one half to three quarters could also work at home.' At Howlett-Packard that would add up to an additional 350 to 520 workers.

If significant numbers of employees in the manufacturing sector could be shifted to the home even now, then it is safe to say that a considerable slice of the white-collar sector – where there are no materials to handle – could also make that transition.

Indeed, an unmeasured but appreciable amount of work is already being done at home by such people as salesmen and saleswomen who work by phone or visit, and only occasionally touch base at the office; by architects and designers; by a burgeoning pool of specialized consultants in many industries; by large numbers of human-service workers like therapists or psychologists; by music teachers and language instructors; by art dealers; investment counsellors, insurance agents, lawyers, and academic researchers; and by many other categories of white collar, technical, and professional people.

These are, moreover, among the most rapidly expanding work classifications, and when we suddenly make available technologies that can place a low-cost 'work station' in any home, providing it with a 'smart' typewriter, perhaps, along with a facsimile machine or computer console and teleconferencing equipment, the possibilities for home work are radically extended.

The campaign for child labour

Children, meanwhile, would also be likely to grow up differently in the electronic cottage, if for no other reason than that they would actually see work taking place. First Wave children, from their first blink of consciousness, saw their parents at work. Second Wave children, by contrast – at least in recent generations – were segregated in schools and divorced from real work life. Most today have only the foggiest notion of what their parent's do or how they live while at work.

The fact is that children today – especially affluent children – are totally divorced from one of the most important dimensions of their parents' lives. In an electronic cottage kids not only observe work, they may, after a certain age, engage in it themselves. Second Wave restrictions on child labour – originally well-intentioned and necessary, but now largely an anachronistic device to keep young people out of the crowded job market – become more difficult to enforce in the home setting. Certain forms of work, indeed, might be specifically designed for youngsters and even integrated with their education.

The alienation of youth today flows in large measure from being forced to accept a nonproductive role in society during an endlessly prolonged adolescence. The electronic cottage would counteract this situation.

Unions (and teachers, whether unionized or not) will lobby for ever-longer years of compulsory or near-compulsory schooling. To the extent that they succeed, millions of young people will continue to be forced into the painful limbo of prolonged adolescence. We may, therefore, see a sharp contrast between young people who grow up fast because of early work responsibilities in the electronic cottage and those who mature more slowly outside.

Over the long pull, however, we can expect education also to change. More learning will occur outside, rather than inside, the classroom. Despite the pressure from unions, the years of compulsory schooling will grow shorter, not longer. Instead of rigid age segregation, young and old will mingle. Education will become more interspersed and interwoven with work, and more spread out over a lifetime. And work itself – whether production for the market or prosumption for use in the home – will probably begin earlier in life than it has in the last generation or two. For just such reasons, Third Wave civilization may well favour quite different traits among the young – less responsiveness to peers, less consumption-orientation, and less hedonistic self-involvement.

Whether this is so or not, one thing is certain. Growing up will be different. And so will the resultant personalities.

The new worker

As the adolescent matures and enters the job arena, new forces come into play on his or her personality, rewarding some traits and punishing or penalizing others.

Throughout the Second Wave era, work in the factories and offices steadily grew more repetitive, specialized, and time-pressured, and employers wanted workers who were obedient, punctual, and willing to perform rote tasks. The corresponding traits were fostered by the schools and rewarded by the corporation.

As the Third Wave cuts across our society, work grows less, not more, repetitive. It becomes less fragmented, with each person doing a somewhat larger, rather than smaller, task. Flexitime and self-pacing replace the old need for mass synchronization of behaviour. Workers are forced to cope with more frequent changes in their tasks, as well as a blinding succession of personnel transfers, product changes, and reorganizations.

What Third Wave employers increasingly need, therefore, are men and women who accept responsibility, who understand how their work dovetails with that of others, who can handle ever larger tasks, who adapt swiftly to changed circumstances, and who are sensitively tuned in to the people around them.

The Second Wave firm frequently paid off for plodding bureaucratic behaviour. The Third Wave firm requires people who are less pre-programmed and faster on their feet. The difference, says Donald Conover, general manager of Corporate Education for Western Electric, is like that between classical musicians who play each note according to a predetermined, pre-set pattern, and jazz improvisers who, once having decided what song to play, sensitively pick up cues from one another and, on the basis of that, decide what notes to play next.

Such people are complex, individualistic, proud of the ways in which they differ from other people. They typify the demassified work force needed by Third Wave industry.

Alvin Toffler, *The Third Wave*. Collins 1980.

SECTION 4 *HOW SHOULD IT BE?*

THE TIMES EDUCATIONAL SUPPLEMENT

Bertrand Russell tried and failed to devise an ideal school.

Can you succeed where he failed?

In this section you will have the opportunity to plan your ideal educational establishment.

A Laying the foundations

1 The whole class should discuss and agree on the following details:
- the location of the planned educational establishment. continent?/country?/area?
- who the target students will be. age?/number?/catchment area?
- available resources. How much?/Where will it come from?

A2 The class should now split into two or three groups for more detailed planning. At this stage you should formulate the principles of your establishment.

Each group should decide on:
- The educational aims of the establishment.
- The subjects to be included in the curriculum and the order of their importance.
- The teaching and learning methods to be adopted.

A3 Once you have decided on the broad outline of your plan, each group should get ready to present their ideas to the whole class.
- Each group should aim to speak for no more than ten minutes.
- In your talk you should make full use of visuals such as charts, diagrams, maps and graphs.
- In order to promote your plan, each group should prepare a brochure outlining the plan in as attractive a way as possible.

A4 Each group should make its presentation to the class as a whole.

B A Utopian establishment?

Following all the presentations there will be a full class discussion, the aim of which will be:
- either to accept one of the proposals
- or to agree on a compromise plan

B1 In your original groups, reassess the whole situation and look again at your own plan to decide in the light of what you have heard:
- if you are going to make any changes
- if you want to approach another group to put your ideas together
- if you are going to stick to your original plan

B2 Organise a full class discussion and agree on a plan acceptable to all.

C **Is it really so different?**

Consider the educational establishment you are now studying in.

Consider the educational establishment that the class has designed.

Write a brief report comparing and contrasting the two.

SECTION 5 *THE EFFECTIVE COMMUNICATOR*

Throughout this unit you have been thinking about your education, career and future environment. It is important to have thought about topics like these since they are likely to arise in future interviews.

In most cases, one of the main purposes of an interview is to test your ability to effectively communicate your ideas on such topics.

It is advisable to take steps to prepare yourself for an interview situation. Below are a set of instructions to guide you in this preparation.

A **What kind of an interview is it?**

What is the purpose of your next interview likely to be?
- to obtain a place for further study
- to get a job
- to take an oral exam

B **Find out as much as you can**

1 Find out what you are likely to be asked.
- by examining any available literature *e.g.* prospectuses, brochures, advertisements, syllabuses etc
- by talking to anyone who may be able to help you *e.g.* careers advisers, tutor, teachers or anyone who has attended or conducted such an interview

B2 Find out if you have to discuss a text, diagram, essay or a piece of work at the interview.

Do you have to bring this with you or is it provided?

B3 Find out what qualities the interviewer will be looking for. Here are some suggestions. Which ones are valid in your case?

confidence	fluency	grammatical accuracy
long answers	initiative	originality
spontaneity	imagination	logical answers
clarity of speech		speaking loudly

Which of these are likely to cause you the most problems in an interview?

C Predict the questions

1 As a result of your investigations, draw up a list of the topic areas that are likely to be covered in the interview.

If you have found it difficult to get this kind of information, consider the following checklist of topics and pick out the ones which you think could be discussed in your interview.

Where you come from Your leisure interests Your present work and study Your future plans and reasons for them Your ability to adapt to new situations Your ability to get on with people Your personal qualities What you know about the organisation you are applying to What you know about the place you are going to Family background Your education

C2 Note down as many questions as you can think of that could be asked on each area you have chosen.

C3 Consider and note down all the points that you would include in answer to each question.

Since you wish to display your ability to communicate, your answers should be well developed. This means that single word answers will not be sufficient.

D Put yourself in the hot seat

1 Working with a partner, practise asking and answering the questions you have prepared.

D2 Most of the problems that you will face in an interview situation are caused by pressure. The interviewee often feels nervous and sometimes panics.

To replicate and overcome this pressure, try the following exercise.

- Form a small group of 3, 4 or 5 students. In turn, each student will be interviewed by the others, who will form a panel of interviewers.
- Set a maximum time for each interview.
- Agree on the qualities that you will be looking for during the interviews.
- The panel should ask their questions in rapid succession giving the interviewee little time to think.
- The panel should be ready to ask supplementary questions if the interviewee's answers are insufficient.
- The panel should ask follow-up questions on interesting points raised by the candidate.
- At the end of the allotted time, the panel should give the interviewee a frank appraisal of his/her performance.
- The interviewee should note any topic areas where he/she has difficulties with the aim of doing some further work on them.

D3 Another way to evaluate the performance is to record the interview and replay it with a teacher/adviser present.

ANSWER KEY

UNIT 1 *HELP YOURSELF*

Section 2

A2 *b* Page 3

(i) the third attempt
(ii) and *(iii)*

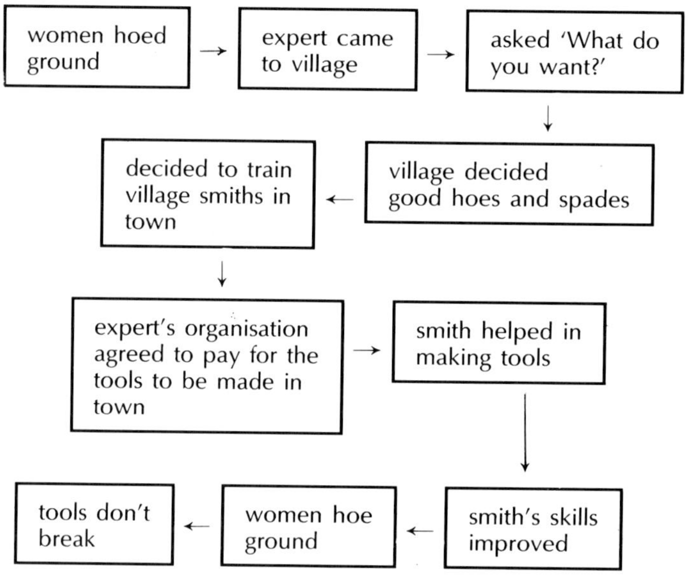

A2 *c* The third attempt was successful because it acknowledged 'local needs, conditions and purses'. The first two did not.

The first expert took no account of any of the above. The second expert did (needs and purses) but not conditions. (In this case, the tradition of men as cyclists. Both of these experts told the people what they needed). The third expert simply asked what people wanted. This approach encompassed all three points mentioned above.

A2 d Page 4

Flowchart:

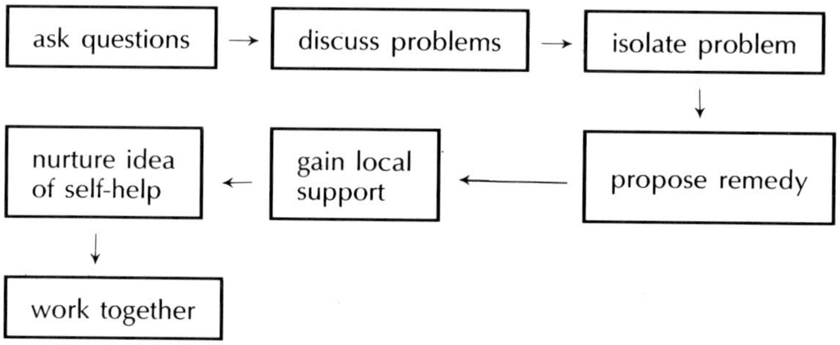

B1 *a* Page 4

they = 100 million people (who have no shelter)
the figure = percentage of urban population living in slums and squatter settlements
this = growth rate of cities in developing countries
these cities = cities in the developing world
these trends = number of people living in cities in the developing world in 1985 *and* the projected number after 14 years
these settlements = squatter settlements (and slums)
they = developing countries
they = developing countries
this situation = all the points in the preceding paragraph
these factors = all the points so far mentioned in the final paragraph

Section 3

A1 *c* Page 7
B establishing a self-help programme

A2 Page 9

Suggested steps:
- man goes to Orangi
- talks to residents
- identifies problem
- investigates possible solutions
- designs cost-efficient sewerage system
- gains acceptance by local population
- oversees inplementation of cost-efficient system

The points could be presented in a flowchart.

A4 Page 9

a B
c City and Industrial Development Corporation (CIDCO)
Madras Metropolitan Development Authority (MMDA)
(Sites and Services Scheme is not itself a planning organisation, it is a project funded by the World Bank).
d Bombay (CIDCO): 36,000 houses since 1970s
several privately-built blocks
44% houses belong to economically weak/low income groups
conventional building standards reduced for economy
planning practices based on Western and Soviet models
centrally determined plans and standards
$500 per site
Madras: residents build own houses
aimed at poverty group (not only low-waged employed)
80% state housing funds to low-waged sectors
$90 per site
communal facilities
employment available near to development area
cheap loans available
30,000 new sites
80,000 improved sites

C1 Page 11

a *(i)* insufficient and inadequate housing especially due to growth of urban populations
(ii) large scale; national/global
(iii) centrally imposed
b final column:

International housing situation
national/global scale
insufficient and inadequate housing
centrally imposed

c (*i*) Yes
(*ii*) the interviewer
(*iii*) acceptable on a small scale, impractical on a large scale

UNIT 2 *ARRESTING STUFF*

Section 2

A1 Page 24

a (*i*) two or more effects stemming from the same source
(*ii*) linked to each other in a direct cause/effect relationship
(*iii*) completely unrelated
b *A* (*i*)
B (*iii*)
C (*ii*)

Section 3

A1 Page 27

'Mummy's boy' – a male who is spoilt by his mother and prefers her company to the company of other people; may be regarded as soft
'run amok' – to go mad or lose control, causing harm to other people

C1 Page 29

The controversy is whether the 26 fans should be extradited from Britain to Belgium or not.

C2
2 very thoroughly
3 frivolous
4 high quality documentary evidence
5 quite obviously the proper place
6 simply shameful xenophobia
7 in no decisive sense inferior
8 hardly

D2 Page 31

Text 1
The writer's attitude is that alcohol produces antisocial conduct. Alcohol abuse is a major cause of crime.
When the Prohibition Law was enforced, there were 'great resulting benefits' and an 'increase in financial saving'.
Since, in the writer's view, 'practically all civilized governments' have tried to restrict the use of alcohol and narcotics, governments which have not are uncivilized.
The writer approves of the National Prohibition Law as it brought great benefits when it was enforced and observed.

Text 2
Drunkenness has decreased because of the increased cost of alcohol, not because of restrictions on its sale.
Restricting the sale of alcohol is not an effective means of decreasing drunkenness.

Text 3
It was fashionable among the privileged classes to promote sociability using alcohol.

This fashion helped to undermine the prohibition law and increased the illegal sale of alcohol.

Thus, the privileged classes were responsible for the increasing level of alcoholism and intoxication.

The writer believes that the American upper classes were promoting alcoholism and intoxication among the American people and that they lacked moral and social idealism.

Text 4

The Prohibition Law failed.

The writer's view is that crime and vice can be eliminated.

The majority did not want the Prohibition Law to be obeyed. Churches and schools did not influence people to obey the law as they should have done.

Text 5

The author believes that law and order can be strictly enforced and that this will lead to an end to most serious crime.

UNIT 3 *A QUESTION OF POWER*

Section 1

B3 Page 46

Suggested answers:
1 energy problems
2 most common world sources
3 problems of nuclear power
4 advantages of nuclear power
5 the future of conventional sources
6 alternative sources

Section 2

A1 Page 48

A tidal B wave power C wind D geothermal
E hydro F tidal G solar

Renewable energy sources are those that do not rely on fuel that is only present on the earth in limited supplies. (Examples of fuels in limited supply are coal, gas, oil and uranium.) Renewable sources may be used again and again, *e.g.* wind, sun and tides, or they may be grown again, *e.g.* timber and crops.

C1 Page 49

Iceland – geothermal
Saudi Arabia – solar
China – geothermal
Uganda – geothermal
Britain – geothermal
The Philippines – geothermal
Australia – thermal
Italy – geothermal and solar

C4 **Table to compare three renewable energy sources**

	Tidal	**Solar**	**Geothermal**
Importance on world scale	Not yet	Not yet – predicted 7% of all EC electricity	Not yet
Suitable location	Estuaries with high tidal variation	World-wide	World-wide, especially seismic areas
Where currently exploited	Few countries – France, USSR, China	France (STEC) US, Australia, S. Arabia, Oman	GB, US, Italy, NZ, Iceland, France, Japan

	Tidal	Solar	Geothermal
Capital outlay	High	High – $20 – 30,000/ kw 2x cost of fossil fuel or nuclear, but may fall	High
Generating costs	Low – compares well with nuclear or oil	Low	Low (2–3p/ kWh) cheaper than wind, solar, oil, small scale nuclear and HEP
Life expectancy of plant	100 years	Not stated	Short – 5–20 years
Advantages	Little environmental impact	Small and large scale possible. Maintenance simple	Can recover salts from waste water
Disadvantages	Intermittent power supply High transmission costs	Technology not yet developed. Intermittent supply – back up needed. Plant takes up large areas	Large scale only. Transport costs high. Environmental problems – sulphur gases → air – warm water → rivers

D1 Page 54

a Similarities – are both similar in that they
compares favourably with
Like

Differences – However
whereas
while
on the other hand
differ . . . in that
In contrast

b These . . .
As far as . . .
As regards . . .
Turning now to . . .
Both . . .

Section 3

B2 Page 58

Text 1 – International Atomic Energy Agency
Text 2 – Foley, G.
Text 3 – Greenpeace Environmental Trust

C1 Text 1 – *f* Text 2 – *d* Text 3 – *b*

D1 safety and cost

D2 *c* *f*

D3 Page 58

	AGR	PWR
Means of heat transfer	Gas	Water under high pressure

Size	Giant core	Compact (used in nuclear submarines)
Safety question	Things go wrong *slowly* – operating fluid CO_2 – giant graphite core SAFE	Same type as Three Mile Island Reactor – people concerned Things go wrong *quickly* BUT – many safety features – works well SAFE
Cost (Capital)	Not clear which better – both cheaper than coal.	

UNIT 4 *RINGING THE CHANGES*

Section 1

C1 Page 68

a Malacca is experiencing a 'fall'.
b high rises have gone up
old buildings demolished
new housing developments
land reclamation (land claims)
port silted up
shipping gone down
warehouses fallen into decay
foreign trade decreased
town diminished in importance for trading
busy business and industrial centre
tourist trade increased

C2 *a* the port has become more and more silted up
the port is becoming less and less important
business has shifted away from the port area
the port, no-one wants to go there any more
b no ships come here any more
shipping has gone down a lot
c all the warehouses there [have] all fallen into decay, [there are] no warehouses there any more
d foreign trade has decreased
the town has diminished in importance as a trading centre
e old buildings [have been] demolished
many of the buildings were ramshackle and falling down
f skyline has changed a lot
g industrial estates have grown up all over the place
h the tourist trade has taken over

C3 *a* **Optimism**
– I think (the) town has picked up a lot
– (the) tourist trade has taken over
– old buildings have been demolished to make way for new housing development and a lot of land claims (=reclamation)

b **Pessimism**
– things have changed you know, not like in the old days
– (the) town has seen better days
– shipping has gone down a lot
– the port is becoming less and less important
– warehouses (have) all fallen into decay
– the town has diminished in importance

Section 2

A4 Page 70

building	deforestation
roads	flooding
soil erosion	climatic change
intensive farming	desertification
using natural organic fertiliser as fuel	overcropping, overgrazing, salinization

B1 Page 70

Threats to arable land

B2 Intensive methods of farming
Desertification
Soil erosion
Building
Deforestation

B3 Page 71

c

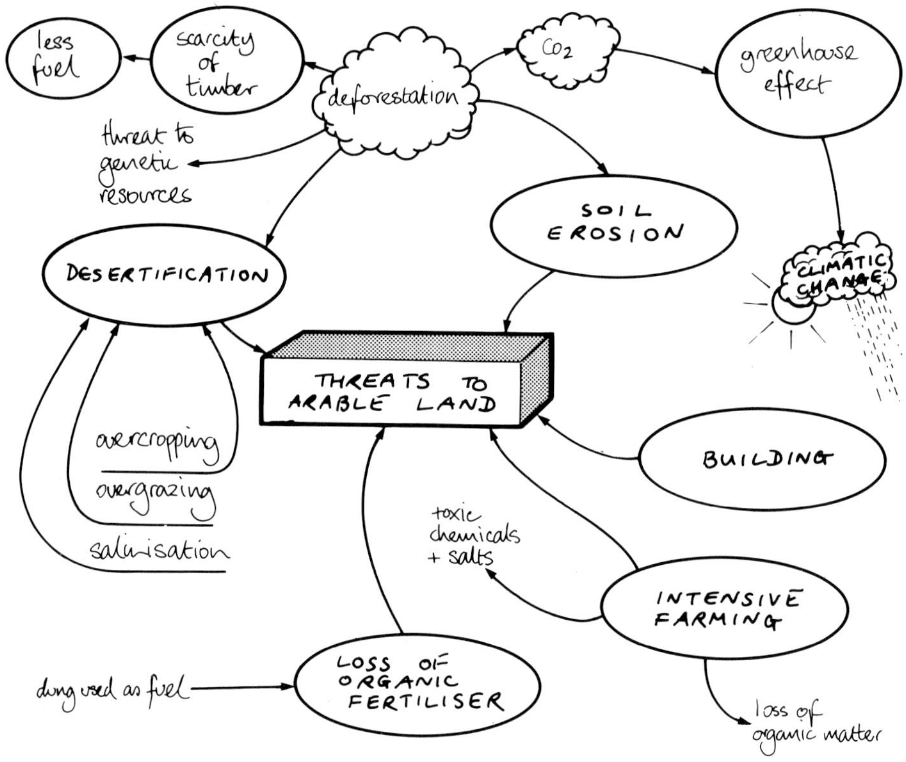

B4 *b* *(i)* False. Deforestation leads to desertification.
(ii) True
(iii) False. Intensive farming is one of the threats to arable land.
(iv) True
(v) True
(vi) False. Deforestation is a threat to the world's genetic resources.
(vii) False. Deforestation results in higher rates of erosion.

C1 *a* It predicts that the amount of good agricultural land area will decrease by about 30% between 1985 and 2005.
b 'At the current rate of land degradation, it is estimated as much as one third of all good agricultural land could be lost within the next two decades.'
c Prediction – at the current rate
– it is estimated that

– could be lost
– the next two decades

Time span calculation – By projecting the present rate of land degradation over the next 20 years

C2 *a* 9 countries will have destroyed all their closed forests within 30 years and a further 13 within 55 years

b – rates of deforestation were not quite as bad as had been feared

– it is thought that...
– on present trends...

c ...for the period up to 1985...
– within x years...

C3 *a* *(iv)*
b *(ii)*
c *(i)*
d *(i)* proceeded
(ii) increase
(iii) steadily
(iv) levelled off
(v) was reduced
(vi) dramatic rise
(vii) reached a peak
(viii) fell
(ix) rate
(x) expected

e *(i)* Paragraphs 1, 2, 3, 4
(ii) Paragraph 6
(iii) Paragraph 5

Section 3

A1 Page 76

b

Products	**Effects**
waste industrial gases	greenhouse effect
carbon dioxide	climatic change
methane	(no specific effect mentioned)
chlorofluorocarbons	ozone layer
	moving the climate outside the natural range

A2 *b* *(v)*, *(ii)*, *(i)*, *(iv)*, *(iii)*

A3

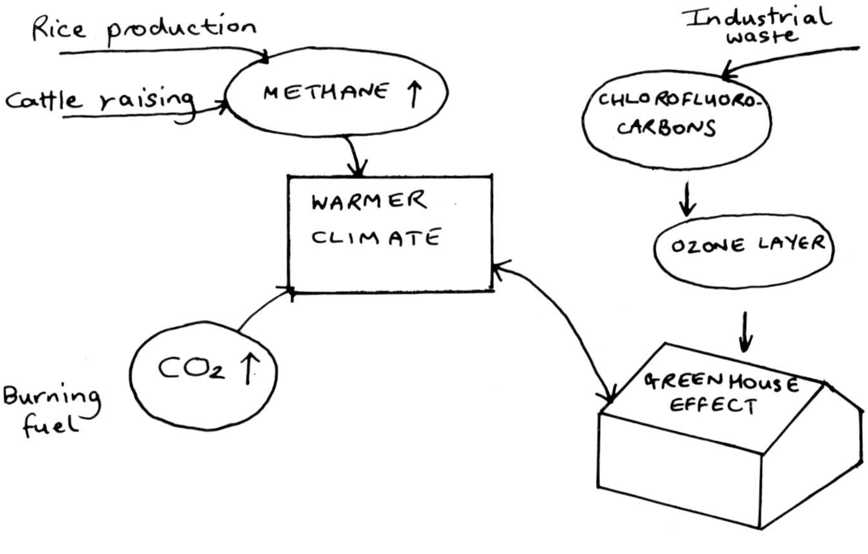

A4 *a* By the end of this century, the level of CO_2 will cross the 600 mark. It's almost inevitable that we will move the climate outside the natural range.
Countries in the North will, on the whole, benefit.
Countries that are reasonably well-off today might suffer.

B1 Page 77

c the extinction of species

B2

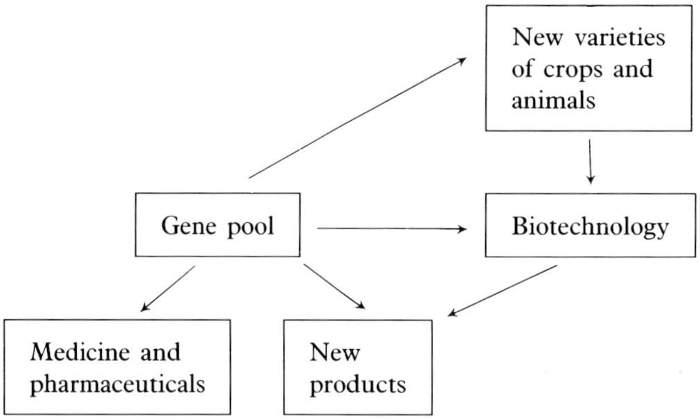

C2 Page 78

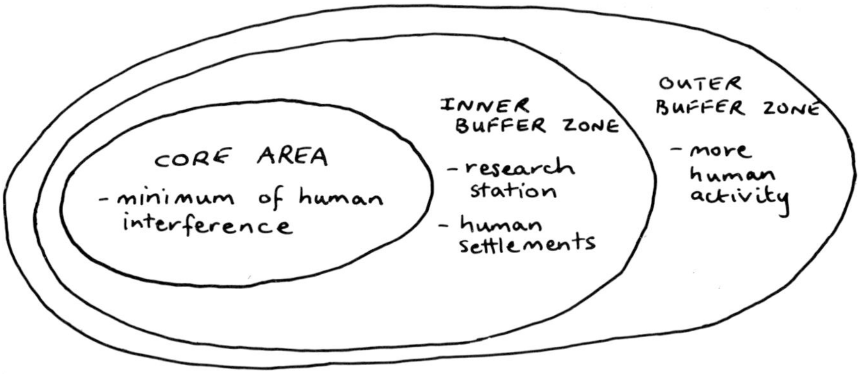

C3

Comparison of biosphere reserves and national parks

	Biosphere reserves	**National parks**
Local involvement	Important	Little
Public image	Good	Not always good
Human settlements	Yes	No
Disruption of traditional lifestyles	No	Yes
Flora and fauna protection	Yes	Yes
Scientific research	Yes	Yes
Stress conservation	Yes, but flexible	100%

E4 *a* Suitable phrases:
(i) I'm going to talk about...
The topic of my talk this (afternoon) is...

I have chosen the topic of. . . for my talk.
This (afternoon) I want to deal with the topic of. . .

(ii) I want to divide my talk into. . . parts.
First of all. . .
I want to start off by. . .

Section 4

A2 Page 81

Text 1: *e*, *f*
Text 2: *b*, *c*
Text 3: *h*, *g*

UNIT 5 *FOOD FOR THOUGHT*

Section 1

B2 Page 91

A Self-sufficiency in food
1 Natural factors
a adequate rainfall
b oil revenue
2 Government policy
a 1/4 of national budget to agriculture
b incentives to farmers
(i) new technology → *(iii)* higher yields
(ii) 1/2 price fertiliser → *(iv)* hour earnings
c encourage women farmers
d international co-operation
e attracted aid

B Effects of self-sufficiency in NW province
1 food output increased by 50%
2 small farms thriving
3 illiteracy down from 80% to 50%

C Export crops
Low prices paid to farmers as disincentive
Encourages switching from coffee/cocoa to food crops

UNIT 6 *A BRAVE NEW WORLD*

Section 1

B1 Page 104

Excerpt 1 – on the way down

Excerpt 2 – on the way down: Overall, the author is pessimistic about the future although he notes improvements that have been made.

Excerpt 3 – on the way down: first sentence.
'We were stealing (wealth) from posterity'.
'The accounting is about to begin'.

B2 Excerpt 1 – *d*, *a*
Excerpt 2 – *c*, *a*
Excerpt 3 – *b*

B3 *a* health and physical well-being
technological achievements

b creation of wealth
man's psychological state
our conduct of social affairs

B4 Page 105

a, *b* Excerpt 1 – Pessimistic: 'on the verge of self-destruction'
'a sordid story'
'unique incompetence'

Excerpt 2 – Optimistic: 'wealthier, stronger, taller, more athletic, longer lives'
– Pessimistic: 'nervous, sleepless, cannot meditate or pray'
'cannot find contentment'
'countries more and more divided'
'the gulf widens between those who have too much and those who have too little'

Excerpt 3 – Optimistic: wealth was created rapidly (though in fact the writer believes this was a mistaken belief)
– Pessimistic: 'We are heading for a period of human misery on a scale quite unprecedented'
'in reality we were stealing (wealth) from posterity'
'The accounting is about to begin.'

C1 Page 106

a Cause and effect: declining food supplies and resources eventually cause a rise in the death rate and a decline in population. Declining industry causes a decline in pollution. An effect of the steeply rising death rate is an increase in the birth rate.
(These may be expressed as either causes or effects.)

Similar shapes: *a* population, pollution, industrial output per capita and food per capita
b birth rate, death rate

Section 2

B3 Page 110

a Some suggestions: 'The Biotechnology Sunrise'
'The Biotechnology Future'
'The Increasing Importance of Biotechnology'

b 'The new field of biotechnology encompasses fields as diverse as genetic engineering, biological prosthetics, new fermentation processes and the use of biological techniques to improve agricultural yields, process waste, and provide energy from biomass.'
'The possibilities of genetic engineering have been opened up by discoveries in two areas.'
'Although the first gene was synthesized in 1964, the technique was improved and during 1978 and 1979 it became possible partially to synthesise the genes responsible for the production of insulin and the human growth hormone and in the latter year these genes were successfully introduced into bacterial cells.'
'The implications of this work were that biological molecules could be synthesised to order by implanting specific genes in various types of micro-organisms.'
'Production of therapeutic chemicals in this way suggests that long and costly toxicity tests for new chemicals may in the future be greatly reduced.'
'The agricultural possibilities of such techniques are almost as exciting.'
'Another field of application concerns the tailoring of certain yeasts and other micro-organisms to do specific jobs in industry, for example, turning the by-products of oil refineries into single-cell protein suitable for an animal feed.'
'Finally, biotechnology is already finding more and more uses in the energy field.'
'The new field of biotechnology offers immediate and attractive prospects for developing countries.'

B4 *a* potentially of great medical importance
agricultural possibilities almost as exciting

savings will be enormous
potential savings immense
benefits. . . the agricultural and rural household
experts are optimistic
biotechnology offers immediate and attractive prospects for developing countries

These extracts all display optimism.

B4 *b* The writer is enthusiastic.

c great, exciting, enormous, immense, benefits, optimistic, immediate and attractive prospects

C1 Page 110

insect spray	cosmetics
weedkiller	paints
washing powder	plastic
food preservatives	medicines

C2 *c* The advertising brochure of a genetic engineering company.

C3

	a	*b*	*c*
Extract 1	biological catalyst	optimistic	will function at standard environmental condition another very useful area nasty chemicals something less harmful preferably harmless economical advantages in every way a good thing
Extract 2	virus resistance	optimistic	really very impressive sounds very exciting (no) question but that it will (change the face of agriculture) very good for the farmer needing less care than what it needed in the past
Extract 3	herbicide resistant plants	optimistic	successfully used with many crop plants the benefit is that one can use better herbicides environmentally more acceptable herbicides weeds can be controlled
Extract 4	putting new genes in animals	optimistic	useful to a farmer the outcome was quite dramatic this has lead to a great deal of interest
Extract 5	genetically engineered vaccines	optimistic	halve the cost of protecting people about 2 million people die of Hepatitis B every year the new (vaccine) costs about half

C4 *b* The speakers feel that genetic engineering can complement the use of chemicals.

Extract 1 – biological catalysts can be used to degrade effluents, that is to take the nasty chemicals out of waste streams or water supplies

Extract 3 – With a plant that is resistant to herbicides one can use environmentally more acceptable herbicides

D1 *a* Text 1 – The Biotechnology Sunrise
Text 2 – Gene engineers fashion giant sheep
Text 3 – Engerix – B: Genetically Engineered Vaccine
c Text 1 – *(i)*, *(ii)*, *(iii)*, *(iv)*, *(v)*
Text 2 – *(i)*, *(ii)*, *(iv)*, *(v)*
Text 3 – *(i)*, *(iv)*

D2 *a* *(i)* imagination
(ii) imagination
(iii) fact
(iv) fact
b *(i)* Imagine...
(ii) We may even come...
(iii) Allows us...
(iv) Catch a glimpse of the power...
c We almost take for granted the endless stream of products from the cornucopia of science and technology.
Miracles of biotechnology come as no surprise.
Imagine a field of crops which manufacture their own fertilizer and fight their own pests.
Imagine replacing green sugar cane, rubber and tobacco by...factories.
The smelly, sad world of human disease.
d A subjective view.

D3 Page 112
a The words are all complimentary. The author is in favour of biotechnology.
b Sober civil servants predict that biotechnology will 'revolutionize' our society, sceptical economists that it is the next 'industrial revolution'.
...a new, more detailed knowledge of the disease process.
...companies hope to do away with the years of expensive, 'shotgun' testing
...do away with or reduce the weakening side-effects
...an infinitely better idea
...harnessing living organisms
...biotechnology's greatest legacy
c *(ii)* the general public
d *(iii)* an overview

D4 *a* already achieved: transgenic sheep, mice – grow larger faster
desired advances: larger, leaner, faster-growing animals
wool growth
disease resistance
b Certain
↓
it will cut
will no longer need
would lead
should soon be possible
Uncertain the technique could produce
c Scientists and interested non-scientists.
d That inserting genes into animals, a process as yet in its very early stages, has recently achieved a breakthrough which could have far-reaching implications for animal breeding.

D5 Page 114
a 'Produced according to 'state-of-the-art' technology and tested to the most stringent international quality control standards...an outstanding profile...highly immunogenic...as demonstrated by the most sensitive methods.
'More than 3000 vaccines have been successfully enrolled into clinical trials.'
'These trials...have confirmed the excellent clinical profile...'
'Reactions were rare, mild and transient.'
'Seroconversion rates of close to 100% have been achieved...very encouraging technical and clinical results...'
'SmithKline scientists...spare no effort to allow the worldwide medical profession to

benefit from Engerix-B, a major medical advance...'
b Members of the medical and pharmaceutical profession.
c The marketing department of Smith-Kline Biologicals.
d To promote sales of Engerix-B.

Section 3

B1 Page 115

c Not in favour, but can see some advantages.

B2

(i) – *(w)*	*(v)* – *(z)*
(ii) – *(s)*	*(vi)* – *(v)*
(iii) – *(y)*	*(vii)* – *(x)*
(iv) – *(t)*	*(viii)* – *(y)*

B3

a	*b*
(i) Agree	in one sense that's true and in another sense it isn't
(ii) Agree	we run the risk
	on the other hand
	exacerbates this problem
(iii) Agree	outrageous experiments
	it's ridiculous – absurd
(iv) Agree	every generation of mice has human hormones
	that plant lights up, day and night

B4 *c* forceful and direct

E1 Page 127

a Because the reply agrees with at least part of the first statement before going on to disagree. 'Surely' also makes a statement more polite as it invites agreement.
b Excerpt 1 – Interviewee: Not at all
Nonsense
Rubbish
Yes, but that's not the point
But that isn't all they are doing
Excerpt 2 – Interviewer: Not at all
Yes, but that's not the point

E2 *a* Disagree
↓
You must be joking.
You can't be serious.
I'm afraid that I don't share your opinion.
Yes, I'm sure you're right but...
I must admit that you've got a point there.
We are obviously thinking along the same lines.
Agree
I couldn't agree more.

UNIT 7 *YOUR GOOD HEALTH!*

Section 1

B2 Page 133

a physical and mental
b

Social ills	**Quality of life**
suicide rate	leisure pursuits
number of murders	cultural activities
road traffic accident rate	sporting activities
juvenile delinquency	climate
drug-taking	length of working day

consumption of tranquilisers
cigarette smoking
average obesity

Section 2

A2 Page 134

From W.H.O.	**From list**
1	government commitment to health policy
2	involvement of the public in decisions on health policy
3	government spending on health
4	distribution of small clinics throughout the country
5	even distribution of resources between town and country
6	availability of resources – from domestic and foreign sources
7	availability of basic health care to everyone
8	average child weight
9	infant mortality rate
10	average life expectancy
11	adult literacy rate
12	country's gross national product

F1 Page 138

a (i)
b (i)
c (ii)
d (ii)
e (i)

Section 3

C Page 141

the houseman is lucky if he gets 18 hours sleep (in a working week)
really hard work
accepted the guidance and advice of her supervisor
don't suffer from verbal diarrhoea (i.e. don't talk too much)
Doctors have to be clear and accurate in their answer (to questions about patients)
accept criticism in the right spirit
She takes the long hours in her stride
remember that patients are human beings
think fast, rely on your theoretical knowledge and act quickly

D1 *a* Smoking has increased most in Egypt.
Smoking has decreased most in the Netherlands.

Both countries have warnings on packets and a partial ban on advertising.

In addition, Egypt has 'weak' bans on smoking in public places while the Netherlands does not ban smoking in public places. Although Egypt has slightly more restrictions on smoking than the Netherlands, cigarette smoking is increasing in the former and decreasing in the latter, leading to the view that government's anti-smoking policies are not the only factor affecting use of cigarettes.

While the table shows the percentage change in use of cigarettes it does not give the proportion of smokers to non-smokers, so we are unable to determine the significance of the percentage for each country. There could be a higher percentage of smokers in the Netherlands than in Egypt, for example.

Section 4

A1 Page 145

fire risks **B**
voluntary anti-smoking campaigns in the private sector **B**
policy proposals to reduce public smoking **A**

economic costs of tobacco-related diseases **A**
compulsory anti-smoking laws **B**
influence on efficiency at work **B**
side effects of passive smoking **A**

UNIT 8 *WHAT'S IT ALL FOR?*

Section 1

B1 Page 152

a target groups: 6th form students at 10 schools in England, Scotland and Wales representing a cross-section of state and public schools.

b 1 How do you see yourself in terms of social class?
What class do you think you belong to?
2 Are you interested in politics?
Do you think that involvement in decision making is important?
3 Do you think your lifestyle will be the same as your parents?
How do you think it will be the same/different?
4 Do you have a hero/heroine?
Who is it?
5 What kind of people succeed in life?
6 What do you think the role of the police is?
Have you had any direct experience of the police?
7 Do you think the legal system is fair?
Do you think that the sentences people get for different crimes are fair?
8 How much influence do you think you can have on government decisions?
Do you think that the British central government represents all parts of the country fairly?
9 How important is religion to you?
Do you have any strong beliefs?
Do you practice your religion?
10 Do you think there are any jobs that only men or only women can do?
11 How will AIDS change people's behaviour?

Section 2

A1 Page 154

Text 1
g to impart a wide scope of knowledge
a to equip the individual with an armoury of facts and figures
c to create an educated workforce

Text 2
c to create an educated workforce
i to teach technological expertise

Text 3
d to give an understanding of values
e to promote involvement in the community

Text 4
b to encourage responsibility towards others
h to instil self-confidence in individuals
l to promote the link between school and community

B1 Page 160

a Alan Fox (3rd speaker)
b Ronald Baker (1st speaker)
c Shirley James (2nd speaker)

B2 *a* interrupting: 'and, sorry, if I could just finish...'
'Can I take you up on that?'
'With respect...'
'Yes, this is all very interesting...'

b Changing direction: 'Can we move on to...'
'If I may continue...'
'Can I remind you of the issues?'

c Agreeing: 'Well, of course...'
'Yes, I'm sure we all agree.'

Note: 'Surely, you must agree' is an invitation to agree with the speaker and does not mean agreement with a previous point.

d Disagreeing: 'Yes, you're talking about...'
'Surely, you must agree...'
'Can I take you up on that?'
'Then surely you are writing about...'
'Let me stress that...'
'But Mr. Fox you're advocating...'
'I have never said that.'
'Let's not forget...'
'Mrs. James, what you are talking about...'
'With respect'

BIBLIOGRAPHY

Anderson, I., 'Drilling Deep for Geothermal Power and Science' *New Scientist, Vol. 1518*

Ashby, A. 'The New Age of Synthetic Biology' in *New Scientist* 25.6.87

Ballantyne, A. & Rose, D. 'Mummy's boy who kept an armoury' in *Guardian Weekly* 30 Aug. 87

British Council, University of Cambridge Local Exam. Syndicate, *English Language Testing Service Specimen Materials Booklet*, UCLES, 1987

Caufield, C. 'Rainforests face Attack of Double Standards', *New Scientist*, 5 June 1986

Clarke, R. *Science and Technology in World Development*, O.U.P./UNESCO, 1985

Connor, S. 'Court overthrows Patent on Gene-Splicing'

Croall, S. *Ecology for Beginners*, Writers and Readers Publishing Co-operative, 1986

Duma S. 'Life for the Fisherman has not improved' in Utusan Consumer, Feb. 1985

Dynes, M. 'Butcher in Shooting is Freed', *The Times*, 27 October 1987

Ellwood, C.A., *Sociology Principles and Problems*, American Book Co., 1924

Foley, G., *Energy* Penguin, 1976

Furnhan, A., 'Growing Up with Computers', *New Scientist*, 26 March 1987

Glantz, M. 'Drought in Africa', *Scientific American Vol. 256, No. 6*, June 1987

Greenpeace Environmental Trust, *Facts you Should Know about Nuclear Power*, 1986

Gribbin, J., *Future Weather*, Pelican, 1982

International Atomic Energy Agency, *Nuclear Power, The Environment & Man*, Vienna, 1984

Ismail, R. 'Where Docs get only 18 hours of Sleep a Week' in *New Straits Times*, Kuala Lumpur, 16 November 1987

Koestler, A. *Janus: A Summing Up*, Hutchinson, 1978

Lord Marshall of Goring, *Power Through the Grid*, CEGB, 1985

Low, A. 'All for IT' *Times Educational Supplement*, 5 June 1987

Madeley, J., 'Cameroon: Food for the People' in *New Straits Times*, Kuala Lumpur, Feb 85

McMillen, L., 'Scholar Decries Cultural Illiteracy in America' The Chronicle of *Higher Education*, April 22, 1987

Monmaney, T. with Hager, M. 'Should Man Make Beast?' in *Newsweek*, May 4, 1987

Moore, P., 'What Makes Rainforests so Special?' *New Scientist* 21 August 1986

Mount, G.R. 'Insect Fighters Gear for War' in *Agriculture Research*, April 1987

Murray, L., 'Computing for Young Superbrains', *New Scientist*, 26 March 1987

O'Brien, J. 'Judge Sympathises with Butcher' *The Daily Telegraph*, October 27 1987

O'Brien, P.M., 'Agricultural Productivity and the World Food Market', *Environment, Vol. 27, no 9*

Ottoson, K., *Thinking About Education*, Lutterworth Educational, 1978

Ratnaike, R.N., O'Neill, P & Chnoweth, R. 'Village Health Workers and Malnutrition: A Project that Failed' *World Health Forum Vol. 6*, 1985

Russell, B. *Education and Social Order* George Allen & Unwin, 1932

Salholz, E. with Michael, R. 'The Morals Mine Field' *Newsweek*, October 20, 1986

Schumacher, E.F. *Small is Beautiful*, Abacus, 1974

Scorer, R.S. *The Clever Moron*, Routledge & Kegan Paul, 1977

Simunek, K. and Stone, P.B. *Sources of New and Renewable Energy* and *New and Renewable Energies*, Earthscan and Development Forum, 1981

Skinner, B.J. (ed.), *Use and Misuse of Earth's Surface*, American Scientist, 1981

Thring, M.W. *The Engineer's Conscience*, Northgate Publishing, 1980

Toffler, A. *The Third Wave*, William Collins, 1980

Ulich, R. *Progress or Disaster?*, London Press, 1971

Van Ormer, C., 'Yuppie Puppies' *Times Educational Supplement*, 7 August 1987

Werner, D. and Bower, B. *Helping Health Care Workers Learn*, Hesperian Foundation, Pato Alto, California, 1983

Willis, R., 'White Collar Crime' *Management Review*, 1987

Yanchinski, S. *Setting Genes to Work*, Pelican, 1985

FOR YOUR NOTES

FOR YOUR NOTES

FOR YOUR NOTES

FOR YOUR NOTES

FOR YOUR NOTES

FOR YOUR NOTES

FOR YOUR NOTES